W9-CEB-634

PREACHERS
PEDAGOGUES
& POLITICIANS

The University of North Carolina Press

Chapel Hill

PREACHERS PEDAGOGUES & POLITICIANS

The Evolution Controversy in North Carolina
1920–1927

by
WILLIAM B. GATEWOOD, JR.

Manufactured in the United States of America

Library of Congress Catalog Card Number 66–15504

Printed by Kingsport Press, Inc., Kingsport, Tennessee

To my daughter

PREFACE

A generation accustomed to missiles and moonshots is likely to consign the evolution controversy of the 1920's to the realm of flagpole sitting, the Coué craze, and other comic mementoes of the decade. But behind the more ludicrous aspects of the conflict lay the deep-seated fears, anxieties, and frustrations of a people who had come to feel alienated from their past. During those first few years following World War I a series of tremors ran through American society as a half century of social, economic, and intellectual changes, as well as a host of new forces unleashed by the war, presented themselves as realities that could no longer be ignored. Traditional formulas for the good life seemed strangely inappropriate in the new America in which old certainties, one after the other, buckled before a rash of social and cultural innovations. The prospects of this new environment set off a spasm of popular disorientation of which the agitation over evolution was one significant manifestation.

This study attempts to contribute to the existing literature on the evolution controversy by exploring the subject in some detail at the grass roots level. For several reasons North Carolina offers an especially appropriate field for such concentration. The controversy raged there throughout most of the 1920's, and perhaps in no other state was the role of the educational leadership more decisive. More significant, the national anti-evolutionist leaders themselves considered the state one of the most critical arenas of their campaign. Failure to enact a statewide statute in North Carolina undoubtedly had an adverse effect upon their crusade in other states. But this work deals primarily with the conflict over evolution in one state within a specified period of time. It includes neither extensive discussions of the origins of regional traditions, which well may be pertinent, nor lengthy speculations about the possible relationship of Puritanism, Jeffersonian philosophy, and the anti-slavery question to the evolution controversy in the South during the twentieth century.

Several institutions and many individuals provided valuable assistance in the preparation of this volume. I am particularly indebted to the American Association for State and Local History and the American Philosophical Society for research grants and to the Social Science Research Institute of the University of Georgia for the proficient typing services of Mrs. Joanna Parsons and Mrs. Sandra Daniels. My research was greatly facilitated by the cordial co-operation of librarians and archivists at The University of North Carolina at Chapel Hill, Wake Forest College, Duke University, North Carolina State University at Raleigh, Atlantic Christian College, the North Carolina Department of Archives and History, and the Presbyterian and Reformed Historical Center at Montreat, North Carolina. To Walter and Susan Gray of the North Carolina Wesleyan College Library, I owe a special debt of gratitude for kindnesses far too numerous to mention here.

I wish to thank the editors of the following journals for permission to use portions of articles which appeared previously, in somewhat different form, in *The North Carolina Historical Review*, *The Wesleyan Quarterly Review*, and *The Journal of Southern History*. I am also grateful to Mrs. Howard W. Odum for permission to use the Howard W. Odum papers and to William Poole, Gerald W. Johnson, Albert Keister, W. T. Couch, and Louis R. Wilson for sharing with me their recollections of the evolution controversy in North Carolina. My friend and colleague, Louis E. Bumgartner, read the entire manuscript and offered excellent counsel about questions of judgment and prose. My wife, Lu Brown Gatewood, maintained a constant interest in the project and is in large measure responsible for its completion.

W.B.G.

CONTENTS

PREACHERS
PEDAGOGUES
& POLITICIANS

1 ∽ THE NEW ENVIRONMENT

". . . it is not improbable, I believe, that the modern mind itself, the spirit of the world in the time in which they lived, had in some imponderable measure touched even the simple also, had all unconsciously entered into them to plant the tiny germ of inward doubt. Perhaps the very Klan and Fundamentalists themselves testify in the end to the beginning of the subtle decay of the old rigid standards and values, the ancient pattern; perhaps they proceeded from the distrust of themselves which I have before noted in Southerners, and represented an ultimately unsuccessful attempt to draw themselves back upon the ancient pattern to escape the feeling that, against their wills, the seeping in of change might claim them also. Perhaps they stood at last, these people, bemused before their own minds, condemned to inactivity by the sweep of current and counter-current through them."

—WILBUR J. CASH

The drowsy little town of Dayton, Tennessee, became the focus of international attention in mid-July, 1925. John Thomas Scopes, the biology teacher in the local high school, was on trial for violating the state's anti-evolution law. That Dayton was the scene of a trial involving such momentous issues was no accident; rather it was the result of a carefully laid strategy by a group of prominent Daytonians motivated by commercial and political considerations.

Consistent with such motives, the trial developed into a first-rate attraction starring two nationally-known figures: Clarence Darrow, a famous criminal lawyer and avowed agnostic who at the time symbolized the secular, urban facet of modern America; and William Jennings Bryan, the folk hero of rural America as unwilling to be crucified on the cross of evolution as on the cross of gold. The American Civil Liberties Union retained Darrow for the defense, and the World's Christian Fundamentals Association arranged for Bryan to assist the prosecution. The fierce forensics of these two star performers regarding the veracity of the Holy Scriptures and the validity of the evolutionary theory largely eclipsed the legal issues of the trial.

A bizarre conglomeration of people trekked into Dayton to witness the spectacle. The town, in fact, assumed the appearance of a crowded circus arena. Leather-lunged vendors of hot dogs and lemonade competed with booksellers hawking Bibles and biological treatises among the gaunt, godly hill people who crowded the streets. Journalists, from all parts of the world, vied for news stories. Internationally famous scientists, on hand to testify for the defense, rubbed shoulders with T. T. Martin, the frenzied, white-maned secretary of the Anti-Evolution League of America, and with Deck Carter, "the Bible Champion of the World" and only person with whom God had communed directly since Joan of Arc. The high priest of irreverence, H. L. Mencken of the *American Mercury*, mingled freely with those whom he delighted in describing as "gaping primates" and "yokels" from the buckle on the Bible Belt. Darrow's cohort, urbane New York attorney Arthur Garfield Hays, listened with utter disbelief as a group of gyrating Holy Rollers screamed: "Thank God I got no education. Glory be to God." And, of course, the monkey motif was everywhere: children dangled toy monkeys in the streets; a circus man displayed two chimpanzees; and a Coney Island sideshow offered its prize exhibit, Bozo, to the defense.[1]

1. See Ray Ginger, *Six Days or Forever? Tennessee v. John Thomas Scopes* (Boston, 1958); Kenneth K. Bailey, "The Anti-Evolution Crusade of the Nineteen-Twenties" (Ph.D. dissertation, Vanderbilt University, 1953); LeRoy Johnson, "The Evolution Controversy During the 1920's" (Ph.D. dissertation, New York University, 1954); Norman F. Furniss, *The Fundamentalist Controversy, 1918–1931* (New Haven, 1954); Frederick Lewis Allen, *Only Yesterday*

The physical setting of the trial, coupled with Darrow's merciless attack on the fundamentalists' religion, made a spectacle of orthodox theology and identified it with bigotry and ignorance. Probably the most tangible result of the trial was the death of Bryan who, ironically, had viewed the event in terms of a nationwide, spiritual revival as well as his own political rebirth. His death, however, bestowed an ambiguous legacy upon the anti-evolution crusade. On the one hand, it furnished the movement with a martyr around whom various forces rallied such as the Bible Crusaders of America. On the other hand, the removal of Bryan from the scene created a vacancy in the leadership of the cause; and though several individuals claimed the Bryan mantle, no one was ever able to co-ordinate the anti-evolution effort as he had.

Behind the farce and comedy of the Scopes Trial lay issues deeply disturbing to the generation of the 1920's. Few failed to recognize, however vaguely, the stirrings that permeated American society. Willa Cather summed up a common reaction to the changes in the postwar era when she observed that "the world broke in two in 1922 or thereabouts." The break left in its wake uprooted emotions, fears, and insecurity; the atmosphere became charged with socio-intellectual tensions and crosscurrents as the cleavage deepened between those who, finding the present frightful, clung tenaciously to a nostalgic past, and those desirous of coming to terms with life in the twentieth century. Indeed, World War I had ushered in a new age characterized by that frenzied ferment and controversy peculiar to periods in which a new order directly challenges the old. In some cases, the war itself had spawned new trends and innovations; in others, it merely brought to fruition various movements long in existence. Revolutionary developments in science, technology, and psychology altered man's views of himself and his universe as well as his way of living. Movies, radios, and automobiles had an immeasurable impact upon American culture and contributed to the revolution in manners and morals. Urbanization gathered such new momentum that during the 1920's more Americans, for the first time in the nation's history, lived in the city than in the country. This

---

(New York, 1959), pp. 138–46; Archibald T. Robertson, *That Old-Time Religion* (Cambridge, 1950), pp. 79–111; Arthur Garfield Hays, *Let Freedom Ring* (New York, 1937), pp. 26–41.

shift in population reflected the upsurge in industrialism that characterized the era and gained for it the epitaph, "second industrial revolution." [2] In some quarters all of these changes came to be associated with the advance of secularism and the breakdown of traditional codes of morality. The "age of amen" seemed to be buckling under the impact of the "age of oh yeah." [3]

But the "age of amen" did not surrender without a mighty struggle against the torrent of novel trends and changing values. "We live in a new world," observed Harry Emerson Fosdick of Union Theological Seminary in 1924, "we picture with increasing clearness the contemporary meanings of an old world, and we feel the incompatibility between them. . . ." [4] Unwilling to accept this view, however true it may have been, the defenders of the old order sought in vain to recapture a past which at a distance appeared far more preferable than the complexities and confusion of contemporary life. In fact, they recoiled from the new world envisioned by Fosdick and often sank into a mire of irrationalism and sullen individualism in their refusals to face the contemporary realities. Theirs became a philosophy of exclusion and escape that prompted a crusade to reject all ideas and concepts held responsible for producing the new world. Such an approach manifested itself in various campaigns of the 1920's. The Red Scare, with its witch hunts and deportations, excluded Communists; the Ku Klux Klan attempted to deny Negroes, Jews, and Catholics the rights of first-class citizens; patriotic groups censored textbooks to weed out all save their own special brands of patriotism; prohibitionists outlawed alcoholic beverages; Congress excluded immigrants; and the religious fundamentalists waged war against modernistic theology.

The widespread disillusionment regarding the outcome of World War I fed this postwar exclusionist temper and strengthened the crusade to eliminate those social and intellectual concepts held responsible for this military disaster. Not only had the war failed to

2. See William E. Leuchtenburg, *The Perils of Prosperity, 1914–1932* (Chicago, 1958), pp. 158–203; Allen, *Only Yesterday*, pp. 112–30; John D. Hicks, *Republican Ascendancy, 1921–1933* (New York, 1960), p. 168.

3. Gaius G. Atkins, *Religion in Our Time* (New York, 1932), pp. 250–52.

4. Harry Emerson Fosdick, *The Modern Use of the Bible* (New York, 1924).

make the world safe for democracy, it seemed to have destroyed old certainties without providing adequate substitutes. The very foundations of the traditional optimism appeared to be dissolving. One of the props of that robust optimism of the prewar years was the Darwinian theory of evolution which implied the existence of a natural order that guaranteed mankind's perpetual progress. The Wilsonian idealism of wartime only intensified the glow of such optimism. But the war, filled with brutality and inhumanity, tended to discredit the prevailing concept of progress and the evolutionary theory per se. Simultaneously, wartime propaganda spawned an anti-German hysteria which held Darwinism responsible for the "destructive rationalism," "brute philosophy of Nietzsche," modernism, higher criticism, and other phenomena responsible for Germany's "demoniac struggle for power." The postwar fruits of such hysteria, coupled with the disillusionment engendered by the collapse of wartime aims, created a climate that nurtured movements to eliminate concepts identified with the causes of the war. Moreover, the defeat of the war aims fostered a vague sense of guilt, particularly among those steeped in the idea of original sin and taught to regard defeats as divine retribution. For them, the signs of the times were clear: the old time religion must be restored and modernism dethroned.[5]

This desperate plunge backward took the form of an offensive, often fanatical in intensity, to fortify the orthodox, traditional order of rural, small town America against the encroachments of the emerging urban-industrial society. The city was anathema to the reactionary for whom it represented immigrants, radicalism, modernistic theology, saloons, and other elements considered alien to the old America. The secular, humanistic manifestations of urban life seemed to threaten the supremacy of the "simple virtues" and old-time religion of the agrarian past; thus, spokesmen for the old order railed against New York City as a sin-ridden "Modern Babylon" and the University of Chicago as "the slaughterhouse of faith." The gulf between rural and urban America which reached a critical stage in the 1920's helped to explain why Arkansas prohibited the teaching of

5. Bailey, "The Anti-Evolution Crusade," pp. 24–31; Ginger, *Six Days or Forever?* pp. 13–16; Furniss, *The Fundamentalist Controversy*, pp. 23–26.

Darwinian evolution by popular vote, while Delaware permitted a similar measure to die in its legislative committee of fish, game, and oysters.[6]

The origin of the warfare between fundamentalism and modernism, which reached a belated climax during the 1920's, lay deep in the history of Christian thought. Late in the nineteenth century the ferment generated by the writings of Charles Darwin accentuated the cleavage: the fundamentalists rejected Darwinian evolution as incompatible with the essentials of divine revelation, while modernists accepted the theory and added it to the intellectual apparatus of the modern Christian. The steady advance of modernism before World War I induced many to consider evolution among the settled issues in theological circles. And even those shocked at the renewal of the late nineteenth-century debate after the war recognized that evolution was but one ingredient, albeit an important one, in the modernist-fundamentalist agitation of the 1920's. It served as a symbol of the gulf between the two theological schools of thought, between the old-time religion and the old-time religion adapted to the demands of modern America.[7]

Protagonists in the evolution controversy held markedly different world views and diverged widely in their interpretations of science, academic freedom and scholarship, and scriptural revelation, inspiration, and inerrancy. While modernists embraced the new scientific discoveries and sought to demonstrate the compatibility between religion and science, fundamentalists viewed the same phenomenon with suspicion and often found the implications emerging from studies in geology, astronomy, and behaviorist psychology even more

6. Leuchtenburg, *The Perils of Prosperity*, pp. 217–21; Maynard Shipley, *The War on Modern Science: A Short History of the Fundamentalist Attacks on Evolution and Modernism* (New York, 1927), pp. 296–97; Reinhold Niebuhr, *Does Civilization Need Religion?* (New York, 1928), pp. 29–88; Maynard Shipley, "The Forward March of the Anti-Evolutionists," *Current History*, XXIX (January, 1924), 578–82.

7. See William Hordern, *A Layman's Guide to Protestant Theology* (New York, 1957), pp. 35–55; John Dillenberger, *Protestant Thought and Natural Science* (New York, 1960), pp. 217–51; John C. Greene, *Darwin and the Modern World View* (Baton Rouge, 1961); Atkins, *Religion in Our Time*, pp. 219–52; Richard Hofstadter, *Anti-Intellectualism in American Life* (New York, 1963), pp. 123–29.

disturbing than those in biology. For example, orthodoxy strongly resisted the encroachment of the natural upon the supernatural that resulted from the psychologists' probings into the process of religious conversion and hypnotic devices of evangelists. Their hostility to a theology that brooked any such encroachments was equaled only by the presumption of those whose faith in science transformed it into a "false messiah," "folk lore in another guise," or an established creed as unrelenting as ecclesiastical dogma.[8] Frequently the modernist-fundamentalist dispute of the 1920's became a conflict "between dogmatic and intolerant religionists and scientists on the one hand, and tolerant religionists and scientists on the other." That the evolution hypothesis became the pivot of the controversy indicates that it was concrete enough and familiar enough to focus the issue between the old and new orders; it required less abstract thought than some of the more recent scientific propositions that appeared no less dangerous to the fundamentalists.[9]

A proper perspective on the evolution controversy of necessity requires a definition of the two major theological schools at the opening of the 1920's. One of these, the fundamentalists, seems to validate Paul Tillich's observation that whenever a movement is under attack, it withdraws into what it considers an impenetrable fortress. Fundamentalism narrowed itself to the famous Five Points: (1) divinely inspired Scriptures which were inerrant "in the original writing"; (2) Christ's Virgin Birth and deity; (3) His substitutionary atonement; (4) His Resurrection; (5) and His "personal, premillennial and imminent second coming." Each of these points possessed a special meaning often misunderstood outside, and even inside, the fundamentalist ranks.[10] This misunderstanding resulted largely from oversimplification and downright distortion of fundamentalist theology particularly at the hands of untutored, sometimes irrational, evangelists who saddled the whole movement with the reputation of

8. C. E. Ayres, *Science: The False Messiah* (Indianapolis, 1927), p. 27. In a similar vein, Reinhold Niebuhr was as critical of the modernists as he was of the fundamentalists. He maintained that the optimism and sentimentality of the modernists threatened to sap religion of its vitality. See his *Does Civilization Need Religion?* pp. 2–17.

9. Johnson, "The Evolution Controversy During the 1920's," pp. 22–23.

10. William B. Riley, "The Faith of Fundamentalists," *Current History*, XXVI (June, 1927), 434–40; William Jennings Bryan, "The Fundamentals," *The Forum*, LXX (July, 1923), 1665–80.

being anti-intellectual. The views of more sophisticated fundamentalists such as J. Gresham Machen of Princeton seldom penetrated the din engendered by fundamentalist zealots who, once they launched their counterattack, narrowed their doctrinal position even further, pinpointed Darwinism as the greatest single menace to Christianity and American society, and offered the choice between God or gorilla as the ultimate ancestor of humanity.[11]

The fundamentalists looked upon evolution as a threat to practically all crucial tenets of their theology. To accept the theory, they argued, was to deny "man's moral responsibility," the "Gospel remedy of sin," and all supernatural elements in Christianity. Equally disturbing to them was the Darwinian principle of laws which worked through chance variation, apparently independent of the Creator. The product, so it seemed, was not man, but man as an animal—a concept that fundamentalists found difficult to reconcile with their idea of a creature in God's own image.[12] Obviously a major reason why evolution evoked such reaction in fundamentalist quarters was its apparent attack on their view of revelation, i.e., how God makes Himself known to man. The fundamentalist emphasized a transcendent God who entered the world in the form of miracles and special acts of revelation such as those recorded in the verbally inspired Bible. To doubt any biblical account of such extraordinary events was, for the fundamentalist, the first step toward a denial of God and the divinity of Jesus, which meant the loss of salvation and the collapse of ethics.[13]

Theological opposition to such views came from those who espoused liberalism and modernism, terms equally difficult to define and disassociate. In general the modernist attempted to restate the substance of Christianity in terms compatible with modern knowledge and refused to accept religious belief on authority alone. In contrast to the fundamentalist, he emphasized the immanence of God—"A God present in all that happens and is." Described as

11. Hordern, *A Layman's Guide to Protestant Theology*, pp. 58–63; see also J. Gresham Machen, *Christianity and Liberalism* (Grand Rapids, n.d.).

12. John W. Porter, *Evolution—A Menace* (Nashville, 1922), pp. 26–89; J. E. Conant, *The Church, The Schools, and Evolution* (Chicago, 1922), pp. 23–44.

13. Dillenberger, *Protestant Thought and Natural Science*, p. 240.

"God's way of doing things," evolution was therefore a vindication of the modernist view of God's immanence. Amid their divergent ideas about revelation, modernists generally agreed that man was *not* absolutely dependent upon special acts of revelation and that even revelation must be tested by reason and experience. Modernism, of course, refused to rely upon the infallibility of the Scriptures solely; it embraced studies in higher criticism which indicated an evolutionary revelation of God reaching its fulfillment in Jesus. To be sure, modernism had its extremists whose thinly-veiled humanism confirmed the worst fears of the fundamentalists.[14]

Undoubtedly the most comprehensive statement of modernism in the 1920's was penned by one of its leading exponents, Shailer Mathews, Dean of the Divinity School of the University of Chicago. Modernism, he said, possessed no confession and "its theological affirmations are the formulation of the results of investigation both of human needs and the Christian religion." According to him, the dogmatists started with doctrines and the modernists with the religion that gave rise to the doctrines; the dogmatists relied on conformity through group authority, and the modernists upon inductive method and action in accord with group loyalty. Mathews defined modernism as

> the use of scientific, historical, social method in understanding and applying evangelical Christianity to the needs of living persons. . . . Its interests are not those of theological controversy or appeal to authority. They do not involve the rejection of the supernatural when rightly defined. Modernists believe that they can discover ideals and directions needed for Christian living by the application of critical and historical method to the study of the Bible; that they can discover by similar methods the permanent attitudes and convictions of Christians constituting a continuing and developing group; and that these permanent elements will help inspire the intelligent and sympathetic organization of life under modern conditions. Modernists are thus evangelic Christians who use modern methods to meet modern needs.[15]

14. Hordern, *A Layman's Guide to Protestant Theology*, pp. 77–177; John Dillenberger and Claude Welch, *Protestant Christianity Interpreted Through Its Development* (New York, 1954), pp. 200–6.
15. Shailer Mathews, *The Faith of Modernism* (New York, 1924), p. 36.

Furthermore, according to Mathews, the modernist accepted the general principle of evolution and made it a part of his intellectual apparatus, "not because he has a theology to be supported but because he accepts modern science." [16]

The modernist embrace of evolution found its most eloquent defense in the powerful sermons of Harry Emerson Fosdick of Union Theological Seminary. He contended that as long as God was the creative power, it made no difference whether man arrived by sudden fiat or gradual process. Fosdick also insisted that the fundamentalists' claim that evolution depreciated the dignity of man by linking him with lower animals was absurd in view of their own belief that man came from dust. Although he shared their fear of the rise of a spiritually sterile generation fed only by materialistic science, he believed that the crux of the problem was whether man would "think of creative reality in spiritual or physical terms," and that any specific scientific theory such as Darwinism was practically irrelevant to the main issue. For him, the fundamentalists' storm over evolution was merely "a red herring across the real trail." [17] The fundamentalists, in their turn, castigated Fosdick and Mathews as city traders in "bootleg theology": the one described as a "renegade Baptist" in Modern Babylon, and the other as the presiding officer of the "slaughterhouse of faith." [18]

Each faction in the controversy possessed organizations that promoted its particular ideas. The spotlight in the twenties focused upon those groups organized in the immediate postwar period which represented the fundamentalist drive to dethrone religious liberalism. In 1919, for example, over sixty-five hundred fundamentalists gathered in Philadelphia for the first annual meeting of the World's Christian Fundamentals Association. Its credo, published under the title of *God Hath Spoken,* was in effect a militant assault upon modernism. Under the direction of a Baptist triumvirate composed of William B. Riley of Minneapolis, John Roach Straton of New

16. *Ibid*., pp. 22–36.

17. See Fosdick, *The Modern Use of the Bible,* pp. 44, 51; Harry Emerson Fosdick, "Evolution and Religion," *The Ladies' Home Journal* (September, 1925), 12, 180, 183, 185; Gail Kennedy, ed., *Evolution and Religion: The Conflict Between Science and Theology in Modern America* (Boston, 1957), p. 33.

18. Shipley, *The War on Modern Science,* p. 107.

York, and Jasper C. Massee of Boston, the Association launched a vigorous campaign to eradicate modernism through a nationwide "religious education program." The plan was to disseminate fundamentalist theology through the distribution of literature, public debates between modernists and fundamentalists, and "Bible Conferences" conducted throughout the United States. By 1922 the Association shifted its strategy and thereafter concentrated almost solely upon the banishment of Darwinian evolution from all classrooms. Numerous other organizations with similar aims sprang up as the anti-evolution crusade gained momentum. The movement found a national leader in William Jennings Bryan.[19]

Modernist theologians, on the other hand, had little need for new organizations with which to meet the fundamentalist challenge, since by 1920 they controlled many of the national religious agencies. One of the most notable societies formed in response to the anti-evolution movement was the Science League of America, which was primarily a body of scientists rather than of theologians. But a view of the conflict solely from the vantage point of national organizations scarcely conveys the full intensity of feelings elicited by the struggle. The controversy often raged most ferociously on the local level among groups little interested in the national organizations.[20]

Few localities felt the crosscurrents and disturbances of the twenties more acutely than North Carolina which, in the phraseology of the times, was in the midst of a "bloodless revolution," a "new day," or a "new regime." The process of closing the gap between the nineteenth and twentieth centuries left many North Carolinians "very much afraid" and haunted by feelings of insecurity, while others optimistically plunged into the task of bringing the state in step with the times. The activities of those reluctant to accept changes often eclipsed the progressive accomplishments of enduring significance. Collisions between the two forces filled the air with controversy, often bitter and sometimes farcical; but in the final

19. Riley, "Faith of the Fundamentalists," pp. 434–36; Stewart G. Cole, *The History of Fundamentalism* (New York, 1931), pp. 298–317.

20. Johnson, "The Evolution Controversy During the 1920's," p. 39; Shipley, *The War on Modern Science*, pp. 371–73; Furniss, *The Fundamentalist Controversy*, p. 32.

analysis the state's "hard-headed sober, canny people," developed a "new sort of vision" under the aegis of their traditional moderation.[21]

A relatively small group of journalists, academicians, politicians, and clergymen spearheaded movements to inject a new spirit into the life of the state. Journalists in particular sought to provide "light for groping minds"; their persistent cry was for a bold and realistic assault on contemporary problems instead of a complacently romantic approach which merely postponed and complicated ultimate solutions. Representing the avant garde in journalism were Gerald W. Johnson, a young Greensboro newspaperman and state university professor; Nell Battle Lewis, a Raleigh newspaperwoman; and William O. Saunders, petulant editor of the Elizabeth City *Independent*. Reminiscent of the muckrakers, their crusade was an attack on the shams, hypocrisies, and parochialism that permeated the North Carolina landscape. Every aspect of society was subjected to their searching analyses; their plain talk, probings, and questions, even in the realms hitherto considered sacrosanct, seemed disturbingly irreverent. Many were shocked by articles bearing such titles as "North Carolina: Militant Mediocrity" and "A Tilt with Southern Windmills." Even more disturbing was the fact that these were works by native writers who claimed that their patriotism impelled them to face the defects as well as the achievements of their patria. Gradually such "patriotic" efforts produced an awareness that "all was not right in the Old North State." [22]

"Incidentally," the weekly column in the *News and Observer* by Nell Battle Lewis, provided a kind of running critique of the changing scene in North Carolina during the 1920's. Allowed virtually complete freedom by editor Josephus Daniels, Miss Lewis consistently produced pungent, pithy analyses of topics ranging from

21. E. C. Brooks, "Development of Social Harmony." Address, June, 1927 (E. C. Brooks Papers, Duke University Library); Gerald W. Johnson, "North Carolina in a New Phase," *Current History*, XXVII (March, 1928), 843–48.

22. See Keith Saunders, *The Independent Man* (Washington, 1962); Gerald W. Johnson, "A Tilt with Southern Windmills," *The Virginia Quarterly Review*, I (1925), 184–92; Robert W. Winston, "North Carolina: A Militant Mediocrity," *The Nation*, CXVI (February 12, 1923), 209–12; Scrapbooks, Nell Battle Lewis Papers, State Department of Archives and History, Raleigh, N.C.; *News and Observer* (Raleigh), November 22, 1922; George B. Tindall, "The Benighted South: Origins of a Modern Image," *The Virginia Quarterly Review*, XL (Spring, 1964), 281–94.

psychoanalysis and poetry to farm tenancy and women's rights. Perhaps her most persistent concern was "the deplorable lack of unprejudiced criticism in this state" and "that type of patriotism which stubbornly shuts its eyes to the patent defects of the patria." For her, the indignation that greeted her criticisms of the prevailing order was but further evidence of the attitude of "what is, is right," a philosophy shouted in "loud refrain" by the boosters and Babbitts.[23] She summed up her advice to the "younger generation" in a little piece of verse entitled, "Tainted Tar Heels":

I thank the Lord that you were never able
To swallow down the patriotic pap,
But for the current local blah and fable
Cared something less, to tote, than a rap;
It is a comfort to me, recollection
That ballyhoos quite naturally absurd
About the glories of your native section
Moved you to thumb your nose at the herd;

I'm proud you wouldn't let them do your thinking;
The noisy boys who set the styles in thought
That, faced by facts which all the rest were blinking,
You held opinions which you hadn't ought
I sing the small perverse minority
That died unsung, unpopular,—and free.[24]

Her answer to the state's "bloated self-glorification" over its economic progress was to expose the "artistic barrenness" and "intellectual inertia" of Tar Heelia. "Outrageous honesty" tinged with occasional mockery characterized her journalistic efforts to arouse North Carolinians to view themselves and their state with a critical intelligence.[25]

The institutions of higher learning were often in the vanguard of movements to rebuild the ancient commonwealth. This was particularly true during the postwar decade; in fact, a majority of the

23. *News and Observer*, July 16, October 1, 1922, November 4, 1923, September 27, 1925.
24. *Ibid.*, June 27, 1926.
25. *Ibid.*, November 26, 1922, January 3, 1926.

journalistic avant garde as well as their counterparts in the pulpits and political arena were products of four colleges in particular. Two of these were sponsored by the Baptists and Methodists respectively, the state's largest denominations. Wake Forest College, the Baptists' institution, flourished under the brilliant direction of William Louis Poteat, a University of Berlin-educated scientist and an outstanding Christian layman whose influence touched practically every Baptist pulpit in the state. The stamp of enlightenment which Poteat's Wake Forest left upon the clergymen who passed through its portals goes far toward explaining why North Carolina Baptists avoided the narrowminded sectarianism that erupted within their denomination elsewhere in the South.[26] Like Wake Forest, Methodist-related Trinity College in Durham took on a new significance in the 1920's when it underwent a spectacular transformation with the aid of the Duke fortune. The metamorphosis of this small institution into Duke University occurred under the guidance of a Shakespearean scholar, William Preston Few, whose impact among Methodist circles had salutary effects comparable to those of Poteat among Baptists.[27] Sharing the academic leadership with the denominational colleges were two state institutions. One of these, North Carolina State College of Agriculture and Engineering, entered upon a new era in 1923 when Eugene C. Brooks assumed the presidency. Within a few years what had been little more than a trade school developed into a technological school of recognized standing where the liberal arts and "elements of culture" undergirded the whole technical curriculum. Among the notable innovations was the Bureau of Social Research directed by Professor Carl Taylor, a liberal sociologist with a knack for irritating reactionaries.[28]

Perhaps the institution most intimately involved in generating

26. The history of William Louis Poteat's administration is covered in the third volume of George W. Paschal, *History of Wake Forest College* (Wake Forest, 1943); see also Robert C. Lawrence, *Here In Carolina* (Lumberton, 1939), pp. 15–19; Gerald W. Johnson, "Billy with the Red Necktie," *The Virginia Quarterly Review*, XXX (Autumn, 1943), 551–61.

27. For accounts of William Preston Few's role in the transformation of Trinity College into Duke University, see Robert H. Woody, ed., *The Papers and Addresses of William Preston Few: Late President of Duke University* (Durham, 1951), pp. 82–141; Earl W. Porter, *Trinity and Duke, 1892–1924: Foundations of Duke University* (Durham, 1964), Chapters VI and VII.

28. See Willard B. Gatewood, Jr., *Eugene Clyde Brooks: Educator and Public Servant* (Durham, 1960), pp. 223–53.

progressive winds during the 1920's was the University of North Carolina in Chapel Hill where the eagerness to hasten the pace of the "New Day" surpassed that of all other academic centers. Entering upon its golden era in the postwar decade, the old university stood in the midst of the spasms that rocked the state in the twenties.[29] At his inauguration as president in 1920, Harry W. Chase, a Massachusetts-born psychologist, clearly indicated in an address entitled "The State University and the New South" his intention to place the University at the head of a movement to hammer out a new civilization "which would fuse in one great creative synthesis the best in both the old and the new." With freedom as its goal, this new civilization would seek to liberate the mind and spirit, "to set men really free, not from responsibility, but through it." To this ideal Chase dedicated the University, and his ten year tenure adequately demonstrated that his inaugural statement was no idle promise of a new college president.[30]

Under his guidance, the University attracted a remarkably able corps of professors, who, firmly committed to his ideal, placed Chapel Hill in the forefront of North Carolina progressivism. Probably no member of the faculty contributed more to the new vision of the postwar period than Howard W. Odum, an owlish-looking sociologist whose various activities placed him squarely in the midst of the treacherous mire of social problems involving race relations, public welfare, and industrialism. Complementing Odum's work and no less disturbing to the *status quo* was that of Professor E. C. Branson in rural social-economics. In the School of Education, Edgar W. Knight not only produced numerous scholarly studies and raised the qualifications of hundreds of teachers who came under his influence but also waged a relentless war against apathy toward public schools. His realistic descriptions of the educational backwardness of the state elicited loud protests among those still basking in the glow of the educational revival under Governor Charles B. Aycock at the turn of the twentieth century. Knight, Odum, and Branson were joined by a score or more of their colleagues in the

29. See Louis R. Wilson, *The University of North Carolina, 1900–1930: The Making of a Modern University* (Chapel Hill, 1957), Chapters XXV–XLI.

30. *Ibid.*, p. 315; see also Louis R. Wilson, *Harry Woodburn Chase* (Chapel Hill, 1960), pp. 2–21; Gerald W. Johnson, "Chase of North Carolina," *The American Mercury*, XVII (July, 1930), 183–90.

various academic areas in launching the "new civilization." Those in the arts and humanities transformed Chapel Hill into a sort of cultural oasis, while graduates of the professional schools carried the spirit of their mentors with them into positions of influence throughout the state.[31] Professor Archibald Henderson, mathematician and Shaw scholar, summed up that spirit when he remarked: "In justice to ourselves, let us scrap these stock excuses, these exculpatory rationalizations . . . and face the cold, relentless truth." [32]

In 1924 Professor W. C. Jackson of the North Carolina College for Women presented a perceptive analysis of the state's contemporary cultural life in his presidential address to the State Literary and Historical Association. Convinced that H. L. Mencken's arraignment of the South for its cultural sterility had at times been overstated, Jackson nonetheless was unwilling to dismiss the charges by the Baltimore sage as the rantings of a prejudiced observer. Instead he used Mencken's critique as a standard for assessing North Carolina's success in establishing "the corollaries of a cultured democracy"—universal education, material prosperity, a democratic social order, and freedom. He was especially disturbed by the lack of progress in achieving that freedom necessary for cultural activity. To determine "how free we are," Jackson posed several questions:

> How long can a minister hold his charge in North Carolina or remain in good standing in his church if he speaks his mind in disagreement with orthodoxy or with the prevalent social and economic order? How long can a teacher hold his professorial chair if he openly advocates an economic system or political program or a scientific theory which is at variance with current thought? How long can an editor survive whose newspaper columns are not filled with orthodox patriotism, orthodox religion, and orthodox economics? How long can the laborer stay by his machine who openly advocates an economic idea at variance with that of his employer? How will the political leader in North Carolina, who presumes to champion an economic or

31. Wilson, *University of North Carolina*, pp. 462–68; Reed Kitchin, "The Story of the North Carolina Club," *North Carolina Club Year Book, 1924–1925;* Jonathan Daniels, *Tar Heels: A Portrait of North Carolina* (New York, 1941), pp. 264–81; George B. Tindall, "The Significance of Howard W. Odum to Southern History," *The Journal of Southern History*, XXIV (August, 1958), 285–307.

32. *News and Observer*, July 8, 1923.

social or political program that is unorthodox, escape without being branded as socialistic, red, bolshevistic? These questions are hard to answer, for these things have been so seldom tried in North Carolina.[33]

Jackson reminded his audience that any culture worthy of the name required that men be free from "ignorance or tradition or bigotry or fear."

While the stirrings in the academic cloister and press reached "feverishly energetic" proportions, the socio-economic developments that began to blossom in the twenties were producing profound effects upon traditional modes of behavior and thought. Industry successfully established itself in the agricultural milieu of North Carolina. By 1920, in fact, the total value of manufactures, principally in tobacco, textiles, and furniture, had reached almost one billion dollars annually. The expansion of hydroelectric projects furnished power for increasing numbers of factories and mills throughout the decade. The advance of industrialization was of course accompanied by major shifts in population; factory towns and villages, especially in the Piedmont region, attracted people from the farms. Although North Carolina possessed no really large metropolitan centers and virtually no foreign-born population, its "new phase" posed problems alien to its rural past as the decade witnessed the largest numerical growth in urban dwellers of any census period in its history. Despite the widespread faith in industrial progress, the encroachment of the bustling factory town upon the farmers' domain brought a feeling of uncertainty to a people accustomed to holding urbanism responsible for a vast assortment of sins. What had once been a distant menace now existed in their midst, and when census statistics failed to impress the populace with the changes in the socio-economic scene, the rise of organized labor and the outbreak of strikes during the 1920's succeeded.[34]

Among the most significant changes that occurred in North

33. W. C. Jackson, "Culture and the New Era in North Carolina," *The North Carolina Historical Review*, II (January, 1925), 13.

34. Gerald W. Johnson, "North Carolina in a New Phase," *Current History*, XXVII (March, 1928), 843–48; Samuel H. Hobbs, Jr., *North Carolina: Economic and Social* (Chapel Hill, 1930), pp. 50–67, 132–50; William H. Richardson, "North Carolina's Recent Progress," *Review of Reviews*, LXVIII (December, 1923), 621–31; Hugh T. Lefler and A. R. Newsome, *North Carolina: The History of a Southern State* (Chapel Hill, 1963), p. 551.

Carolina during the postwar decade was a veritable revolution in public education. The outstanding accomplishments included implementation of the six months' school term, the establishment of a uniform teacher certification plan and salary schedule, a rapid expansion in school plant facilities, and a sweeping change in the method of financing public schools. School consolidation radically reduced the number of one-teacher schools. "Moonlight schools" tackled the problem of adult illiteracy. Despite its achievements, however, North Carolina fell far below national standards. The state continued to be plagued by an appallingly high rate of illiteracy. It possessed woefully inadequate library facilities and numerous one-room school houses. Certainly, too, one of the state's most acute needs in the postwar era was for qualified teachers. Although State Superintendent Eugene C. Brooks initiated a crash program in teacher training in 1919, the number of teachers who lacked the necessary academic qualifications for the advanced certificates remained distressingly low. Hundreds of teachers did not even possess the equivalent of a standard high school education during the 1920's.[35]

Nevertheless, most North Carolinians took great pride in their progress and in their recently acquired reputation as the "Wisconsin of the South." Yet, one observer maintained that "the typical Tar Heel," for all his progress, was still one who "chews tobacco, belongs to an evangelical religious sect, thinks William Jennings Bryan is inspired, considers the largest hosiery mill in the world a sign of Progress, admires Andrew Volstead and drinks hard corn, claims to 'know niggers,' and considers New York provincial." [36] This description, despite its exaggeration and cynicism, does convey some notion of the complex reactions of a basically rural, conservative people caught in the throes of social and economic changes. For many, progress meant little more than the "world's largest hosiery mill" and progressivism little more than the application of a few business principles to government. Moreover, their pride in the state's new reputation, stroked by chambers of commerce and other "boosters,"

35. Gatewood, *Eugene Clyde Brooks*, pp. 113–49; Hobbs, *North Carolina*, pp. 252–65; Edgar W. Knight, "The Contributions of the University to Public Education," *The Chronicles of the Sesquicentennial*, ed. Louis R. Wilson (Chapel Hill, 1947), pp. 174–75.

36. *News and Observer*, November 4, 1926.

tended to spawn a "childish hypersensitiveness" resentful of any suggestion of backwardness in any area. On occasion it acted as a general deterrent to deeds likely to "make the state ridiculous in the eyes of the civilized world." The popular pride in the state's achievements in education, roads, and business expansion, therefore, contributed indirectly to the advancement of social justice during the 1920's. A pioneer in this field, the Conference for Social Service, helped to create a climate conducive to the success of penal reforms, child welfare crusades, and other social justice movements. The activities of the State Inter-Racial Commission, the Division of Negro Education which was established in the Department of Public Instruction in 1921, and several other bodies were designed to allay racial friction. Their efforts enabled North Carolina to avoid the outbreak of racial violence that characterized the postwar scene and to eliminate the cruder manifestations of racial prejudice.[37]

Elements of the old order blended with newer trends to produce "business progressivism," a term applied to the dominant tone of North Carolina politics in the 1920's by Professor George B. Tindall.[38] This particular brand of progressivism which emphasized efficiency and public service in government found eloquent expression in the administrations of Thomas W. Bickett, Cameron Morrison, and Angus W. McLean, the state's three governors during the decade. Their names became linked with "good roads" and significant reforms in taxation, county government, and fiscal management in an era when the South was attracting attention as the home of the Ku Klux Klan and the anti-evolution crusades.[39] The

37. See Gatewood, *Eugene Clyde Brooks*, pp. 161–71; Paul Benjamin, "The North Carolina Plan," *The Survey*, XLVII (September, 15, 1922), 705–7; William H. Richardson, "No More Lynchings: How North Carolina Has Solved the Problem," *American Review of Reviews*, LXIX (April, 1924), 401–4; C. Chilton Pearson, "Race Relations in North Carolina: A Field Study of Moderate Opinion," *The South Atlantic Quarterly*, XXIII (January, 1924), 1–9; "North Carolina's Negro Program," *The American Schoolmaster*, XV (May 15, 1922), 192–93.

38. See George B. Tindall, "Business Progressivism: Southern Politics in the Twenties," *The South Atlantic Quarterly*, LXII (Winter, 1963), 92–106.

39. The programs of Governors Bickett, Morrison, and McLean are sketched in Robert B. House, ed., *Public Letters and Papers of Thomas Walter Bickett, Governor of North Carolina, 1911–1921* (Raleigh, 1923); D. L. Corbitt, ed., *Public Papers and Letters of Cameron Morrison, Governor of North Carolina, 1921–1925* (Raleigh, 1927); D. L. Corbitt, ed., *Public Papers and Letters of Angus Wilton McLean, Governor of North Carolina, 1925–1929* (Raleigh,

fact that Cameron Morrison was known, on the one hand, as a champion of improvements in highways, schools, and ports, and, on the other, as a militant anti-evolutionist indicates more than the work of a facile politician. His seemingly paradoxical actions reveal something about the nature and limitations of "business progressivism." Actually it was a kind of step-child of the earlier Progressive Movement, whose complexion bore the marks of the times and the region. The North Carolina progressive of the 1920's embraced a new business mentality, while at the same time he held fast to a morality and theology characteristic of a rural culture steeped in evangelical Protestantism. By its very nature "business progressivism" was an ambivalent philosophy that fostered what appeared to be an endless round of anachronisms. For example, when the progressive faith in the efficacy of democracy was utilized to cleanse the moral and religious order, the result was a rash of morality legislation and an inclination to equate religious truth with the majority vote. Viewed from this standpoint, the anti-evolution bills and the Scopes Trial represented new levels of democratic achievement. The peculiar cast of the socio-religious foundations of "business progressivism" imposed limitations upon its ideological spaciousness and helped to promote its anachronistic manifestations. Therefore, appearing alongside the advocates of social and economic changes were those highly vocal elements in the state who tenaciously defended the old order against the intrusion of undesirable modern innovations. Perhaps these forces represented what some have described as a degradation of the progressive ideals.[40] At any rate, their crusades of a moral and religious nature enlisted widespread support among those closely identified with "business progressivism."

Among the most notable organizations bent upon holding back the twentieth century was the Ku Klux Klan, whose Imperial Wizard William J. Simmons made a whirlwind tour of the state in 1921. In an address at the Baptist Tabernacle in Raleigh before a crowd of two thousand, Simmons outlined the principles and strategy of the Klan and promised to wipe "every evil-doer from the face of the

1931); Mary E. Underwood, "Angus Wilton McLean, Governor of North Carolina, 1925–1929," (Ph.D. dissertation, University of North Carolina, 1962).

40. Richard Hofstadter, *The Age of Reform: From Bryan to F.D.R.* (New York, 1955), pp. 280–300.

earth" by moral suasion if possible or by use of "real men" if necessary. The Klan flourished in North Carolina for a time under the leadership of Superior Court Judge Henry Grady, but its influence in statewide political circles apparently was not very great until the presidential campaign of 1928.[41] For the most part, the Klan's role in politics was restricted to a few localities where municipal officials catered to its whims. From the very beginning, the press as well as educators, clergymen, politicians, and civic leaders heaped scorn upon the organization as "stalking cowardice that operates under the cover of darkness behind a craven's mask." In 1927, when the legislature almost passed an "unmasking" bill, Judge Grady resigned as Grand Dragon of North Carolina, ostensibly because of a squabble with Hiram W. Evans, the new Imperial Wizard. But just as the Klan appeared to be near collapse, the election of 1928 with its issues of prohibition and Catholicism stimulated its temporary revival in North Carolina.[42]

The Ku Klux Klan was by no means the only agency to consider itself the protector of the old order and custodian of public morals. Various groups seized upon censorship as a favorite device for shutting out undesirable or alien ideas held responsible for the contemporary ferment. The United Daughters of the Confederacy kept a constant vigil over schools and textbooks to insure that they imparted "*whole-souled* sympathy for our men who wore the grey." Muzzey's *American History*, a state-adopted textbook, bore the brunt of their ire and was ultimately removed from some schools by local chapters of the UDC.[43] The American Legion, another organization busily engaged in patriotic activities, pursued similar tactics. Gripped by the fears and insecurity spawned by the postwar Red Scare, the

41. *News and Observer*, January 3, 23, February 19, July 3, 1921, January 23, 1924; *Charlotte Observer*, January 23, 1924; *Gastonia Gazette*, January 21, April 24, 1924.

42. *Charity and Children*, XXXV (February 10, 1921), 5; *North Carolina Christian Advocate*, LXVIII (February 15, 1923), 3, 5; *Methodist Protestant Herald*, XXVII (August 11, 1921), 1; *News and Observer*, July 27, 1924; Arnold Rice, *The Ku Klux Klan in American Politics* (Washington, 1962), pp. 34–35, 48, 87; Underwood, "Angus Wilton McLean, Governor of North Carolina, 1925–1929," p. 230.

43. *Minutes of the Twenty-Seventh Annual Convention of the United Daughters of the Confederacy, Greensboro, N.C., October 4–6, 1923*, p. 43; *Charity and Children*, XXXVI (January 5, 1922), 4; *News and Observer*, November 27, 1921.

North Carolina Legionnaires tended to identify virtually any new stirring in the state with an ideology alien to the American Way. Their remedy was twofold: exclude books, teachers, and other conveyers of ideas suspected of disturbing the *status quo;* and fasten the patriotic credo of the Legion upon the new generation in order that it might be spared the pitfalls of the present. The Legion's crusade bore fruit in 1923 when the North Carolina legislature passed a law requiring all high schools to offer instruction in Americanism. State Superintendent of Public Instruction Eugene C. Brooks exerted every effort to make the course a worthwhile study of American institutions and political theory rather than a platform from which a private fraternal society might expound its particular creed. Brooks himself wrote a little volume that was later adopted by the State Board of Education as a textbook for the course.[44]

Once the patriotism of school children was insured by statute, the Legion focused its attention upon outside forces which posed a threat to North Carolina. It branded such organizations as the Federal Council of Churches of Christ and the National Parent-Teacher Association as unpatriotic, pacifist bodies with "Communist leanings" and mapped out a plan for cancelling speaking engagements of outsiders whose views the Legion considered undesirable. General Albert J. Bowley, the commandant of Fort Bragg, reinforced the fears of the Legion by persistently warning that North Carolina was in imminent danger of a Soviet-inspired revolution. The state's "social welfare legislation" was, in his opinion, the forerunner of complete domination by the Soviets. More sensational, however, was his linking of the Red Scare and the Negro problem. "These Soviet emissaries," Bowley declared in 1924, "have subsidized some of the yellow negroes who have more sense than the others, and have brought about the movement north in preparation for a black revolution." North Carolinians were assured that the Red menace was all the more dangerous because of its black implications.[45]

On many issues the views of the Daughters of the American

44. Gatewood, *Eugene Clyde Brooks*, pp. 249–50.

45. *News and Observer*, November 28, 1926; O. G. Villard, "What the Blue Menace Means," *Harper's*, CLVII (October, 1928), 535; for the position of the reactionary *Textile Bulletin*, see Tindall, "The Significance of Howard W. Odum to Southern History," p. 290.

Revolution coincided with those of the Legionnaires, and occasionally the two organizations worked in concert to eliminate contaminating influences. The Daughters endorsed movements to censor school books and launched campaigns to alert North Carolinians to the dangers in their midst. In 1926 the State Regent, Mrs. Edwin C. Gregory, sounded the keynote of the crusade when she publicly stated: "North Carolina today is the target of the most desperate efforts of the Soviet propagandists seeking the overthrow of American government and planning a Red Russian invasion of the South." Following this clarion call, the Daughters initiated a "blacklisting" campaign against speakers whom they considered "unsafe" and resolved to support efforts aimed at requiring all public school teachers in the state to confirm their loyalty to the principle of private ownership of property.[46]

The heresy-hunting of those disturbed by certain manifestations of the "new day" was equalled only by their faith in the efficacy of legislation to regulate the morals and mind of the public. During the 1920's the state legislature was forced to consider numerous "morality" bills, including anti-flirtation and anti-petting measures. In 1927 Representative Oscar Haywood, a Baptist evangelist turned Ku Klux Klan Lecturer, sponsored a bill "to prohibit sexual immorality," which was defeated only after a lengthy debate in the House. A statute to censor movies was also a durable topic of discussion throughout the decade. Although the legislature defeated such a measure in 1921, various civic and religious organizations continued to champion its enactment.[47] But prohibition provided the classic example of the popular faith in the efficacy of legislation. Moreover, it was the "reform" that united widely divergent forces in a common cause. For those preoccupied with preserving moral purity, it became a virtual obsession. It was their singular achievement on the national level which stood as an example of what they might conceivably

46. *Goldsboro News*, September 30, 1926; *News and Observer*, October 1, 3, 7, 8, 1926; Villard, "What the Blue Menace Means," p. 533.

47. *News and Observer*, March 2, 1921, February 26, 1925; *Journal of the House of Representatives of the General Assembly of the State of North Carolina, Session*, 1927, pp. 52, 173; *Journal of the Ninety-Fifth Session of The North Carolina Annual Conference of the Methodist Protestant Church, November 24–29, 1920*, p. 78; *Journal of the North Carolina Annual Conference of the Methodist Episcopal Church, South, November 17–22, 1920*, p. 81.

accomplish through legislation in other spheres.[48] Certainly if alcohol, sex, movies, and Communism became the subject of restrictive legislation, a similar fate awaited any phenomenon that appeared as a direct menace to orthodox religion and to traditional concepts of morality. Such a fate awaited the theory of biological evolution.

48. For an account of prohibition in North Carolina, see Daniel J. Whitener, *Prohibition in North Carolina, 1715–1945* (Chapel Hill, 1945).

2 ∽ CALL TO ARMS

"The Southerner is reared with a consciousness of the Bible. His region historically has been subject to Calvinist and other fundamentalist doctrine. The Southerner is apt frequently to quote Scripture and to have a fondness for the more articulate charlatans in religion as he has for his more preposterous, rascally politicians."

—RALPH MCGILL

The campaign to rid North Carolina of the theory of biological evolution represented far more than an attempt to eliminate a scientific hypothesis. Rather it was an effort to preserve evangelical religious traditions from the onslaught of secularism. Evolution conjured up in the minds of many a host of modern evils; therefore, it was not a single issue but a conglomeration of issues, all existing in a single framework. A feeling, however vague, that something had gone wrong gave rise to a movement to lead society back to its old moorings. For a large segment of the population, the most vital stabilizing force in American society was a morality undergirded by Christian theology. Since evolution was identified with science, the "new theology," and other forces held responsible for the departure from orthodoxy, it provided a convenient focus for the anxieties of those determined to recapture the comfortable certainties of the past. According to one observer in North Carolina, the war of the anti-evolutionists was as much a struggle against an "attitude of mind" as it was a fight against a biological theory.[1]

North Carolinians, like most Southerners, prided themselves on being a people of piety and tradition. Theirs was a religion bequeathed by frontier revivalism and perpetuated by clergymen whose ministerial training was little, if any, more sophisticated than that of their frontier forebears. The vast majority of the laymen were relatively poor, theologically untutored farmers. Their close relation to the natural world created in them a reverence and fear of the God who presided over it. Denominational differences existed, to be sure; but beneath this outward diversity there was within the Protestant community basic agreement on "theological fundamentals." These fundamentals, according to one clergyman in 1923, left no room for the interpretations of "broadminded Christians" in North Carolina. Indeed, the commitment to religious orthodoxy tended to discourage excursions into the newer theological concepts and to impede denominational involvement in social and economic reforms. Solidarity in religion appeared to be as much a virtue to many North Carolinians as fidelity to the Democratic party. In fact, political and theological orthodoxy often emerged as Siamese twins: politicians proclaimed North Carolina "an old-fashioned Christian Commonwealth," and clergymen boasted that their loyalty to Democracy was second only to their allegiance to the Christian faith. "No government on earth in the short span of twenty-five years," proclaimed the Democratic politician O. Max Gardner in 1926, "has written and incarnated in the life of the people more of the platform of Jesus Christ than has the Democratic party in North Carolina." In view of the "mighty mixing of politics and religion in the state," many undoubtedly assumed that the party could be enlisted in maintaining religious orthodoxy.[2]

1. *News and Observer,* December 12, 1926; W. J. Cash maintained that Darwinism was "no more than a focal point of an attack" prompted by a "whole body of fears," and that in the Southern mind "Darwin, Huxley, Ben Butler, Sherman, and Satan" existed as a single person.

2. *News and Observer,* September 13, 1923, October 31, 1926; *Gastonia Gazette,* December 8, 1924; see also Kenneth K. Bailey, "Southern White Protestantism at the Turn of the Century," *The American Historical Review,* LXVIII (April, 1963), 618–35; Edwin M. Poteat, Jr., "Religion in the South," in *Culture in the South,* ed. W. T. Couch (Chapel Hill, 1935), pp. 248–69; Jesse M. Ormand, *The Country Church in North Carolina* (Durham, 1931),

Those North Carolinians disturbed by the advances of secularism found reason to become alarmed about the state of affairs after World War I. Industrialism and scientific developments appeared to emphasize material values at the expense of spiritual ones. This reorientation of values seemed to have permeated all areas of North Carolina life: ministers were concerned with saving society rather than individual souls; laymen had forsaken the Wednesday night prayer meetings for sinful "joy rides;" and denominational groups had been eclipsed by the civic clubs that were so concerned with "material wealth and commerce until moral and spiritual values are the last things to be thought of in North Carolina." Secular education in state schools had largely replaced religious instruction in denominational institutions. The bitter warfare between state and denominational schools in the late nineteenth century had left deep scars despite the *modus vivendi* which had been reached by the opening of the twentieth century.[3] In the 1920's the lingering hostility toward secular institutions of learning became increasingly obvious in the attacks on the state university during the evolution controversy.

Finally, a religiously orthodox, rural people viewed with utter alarm what they believed to be the flourishing of modernism in the major Protestant denominations. For them nothing provided greater evidence of the triumph of secularism. Their reaction to this condition was an immediate plunge backward to the security offered by the religion of their fathers. The "old-time religion" seemed to provide the only bulwark against secularism; its creeds were the only unchanging, infallible guides. Any relaxation of creedal standards opened the way for secularized religion and the destruction of old certainties. Orthodoxy's quarrel with modernism was precisely at this point: modernists were accused of so completely accommodating the church to secular forces as to destroy the very essence of the Christian faith. The "vague" and "nebulous" language attributed to the modernist theologians confirmed the belief that modernism had

---

pp. 28–34; the most comprehensive account of twentieth-century Protestantism in the South is Kenneth K. Bailey, *Southern White Protestantism in the Twentieth Century* (New York, 1964).

3. *Gastonia Gazette,* May 6, 1924; *Greensboro Daily News,* January 31, 1927; see Luther L. Gobbel, *Church-State Relationships in Education in North Carolina Since 1776* (Durham, 1938), pp. 132–71.

destroyed old religious certainties without creating adequate substitutes. The fundamentalists feared that the power and validity of the moral prescriptions of the Bible would be destroyed by the modernists' challenge of its historical and scientific pronouncements.

The opening volley of the fundamentalist-modernist conflict in North Carolina was fired early in 1920 by a Mississippi evangelist in a Baptist paper published in Kentucky. Thomas Theodore Martin, a preacher from Blue Mountain, Mississippi, wrote a series of articles in the *Western Recorder* concerning the "fatal teachings" of President William Louis Poteat of Wake Forest College. Martin not only launched the evolution controversy in North Carolina with the publication of these articles, but also plummeted himself from relative obscurity to the center of one of the fiercest struggles of the postwar era. Educated at the Southern Baptist Theological Seminary, the "Blue Mountain evangelist" had pursued a varied career in teaching and preaching. In 1919 he became Dean of the School of Evangelism at Union University, a struggling Baptist institution in Tennessee, which oddly enough, bestowed an honorary degree upon Harry Emerson Fosdick in the same year. Throughout the 1920's, however, Martin waged a relentless campaign against modernism and evolution as an official in several fundamentalist organizations. His often quoted volume, *Hell and the High Schools,* was a bitter indictment of the evolutionary hypothesis and its corrosive effects upon the moral and spiritual welfare of children educated in tax supported schools.[4]

The subject of his verbal assault in 1920 was the "teachings" of William Louis Poteat of Wake Forest College. Both the man and the institution had long occupied positions of leadership in Baptist circles in the South as well as in North Carolina. The short, slightly rotund "Billy" Poteat, with his red necktie, was a native of Caswell County and an alumnus of the college that he headed. He had served as president of both the Baptist State Convention and the North Carolina Academy of Science. Even H. L. Mencken stood in awe of the unusual qualities of this Southern Baptist biologist whom he described as a "liaison officer between Baptist revelation and

4. Albert N. Marquis, ed., *Who's Who in America, 1928–1929* (Chicago, 1928), p. 1387; T. T. Martin, *Hell and the High Schools: Christ or Evolution, Which?* (Kansas City, 1923).

human progress" largely responsible for making North Carolina "the most intelligent of the Southern states." Indeed, Poteat had rejected offers from famous universities in order to labor in the struggling Baptist institution of his native state. By 1920 he had been at Wake Forest for forty years in various capacities as student, biology professor, and President. His broad scholarship, tenacious defense of freedom of the mind, and deep religious convictions had enabled him to pick "a little path of light into the surrounding darkness." Few individuals exerted so great a liberalizing influence among ecclesiastical quarters in North Carolina. Yet his graduate training in zoology at the University of Berlin tagged him as a product of German rationalism, a term synonymous with a variety of evils in the 1920's. Actually, his liberal theology and advanced scientific ideas had provoked "rumblings" among Baptists for some time before the outbreak of the evolution controversy after World War I.[5]

As early as 1907 Poteat had been accused of being a "higher critic" unwilling to accept a theory of biblical inspiration which required him to embrace scriptural pronouncements on science and history as infallible. At that time, D. F. King, a prominent Baptist layman in North Carolina, raised objections to Poteat on the grounds that his acceptance of higher criticism and biological evolution made him unfit for the presidency of the denominational college. When the college trustees refused to endorse his view by firing Poteat, King cut off his financial contributions to the college but promised a donation of five thousand dollars if higher criticism were removed from the campus. King maintained the same attitude regarding financial support to Wake Forest when the Southern Baptists launched their seventy-five million dollar Campaign for Christian Education shortly after the war. In 1919 he wrote an article on Poteat's unorthodox views for publication in the *Biblical Recorder,* the organ of the Baptist State Convention; but the editor rejected it because of its "offensively personal" remarks about the college president. King's article had relied heavily upon an address delivered

5. W. B. Royall, "William Louis Poteat," *Biographical History of North Carolina,* ed. S. A. Ashe (Greensboro, 1906), V, 321–26; Suzanne C. Linder, "William Louis Poteat and the Evolution Controversy," *The North Carolina Historical Review,* XL (April, 1963), 135–38, 155–56; Gerald W. Johnson, "Billy with the Red Necktie," *The Virginia Quarterly Review,* XXX (Autumn, 1943), 555.

almost twenty years earlier by Poteat to a Baptist congress in Richmond. Shortly after the *Recorder* refused his manuscript, King printed Poteat's address, entitled "Wherein Lies the Efficiency of Jesus' Work in Reconciliation," in pamphlet form and distributed it widely among Southern Baptists. This pamphlet provided the basis for Martin's attack in 1920.[6]

Through the columns of the *Western Recorder* the Mississippi evangelist charged that Poteat belonged to that "fatal, Bible-warping, soul-destroying" conspiracy against the gospel which emanated from the University of Chicago. Sixteen excerpts lifted from Poteat's twenty-year-old Richmond address were offered as proof of this accusation. A primary target of the Martin assault was Poteat's interpretation of the atonement and his conception of the reconciliation between God and man which drew heavily from the theology of Horace Bushnell. In the course of his Richmond address, the Wake Forest president had insisted that if God were the father of men, then men were the sons of God. Therefore "trouble between God and man is a family trouble," Poteat said. His God was an immanent deity who, rather than residing "in cold clouds" and imposing arbitrary legislation upon men, took a paternalistic view of the sinner. For Martin, the crowning blow had been Poteat's declaration regarding the method of reconciliation between God and man: "The essential and sufficient condition of reconciliation [Poteat had said] is the change of man's attitude toward God—that is, repentance—God's attitude being already favorable. God was in Christ reconciling the world unto himself. The work of Jesus in reconciliation therefore must be concerned with a change of man's attitude only." Martin condemned this statement on the grounds that it "took from this sin-cursed world its only hope through Christ dying for our sins." Furthermore, Poteat's heretical theology allowed "the Jew, the infidel, and the Mohammedan to go to heaven if only they quit sinning." Martin denounced Poteat for "waving aside with a slur all of the Apostle Paul's teachings on the subject of reconciliation" and cited

6. D. F. King, "The Salvation of the World Depends on Eliminating the Higher Critics from Our Christian Schools," *Biblical Recorder*, LXXXV (March 24, 1920), 3; *Biblical Recorder*, LXXXV (March 24, 1920), 6; Linder, "William Louis Poteat and the Evolution Controversy," pp. 138–39.

a long list of scriptural references to prove that "God's dealing with sinners" was of a judicial, rather than of a paternal, nature.[7]

In a second broadside against the President of Wake Forest, Martin again attacked his idea of the fatherhood of God and attempted to identify him with Thomas Paine, Mary Baker Eddy, and other "infidels." Poteat's idea was subversive because it held that God was the father of unredeemed sinners, such as harlots and drunkards, as well as the father of "saved sons," a concept which in Martin's view precluded "any real redemption, substitution, law, right or justice." Not only did the idea that "God is the father of sinners flatly contradict God's word," but it also spread abroad among sinners a sense of complacency which condemned them to death unredeemed and unsaved. Martin maintained that sinful man could at best become the "adopted son" of God and that such a status could be achieved only through faith in Christ and in his redemptive powers. His main quarrel with Poteat, therefore, was that the latter's theology blinded sinners to the need for redemption by holding that God was already their father without it.[8]

The third salvo fired by Martin focused upon Poteat's avowed espousal of biological evolution which, according to the fundamentalists, relegated the Wake Forest president to the domain of the "rank infidel." Since the 1880's, to be sure, Poteat had included the theory of evolution in his biology courses and had persistently maintained that it was thoroughly compatible with the basic tenets of evangelical Christianity. And he refused to believe that either religion or science had to be compromised in order to achieve this compatibility. According to one of his colleagues on the Wake Forest faculty, he possessed a Christian mysticism that distinguished faith from belief and recognized faith as an "independent organ of spiritual knowledge as supreme and authoritative in its sphere as sense and reason are in theirs." In short, Poteat interpreted his mission, whether in the laboratory or in the pulpit—and he was competent in both—to be

7. T. T. Martin, "The Three Fatal Teachings of President Poteat of Wake Forest College," *Western Recorder* (January 22, 1920), 4–5.

8. T. T. Martin, "The Three Fatal Teachings of President Poteat of Wake Forest College," *Western Recorder* (January 29, 1920), 4–5.

the saving of Christians from skepticism on the one hand and from obscurantism on the other.[9]

But, for fundamentalists like Martin, evolution was totally irreconcilable with the Christian faith. "Every honest man knows," Martin declared, "that accepting evolution means giving up the inspiration of Genesis; and if the inspiration of Genesis is given up, the testimony of Jesus to the inspiration of the scriptures goes with it; and if his testimony to the scriptures is given up, his deity goes with it, and with that goes his being a real Redeemer and we are left without a Savior and in the darkness and in our sins." Furthermore, the theory was "sheer nonsense" and had been repudiated by all reputable scientists. At least the twenty-five scientific treatises quoted by Martin had consigned the theory to such a fate. Valid or not, the "soul-destroying doctrine" had already proved its nefarious influence in the case of Germany where evolution served as the main prop of the Germanic belief that "might makes right." In brief, evolution "caused the horrible world war" since it motivated Germany's drive "for world power." The obvious implication was that Poteat had predicated his so-called Christian theology on an erroneous and unchristian doctrine imported from Germany and useful only for fostering immorality. Martin's final lash struck at the personal integrity of William Louis Poteat who was accused of accepting money under false pretenses and of misappropriating funds designated for the teaching of Baptist doctrines when he never intended to do so. Martin concluded that the only way to deal with Poteat was for the Baptists in North Carolina and the college trustees to drive him from the Wake Forest presidency.[10]

The publication of Martin's articles provoked an immediate and loud reaction in North Carolina. The editor of the *Biblical Recorder*, Livingston Johnson, a friend of Poteat and a college trustee,

9. George W. Paschal, *History of Wake Forest College* (Wake Forest, 1943), III, 119–23. Poteat declared in 1926: "I think of science as walking to and fro in God's garden, busying itself with its forms of beauty, its fruits and flowers, its beast and bird and creeping thing, the crystals shut in its stones and the gold grains of its sands, and coming now at length in the cool of the long day upon God himself, walking in this garden." Quoted in Johnson, "Billy with the Red Necktie," p. 561.

10. T. T. Martin, "The Three Fatal Teachings of President Poteat of Wake Forest College," *Western Recorder* (February 5, 1920), 4–5; *ibid.*, (February 12, 1920), 5.

refused to reprint the articles in his journal; but "two Baptist deacons" published them in a pamphlet edition that circulated widely, especially among Baptist ministers in the state. Martin's assault upon Poteat was well timed, for the Baptists had just launched their "Seventy-Five Million Campaign" to raise funds for their educational institutions. Under the aegis of this financial crusade, Baptists became acutely conscious of their control and ownership of colleges. They became more inclined to scrutinize the fidelity of these institutions to Baptist ideals. Martin's accusations and the quickened interest in Baptist schools provided the long-awaited opportunity for Poteat's old critics to speak publicly.[11]

D. F. King in particular rose to the occasion by denouncing Poteat as a "higher critic . . . of the most destructive sort." King renewed his charges that Poteat was untrue to Christian fundamentals and held up as proof of this infidelity Poteat's reaffirmation of his "heretical" views on atonement made in a speech in 1919 at the launching of the "Seventy-Five Million Campaign" in North Carolina. Others who shared King's anxiety suggested that Poteat publicly clarify his position on scriptural inspiration and explain how the theory of evolution could be harmonized with Genesis. One Baptist layman considered such explanations necessary in view of the commonly held belief that "it is impossible to belittle the intellectual integrity of the Scriptures without belittling the spiritual integrity." Some critics were candid enough to say that Poteat should either retract statements that they considered unorthodox or resign his post.[12]

The chorus of those who rushed to Poteat's defense virtually drowned out the critical voices. From almost every corner of the state, Baptist ministers and prominent laymen, most of whom were Wake Forest alumni, rallied to the support of their college mentor and roundly denounced any suggestion that he air his theological views in a series of articles. Such action, they argued, would merely provide additional opportunity for their untutored brethren to misconstrue his ideas and to ignite a harmful agitation. One Baptist

11. Paschal, *History of Wake Forest College*, III, 123–25; *Biblical Recorder*, LXXXV (March 3, 1920), 7.

12. *Biblical Recorder*, LXXXV (March 10, 1920), 8; *ibid.*, LXXXV (March 24, 1920), 3.

clergyman refused to believe that Martin's assault would be taken seriously; another described the Blue Mountain evangelist as a "modern inquisitor" whose name would forever be notorious in North Carolina because of its connection with an "unrighteous crusade against the college president whom all the state delights to honor." [13] C. C. Brown, a Baptist official acquainted with Martin and his career, viewed his attack on Poteat as an effort "to win a doubtful kind of notoriety" by assailing one of the outstanding denominational leaders. Brown's impression was that Martin had based his articles on "books that he has never read" and on "witnesses about whom he knows nothing." Other Baptist laymen who had studied under Poteat attested to his orthodoxy and broad vision. One of these, Ivan L. Bennett, declared publicly: "He [Poteat] taught me to marvel at the mighty works of God, to wait and trust with more implicit faith, as we look for a fuller peace and knowledge of the infinite beyond." Still others defended the college president on the grounds that his views of the atonement had changed significantly since his Richmond address in 1900 and no longer provided any cause for alarm.[14]

The two major Baptist periodicals in North Carolina also took up the cudgels in behalf of Poteat. *Charity and Children,* edited by Archibald Johnson, voiced a common sentiment by reminding Martin that he was neither "running affairs in North Carolina" nor "doing the thinking of our folks." [15] Both Archibald Johnson and his brother, Livingston, editor of the *Biblical Recorder,* were orthodox to the core; neither of them subscribed to evolution or modernism, but their sturdy faith in freedom of the mind precluded any attempt by either to "compel the conscience of an honest man who disagreed with them." [16] While editor Johnson of the *Biblical Recorder* readily admitted theological differences between him and Poteat, he described the Wake Forest president as a man of "unimpeachable

13. *Biblical Recorder,* LXXXV (February 18, 1920), 1; *ibid.,* LXXXV (March 10, 1920), 1; *ibid.,* LXXXV (March 17, 1920), 8.

14. C. C. Brown to Brother Alderman, February ?, 1920, copy (William Louis Poteat Papers, Wake Forest College Library, Winston-Salem, N.C.); *Biblical Recorder,* LXXXV (March 17, 1920), 6; *ibid.,* LXXXV (March 24, 1920), 3.

15. *Charity and Children,* XXXIV (February 26, 1920), 3.

16. Gerald W. Johnson to the author, April 21, 1963.

Christian character" and severely reprimanded his old acquaintance, T. T. Martin, for attempting to set off a religious controversy in North Carolina. "One can almost hear the crackling of the fagots," declared the *Biblical Recorder,* "as he reads the words by which this far-away defender of the faith consigns to outer darkness Dr. Poteat and all those who have sat at his feet." [17]

Refusing to enter a debate directly with Martin, Poteat contented himself with a few concise statements designed to explain the essence of his religious thought. The dignity and simplicity that generally characterized his pronouncements marked his letter in the *Biblical Recorder* on February 11, 1920:

Of course, I accept the New Testament as the law of my life and the standard of my thinking. To find its meaning and to extend its power have been the business and joy of these forty years. Jesus knows I am frail and blind, but He knows too, that my heart is set to follow Him where I cannot see, if He will only let me hear His voice. The mystery of His compassion and His redemption I do not understand, but to His sacrificial life and atoning death I look for forgiveness of sin and the life eternal. My savage critic [Martin] doesn't know me, and that, I think is why he raves. I think he has the same reliance I have, and I hope it sheds in him, when he is calm, the same great peace.[18]

Such simple, open statements of his faith disarmed the critics of the Wake Forest president. Even Martin recoiled in the face of Poteat's testimony. "And now that your editorial and Pres. Poteat's letter make it known to me where he now stands," Martin wrote Livingston Johnson, "I would look on it as a calamity for the denomination for him to leave Wake Forest." [19]

By April, 1920, the initial disturbance seemed to have subsided. But the calm that followed was short-lived. The attack on Poteat had unleashed various forces long concerned about the "creeping influences" of modernism in churches and church-related colleges. Once aroused, these forces were not easily deterred from achieving their ultimate aim of restoring the old-time religion. Martin made another

17. *Biblical Recorder,* LXXXV (February 4, 1920), 6.
18. *Biblical Recorder,* LXXXV (February 11, 1920), 6.
19. *Biblical Recorder,* LXXXV (March 24, 1920), 3.

volte-face within a few months and resumed his war on Poteat with renewed zeal. At the Wake Forest commencement exercises late in May, 1920, several incidents indicated that the initial agitation sparked by Martin had not yet run its course. Among the most conspicuous participants in the commencement program was Dr. Amazi C. Dixon, a native North Carolinian who had achieved national prominence as a spokesman for fundamentalist and anti-evolutionist causes. Dixon had edited the *Fundamentals,* a multi-volume statement of the fundamentalist credo published in 1910, and had figured prominently in the launching of the World's Christian Fundamentals Association in 1918. His public addresses on the campus of his alma mater in May, 1920, were essentially designed to expose the fallacies of evolution and the infidelity of evolutionists. Germany, he said, was the prime example of the immorality that resulted from the acceptance of Darwinism; he urged the graduating classes to "hold to the old faith in regard to Creation, and to accept the Genesis account of it at its face value." Even the *Biblical Recorder* praised his sermon as "worth far more than the ornate essays on Social Service which are frequently palmed off on commencement occasions as Gospel Sermons." [20] Dixon must have also been pleased by what he heard at the faculty-trustees banquet on May 26. Professor E. W. Timberlake, speaking for the faculty, pledged loyalty "to the faith of the denomination" and "to the teachings of the Bible." The spokesman for the trustees, Stephen McIntyre, promised that "no German rationalism" would be allowed within the college walls and regretted that before World War I "any teacher who had a Berlin Diploma was at a premium." He expressed the hope that "we are done with German kultur." Poteat, an alumnus of the University of Berlin, sat across the table and within easy earshot of McIntyre.[21]

The specter of disloyalty to traditional religion raised by Martin in his attack on Poteat in 1920 was kept constantly before North Carolinians by free-lance evangelists and spokesmen for national

20. A. C. Dixon, "The Menace of Evolution," *Biblical Recorder,* LXXXV (June 16, 1920), 4–5; *ibid.,* LXXXV (June 2, 1920), 4.

21. *Biblical Recorder,* LXXXV (June 2, 1920), 4–5.

fundamentalist organizations who descended upon the state after World War I. Both championed a fundamentalist religion and waged a relentless war on modernism and other phenomena held responsible for contemporary evils. The theory of evolution was the target of their most persistent and vicious assaults. Darwinism was singled out as the cause of Germany's guilt in bringing about the World War. Germany, so the argument ran, had replaced the standards of Christ with those of the evolution-oriented philosophy of Nietzsche. German universities, gripped by the evolutionary credo, had divested Christianity of its essential supernatural qualities and moral precepts by embracing higher criticism, modernism, and rationalism. The obvious implication of the fundamentalist crusaders' argument was that the continued deviation from the old-time religion would lead America to the same catastrophic fate that had engulfed Germany. But the revivalists not only capitalized on the wartime hatred of Germany and all things German; they also found the mood engendered by the Red Scare useful in the promotion of their cause. They argued that a belief in biological evolution led inescapably to atheism, and modernists were therefore atheists who clothed their infidelity in a garb of high-sounding phrases borrowed from Christian theology. Since the Red Scare had pointed up atheism as an essential characteristic of Communism, it was easy to identify modernism with Communism and modernists with Bolsheviks. The less sophisticated revivalists placed evolution, German rationalism, and Communism in a single package and characterized it as the major menace to "the vitals of Christianity and democracy." By blurring any distinction between the three phenomena, the crusaders could expect enthusiastic support for their cause from civic and patriotic groups whose primary concern was not ordinarily the protection of religion. Small wonder then that when Communists appeared in the Gastonia strike of 1929, they were more widely denounced for their atheism, advocacy of race equality, and alleged free love heresies than for their economic doctrines.[22]

Immediately after World War I, North Carolina witnessed a rash of revivals conducted by itinerant evangelists dedicated to cleansing

22. Benjamin B. Kendrick and Alex M. Arnett, *The South Looks at Its Past* (Chapel Hill, 1935), p. 172; Thomas Tippett, *When Southern Labor Stirs* (New York, 1931), p. 92.

the state of the evil influences being spread by the modernists and evolutionists. Most of the popular evangelists employed similar methods in launching and conducting their religious crusades. They combined techniques borrowed from the businessman, psychologist, and actor. The evangelist's "advance man" first surveyed the prospective site of the crusade, then opened a publicity campaign in preparation for the arrival of the main attraction. Most of the services took place in large tents or in hastily constructed "tabernacles," since presumably no ordinary church sanctuary would accommodate the crowds. The "free-will offerings," collected in washtubs or other large containers, formed a significant part of each revival service. Chief among the evangelist's assistants was a singer who opened each service with music noted primarily for its quick tempo and strong rhythm and who encouraged full participation by the audience in the singing. The evangelist entered the pulpit immediately following the "song fest" to deliver a sermon usually marked by strong, if not extravagant language, detailed accounts of the evangelist's own sinful past before conversion, and highly simplified versions of complex phenomena. Dramatic oratory largely compensated for whatever he lacked in theological profundity. The climax of the revival was the call to the altar, and the success of the service was measured by the number of people who responded to this call. Many thousands witnessed such performances in North Carolina after World War I, and a few believed that "the Second Reformation" was at hand.[23]

Among the most ubiquitous revivalists who swept across North Carolina in this period was Baxter F. McLendon, formerly a barber from Bennettsville, South Carolina. Known professionally as "Cyclone Mack," he acquired a reputation as a kind of whirling dervish of the pulpit. His gyrations, gesticulations, and impersonations left him in a frothy sweat by the end of a service. His performance was always dramatic and sometimes grotesque. On one occasion Cyclone Mack interrupted his crusade in Clinton to accept the challenge of a carnival wrestler who usually demonstrated his prowess with apes rather than evangelists. He returned to the pulpit after a few minutes on the mat, fifteen dollars richer for having defeated his opponent.

23. Gerald W. Johnson, "Saving Souls," *The American Mercury*, I (July, 1924), 364–68; *News and Observer*, July 20, 1924; see also Bernard A. Weisberger, *They Gathered at the River: The Story of the Great Revivalists and Their Impact upon Religion in America* (Boston, 1958), pp. 271–74.

McLendon had originally been a Methodist; but when his "dramatic Christianity" brought criticism from the church hierarchy, he affiliated with the Baptist church in 1922 with the assistance and encouragement of J. Frank Norris, a fiery Baptist preacher of Fort Worth, Texas, whose relentless war on evolutionists at Baylor University received national notoriety. The South Carolina evangelist claimed that the Baptist belief in "the Bible from Genesis to Revelation" was in accord with his own desire to preach "the old-fashioned backwoods religion." [24]

During the 1920's Cyclone Mack conducted numerous revivals in North Carolina, some of which lasted for several weeks at a time and attracted thousands of people. He often described the social gospel as a clear-cut deviation from the church's essential task of saving souls; he denounced European immigrants as "immoral paupers" whose presence in America posed a serious threat to the nation's traditional concepts of morality and democracy. But those North Carolinians who flocked to McLendon's "tabernacles" soon realized that his most extravagant diatribes were reserved for modernists and evolutionists. With a vigor and enthusiasm that would have befitted his "wild and woolly" past, McLendon heaped upon them a succession of his so-called "Mack-o-grams" such as "Evolution is at every step a contradiction or a monstrosity," "Fundamentalism is fighting for the Book, Modernism is undertaking to de-heart it," and "According to the evolutionist a man is only a bankrupt monkey." He repeatedly warned his congregations that unless modernism were soon checked, it would destroy "New Testament Christianity" and enthrone unitarianism. Modernists were already shunting aside the Bible "by ignoring its standards, rejecting its authority, and ridiculing its doctrine." "They deny the literal teaching of the Word of God," he thundered, "and say it does not mean what it says, and does not say what it means, and therefore, it is legendary, mythical, allegorical or anything else other than the Word of God." [25]

Cyclone Mack assured his audience that modernists, appearing as

24. For a biography of McLendon, see Walter Barr, *Baxter McLendon: A Biography* (Bennettsville, S.C., 1928); see also Baxter F. McLendon, *The Story of My Life and Other Sermons* (Bennettsville, S.C., 1923); *News and Observer*, November 19, 1922.

25. *News and Observer*, August 15, September 13, 1921, February 24, November 19, 1922; *Goldsboro News*, August 3, 4, 5, 6, 8, 9, 10, 14, 24, 25, 1926; Baxter F. McLendon, *Defending the Faith and Other Sermons* (Clinton, S.C., 1925), pp. 11, 23, 28.

"wolves in sheep's clothing," already infested the church colleges and seminaries where they were preaching "damnable heresies and bloodless salvation." Among these heresies none was more dangerous than evolution, that "bloody and treacherous infidelity," which fastened "moral leprosy" upon society. "I would rather have saloons, dance halls, and gambling halls on every corner," he exploded at one point, "than one of these slick, mild-mannered, artful, designing, scheming professors destroying the faith of our boys and girls." The evangelist repeated his famous definition of evolution before audiences throughout North Carolina:

In the beginning [McLendon declared] the amoeba begat earthworms; earth worms begat skull-less animals; these animals begat other kinds of animals; these other kind of animals begat some kind of fish, away back in the dateless date; and the fish away beyond the gates of morning begat some kind of gilled amphibian; and these begat tailed amphibians that lived away back when ages were but drifts of foam on the mighty sea of time; and these begat primeval amniota; and these begat mammals; and these begat kangaroos; and kangaroos begat apes; and apes begat gorillas; and gorillas, thank God, begat pin-whiskered, top-heavy college professors who draw their breath and salary and use great big jaw-breaking words, and talk about the Bible being allegorical, figurative, probable, inferential, and hypothetical.[26]

To emphasize his point, he usually charged that evolution was being taught in the public schools of the very village or hamlet in which he was then preaching and to the children of those listening to him. He confirmed the worst fears of his followers regarding their public educational institutions and aroused the suspicions about their denominational colleges.[27] His repetitious charges of infidelity throughout the 1920's fanned the sputtering fires lighted by Martin at the opening of the decade.

Even more sensational and perhaps more influential than Cyclone Mack was a spell-binding evangelist from Louisville, Kentucky, by the name of Mordecai F. Ham. The husky voice of this tall, rather handsome man, who had a smoothly bald head, closely cropped grey moustache, and "keen brown eyes," became familiar to thousands of

26. *North Carolina Lutheran,* I (September, 1923), 4.
27. *News and Observer,* May 6, 1923.

North Carolinians during the 1920's. His organization, skillfully managed by W. J. Ramsey, staged revivals in numerous towns and villages throughout the state. Few if any outside evangelists equalled his record.[28] One of the earliest and most successful Ham "crusades" took place in the summer of 1921 in Goldsboro where he gained twelve hundred "converts for Christ" and forty-five hundred dollars in "free-will offerings." So successful in fact was this performance that a Ham revival became an annual affair in Goldsboro for some years thereafter.[29]

By 1924 Ham had achieved considerable fame in the state as a flamboyant dispenser of the old-fashioned religion that emphasized individual salvation and condemned "welfare work." "Show me one word in the New Testament that exhorts Christians to make the world a better place in which to live," he declared, "and you may hang me from a telephone pole." [30] His verbal lashing of the social gospel was equalled by his anti-Semitic diatribes, which reached a new high in intensity in 1924 when he publicly accused Julius Rosenwald of Chicago, the millionaire philanthropist, of being party to a vice ring engaged in prostitution and white slavery. His accusation triggered a prolonged and acrimonious controversy between him and William O. Saunders, editor of the Elizabeth City *Independent* who attempted to disprove Ham's charge and denounced his kindling of anti-Semitism in a region already beset by racial and religious antagonism. Aiming his acid pen at the "meddlesome" evangelist, Saunders characterized him as "a shekel-gathering pulpiteer" and as an ecclestiastical demagogue gifted in "the art of making people hate." Although the *Independent*'s vigorous editorial campaign against what it considered the evil influences of a perverted Christianity probably did no permanent damage to Ham's reputation, it did cause the evangelist to retire from North Carolina until the furor had subsided.[31]

For three years before his collision with the Elizabeth City editor, Ham had repeated his "sermon on evolution" before thousands of North Carolinians in virtually every section of the state. He ridiculed

28. *Ibid.*, November 6, 1923; Johnson, "Saving Souls," pp. 364–65.
29. *News and Observer*, June 15, 21, July 27, 1921.
30. *News and Observer*, February 14, 1924.
31. Keith Saunders, *The Independent Man* (Washington, 1962), pp. 188–204; *News and Observer*, March 3, 1924.

the biological theory as an utter hoax and insisted that it was no more scientific than a proposition that stated: "A piece of iron ore one day got to wiggling around and evolved itself into a Ford automobile." The orderly design of the universe was, according to the evangelist, sufficient evidence to explode a theory which relied so heavily on chance and chance variations. Ham delighted in discussing heptads and the prevalence of the "perfect number seven in all works of creation" as a means of disproving evolution. He traced the number "through nature, the snowflakes and the elements of chemistry on up to the godhead itself" and claimed that the earth had revolved about the sun in a perfect 360° circle "until sin was born."

Ham's "evolution sermon" not only reduced the biological hypothesis to "a mere guess," invalidated both by the Bible and by nature, but it also contained an elaborate argument to show that practically all major ills of the postwar era stemmed from evolution and Darwinism. For the uncritical audiences that flocked to hear him, his argument was all the more convincing because of its simple logic and dramatic presentation. He began by declaring: "Evolution is a lie out of Hell that has never produced anything but infidelity." Then, to prove the validity of this generalization, he argued that the Germans had "mixed the Bible and Darwinism" to get higher criticism which in turn "was responsible for destroying their faith" and for their acceptance of militarism. With comparable simplicity he identified evolution with the "anti-Christ Bolshevism," since in his view both evolution and Communism were atheistic. Never in his sermons did the evangelist distinguish between the theory of biological evolution and Darwinism; in fact, he used scientific and philosophical terms interchangeably. For him, one was as dangerous to the public morality as the other. The usual conclusion to his "evolution sermon" was his frequently repeated warning: "The day is not distant when you will be in the grip of the Red Terror and your children will be taught free love by the damnable theory of evolution." [32]

In order to forestall such a fate, Ham urged all loyal Christians in North Carolina to terminate financial aid to the "so-called Christian

32. *News and Observer*, November 6, 16, 1923, February 14, 15, 20, 29, March 14, 1924.

colleges" which surreptitiously taught evolution in any form. By 1924 his revival services concentrated almost exclusively upon the evolution theme. Those who thronged to his tent in Elizabeth City heard him say "twice daily for six weeks that anyone who believes in evolution is a fool." In Raleigh, he produced numerous letters from "mixed-up" students seeking his counsel and comfort because of the disturbing doctrines being voiced by their professors. Such letters provided tangible proof to bolster Ham's charge that "learned gentlemen" in Christian colleges were teaching evolution and other obnoxious doctrines "under the guise of science." The evangelist insisted that science, "properly taught," might well be offered in Christian schools, but, he concluded, "to hell with your science if it is going to damn souls." [33]

Certainly the most famous evangelist to tour North Carolina in the post-World War I era was the indefatigable Billy Sunday, who hit the sawdust trails in the villages of rural America when he no longer received urgent calls to hold crusades in the great cities. A former baseball player, Sunday continued to employ antics and language more appropriate to the mound than to the pulpit. His sojourns in North Carolina were less frequent than those of Ham and McLendon, but his influence in the state was no less profound than theirs. A Presbyterian who described himself as an "uncompromising fundamentalist," Sunday waged an unrelenting fight against Darwinism, dancing, "wets," Bolshevism, flappers, and many other phenomena that he considered manifestations of modern secularism. When he unleashed his repetoire of invectives against these "evils," the Sunday "tabernacles" resounded with "tumults of cheering." Dancing, he said, was nothing more than "a hugging match," and Darwinism was rank atheism. "Nobody can tell whether a man came out of the Garden of Eden," he told an audience of four thousand in Wilson in 1923, "or a zoological garden when you are done listening to these ———." The remainder of his description of the evolutionists was lost in the roar of applause. Later in the same year he opened a "gigantic campaign" in Charlotte, where local citizens as well as those from nearby towns who had organized "Billy Sunday Excur-

33. *News and Observer*, February 20, March 3, 1924; Stephen Gardner to Robert Winston, December 5, 1924 (Robert W. Winston Papers, Southern Historical Collection, University of North Carolina).

sions" heard him reiterate time and again his charges against Harry Emerson Fosdick, Percy Stickney Grant, and other theological defenders of biological evolution. Upon the evolutionists he placed the blame for the moral shabbiness of the era, and he warned North Carolinians that any further delay in returning to the "old ways" and old-time religion would mean utter disaster.[34]

The wave of revivalism that swept North Carolina in the wake of the Great War attracted many lesser lights than Sunday, Ham, and McLendon. A host of local evangelists joined the ranks of these fundamentalist crusaders so that virtually every hamlet and village had its "campaign." The revivalists, whether famous or obscure, placed evolution alongside alcohol and sex as a cardinal sin of the day and linked it to Bolshevism, German militarism, materialism, and disintegration of the family. Most of them depicted it as the nexus of a host of modern infidelities. They allowed no equivocation or reservation whatever regarding evolution; either one subscribed to the teachings of the Bible or to evolution and atheism. The theistic evolutionist was characterized as "the very worst sort of infidel," because his sin included deception as well as unbelief. The revivalists repeatedly fixed the responsibility for the sad state of affairs upon the intellectuals, especially the "pin-whiskered professors" whose teaching of evolution was producing infidelity and moral bankruptcy. According to their descriptions, intellectuals were clandestine conspirators engaged in a nefarious plot to destroy the underpinnings of the Christian faith.[35]

By dramatizing evolution, the evangelists made their audiences conscious of the existence of such a phenomenon. Undoubtedly many North Carolinians were unfamiliar with Darwin's theory, much less aware of its implications, until they heard the revivalists. The pulpit exhortations to obliterate the menace of evolution produced several obvious results: first, the controversy over the evolutionary teachings of William Louis Poteat was revived as public interest in evolution quickened; second, there emerged a drive to

34. *Charlotte Observer*, December 30, 1923, January 24, 26, 1924; *News and Observer*, March 27, December 31, 1923; *Gastonia Gazette*, January 3, 11, 18, 1924; David Ovens, *If This Be Treason* (Charlotte, 1957), pp. 46–47; *Presbyterian Standard*, LXV (January 2, 1924), 1.

35. See especially the *North Carolina Lutheran*, I (September, 1923), 4; *News and Observer*, March 3, 1924.

counteract the paganism spawned by evolutionary science by placing Bible courses in the public school curriculum; and third, when the Bible courses failed to receive statewide adoption and Darwinism remained unchecked, the fundamentalists launched their crusade to eliminate evolution and its destructive influences by prohibitory legislation, the device by which demon rum had presumably been eliminated.

Although the activities of the revivalists were generally greeted with popular approval, they aroused rather severe criticism in several quarters. In 1921, the influential Baptist paper *Charity and Children* described Mordecai F. Ham as a sensational preacher who "makes extreme statements and takes a crack at creation." Less than three years later, the paper's editor Archibald Johnson attended a Ham revival and came away enthusiastic about the "great and mighty work" of the evangelist. Other critics underwent no such change of heart.[36] The *Mission Herald*, organ of the Episcopal Diocese of East Carolina, remained steadfast in its opinion that Ham and Sunday had "piled many fagots on the flame by consigning evolutionists and liberal thinkers to Hades." Ham in particular was criticized for preaching a gospel distinguished for "its distrust of learning and fanatical hatred of science." [37] Nell Battle Lewis, through her column in the Raleigh *News and Observer*, characterized the evangelical orations as "strangely unlike the Gospel of Jesus" and the tabernacle orators as "egocentric poseurs" unable to distinguish between their own prejudices and the divine will. She found their "dissonant and barbaric harangues" so filled with blasphemy that their confused, credulous audiences could no longer hear that "guiding Voice described as 'still and small.' " The gravest error of the fundamentalist leaders, in her opinion, was their denial of the fact that "many people who refuse to have their religious instinct cooped up in a traditional creed are among those in whom the instinct is strongest." [38]

Unquestionably the most outspoken critic of the evangelists was Gerald W. Johnson, professor of journalism at the state university whose father edited *Charity and Children*. He credited the success of

36. *Charity and Children*, XXXV (August 4, 1921), 4; *ibid.* (September 22, 1921), 4; *ibid.*, XXXIX (April 13, 1924), 3.
37. *Mission Herald*, XXXIX (June, 1925), 8.
38. *News and Observer*, August 5, 1923.

the evangelists to the absence of any decent public amusements and likened them to witch-doctors. They provided people with an emotional escape from their drab existence by arousing in them a "fear of Hell and a wrath against the wicked." While congregations usually looked to clergymen for the bread of life, the followers of the evangelist looked to him "for red meat." Johnson characterized the professional revivalist as a high-pressure peddler of psychological gimmicks such as hypnosis and "tricks of terrorization" in a carefully staged atmosphere likely to produce the desired pecuniary returns. He reaped large cash remuneration "for no more distasteful labor than bullying his audiences and abusing people he dislikes." And although the evangelist might not believe in all of his own tricks, Johnson acquitted him of being a doctrinal hypocrite. Of all the revivalists in North Carolina, Mordecai F. Ham, according to the state university professor, demonstrated the greatest talent for sowing seeds of anti-Semitism, anti-Catholicism, and community strife. Preached "in the most unbridled language," his "demoniac religion" vilified any group, especially intellectuals, which failed to meet his transient approval.[39] In assessing the net results of the revivalists' activities, Johnson remarked: "Certainly it is true that the evangelist's work tends toward the suppression of such evils as the spread of syphilis and cirrhosis of the liver, fractured skulls, and involuntary bankruptcy. By providing bored communities with a better show attended by less personal danger, it tends also to discourage lynching. By exhausting the honest workman's capacity for emotion of any sort it tends to discourage strikes, as astute cotton manufacturers in the South have discovered." [40] In short, the positive accomplishments of the evangelists were scarcely sufficient either to justify their methods or to outweigh their negative results.

The activities of the World's Christian Fundamentals Association constituted a significant aspect of the postwar religious revival in North Carolina. It was, however, only one of several similar organizations which came to consider the state as one of the most critical arenas in the struggle over evolution. Aware of North

39. Johnson, "Saving Souls," pp. 364–68.
40. *Ibid.*, p. 368.

Carolina's position of leadership in the South, the fundamentalist strategists believed that the state held the key to the success of their crusade in the region. Most of them agreed that if Tar Heels could be induced to outlaw Darwinism, the accomplishment of their goal in other southern states would be easier. The fact that such groups as the World's Christian Fundamentals Association viewed North Carolina as a "pivotal" area helps to explain the intensity of the conflict in the state.

Beginning in 1920, the Association held annual Bible conferences at the Baptist Tabernacle in Raleigh which attracted statewide attention. Conducted by an impressive array of nationally known evangelists, these conferences complemented the revivalistic crusades of the free-lance evangelists and quickened still further the public interest in the "perils of evolution and modernism." The Bible Conference held in the spring of 1920 was conducted by William B. Riley, the Minneapolis minister who headed the World's Christian Fundamentals Association. The primary aim of his sermons was to awaken in North Carolinians "a sense of sin." Riley claimed that Christian Scientists, Roman Catholics, and modernists were contributing to the moral delinquency of the generation because they sidetracked the problem of individual sin. The preoccupation with saving society impeded the salvation of the individual sinner. The hope of the nation, according to him, lay in the religiously orthodox South because the northern seminaries, under the influence of rationalistic theology, had already compromised the deity of Christ and thus set in motion the destruction of the underpinnings of the Christian religion.[41]

The second of these conferences that took place in January, 1921, brought to Raleigh a group of distinguished fundamentalists whose primary focus was upon the inerrancy of the Holy Scriptures. In addition to Riley, the group included W. Leon Tucker, a New York preacher and religious journalist, and Amazi C. Dixon. All three attempted to prove the inerrancy of the Bible on the basis of its divine inspiration. The Scriptures, Riley said, were "God-breathed" and were therefore accurate. But the Minneapolis crusader refused to adhere to a strictly literal interpretation of all the Scriptures. In the

41. *News and Observer,* May 4, 7, 8, 9, 12, 1920; *Biblical Recorder,* LXXXV (May 12, 1920), 4.

course of his explanation of the scientific accuracy of the biblical account of creation, he remarked: "There is not a hint in the Bible of the twenty-four hour day. One argument alone dispels this contention, for there was no sun, no moon or stars until the fourth day, and the first three days could not have been solar days. The Lord had a right to define his own day, and one day in the period of creation could have been a thousand years or more." The statement indicated that Riley was not a blind literalist of the common variety; in fact, he was a rather sophisticated fundamentalist who insisted that the scriptures were inerrant only in their "original" writing.[42]

Both Dixon and Tucker pursued arguments similar to those advanced by Riley to demonstrate the accuracy of the Bible. "I tell you," Tucker declared, "it is not a question of the Bible accommodating itself to science, but of science catching up with the Bible." During one session of the Bible conference he used a large chart to "trace every truth" in the Bible. Among the truths which Tucker traced on his chart were the infallibility of the scriptures, the deity of Christ, the atonement, and the "imminent return of our Lord." Tucker's sermons contained numerous references to the contemporary scene which he believed to be dominated by an immorality unmatched in American history. One ray of hope in this darkness was President-elect Warren G. Harding, "a believer in the Book and in the second coming of Christ." Tucker interpreted Harding's election as a "protest against the eight years when a man [Wilson] who favored Romanism had the country at his command." [43]

The third Bible conference, held for ten days in May, 1922, under the direction of William B. Riley and heralded as "one of the biggest religious events of the year," exemplified the tactical shift that had been made by its sponsors. This shift had already been indicated by the Association's efforts in Kentucky earlier in the same year in behalf of a law to prohibit the teaching of evolution in public schools. The first half of the Raleigh Bible conference in 1922 was dominated by Jasper C. Massee of the Tremont Temple in Boston. Formerly a pastor in North Carolina, he was already well known in the state as a militant fundamentalist and as a pulpit performer of

42. *News and Observer*, January 5, 22, 1921; *Biblical Recorder*, LXXXVI (January 26, 1921), 6.

43. *News and Observer*, January 17, 18, 19, 21, 1921. See also *ibid.*, September 11, 12, 1921.

unusual ability. In his keynote sermon he plainly stated that "evolution causes the nation's ills" because it spawned a "morality without Christ," which in turn bred a "multitude of modern infidelities." He then proceeded to "expose" the fallacies of the Darwinian hypothesis and concluded that it was utter fiction, without scientific foundation. By omitting the supernatural elements, evolution jeopardized the "very fabric of the Christian religion." "It is impossible," he thundered at one dramatic point in a sermon, "for a man to be a Christian and believe in a theory that denies the supernatural and makes Jesus Christ the bastard son of illegitimate intercourse between Mary and Joseph." Perceiving the impact of his declaration, Massee seized the opportunity to advise his audience on the best means of preventing the spread of "this damnable heresy." He called upon all Christians in North Carolina to terminate their support of all schools that tolerated the teaching of evolution and warned that unless the menace were removed immediately, both Christianity and democracy would "topple in ruin." [44]

Massee, however, reserved his most vitriolic remarks for science, scientists, and the scientific mind which he held collectively responsible for the widespread acceptance of evolution and the existence of its evil offspring. He accused the scientists of being so blinded by their own arrogance and egotism that they refused even to consider the possibility of supernatural elements. He also contended that scientists, in spite of their claims to a monopoly on knowledge and wisdom, failed to appreciate the simple fact that a finite being "cannot by intellectual inquiry grasp an infinite God." Thus, he concluded: "The scientific mind cannot pray. The scientific mind cannot approximate God." [45]

Massee's declarations prompted a lengthy reply by the members of the science faculty at North Carolina State College, a publicly supported technological institution located a few blocks from the Baptist Tabernacle where the Bible conference was held. The faculty statement challenged the validity of Massee's assertions and sought to refute the idea that science and religion were incompatible. All six signers of the statement professed to be Christians; several of them pointed to the important lay positions that they occupied in their

44. *News and Observer,* May 7, 8, 9, 10, 11, 12, 13, 1922.
45. *News and Observer,* May 11, 12, 1922.

churches as evidences of their Christianity. Their reply insisted that "every biologist in the world today recognizes evolution as the central *fact* of his science," but confusion in the public mind had resulted from a failure to distinguish between the *fact of evolution* and the theories, including Darwin's, which had been advanced to explain how evolution worked. The scientists further maintained that to follow Massee's advice by terminating all support of institutions that taught evolution would mean "the instant abandonment of all investigation related to the improvement of field plants, fruit crops, vegetables, dairy cows, chickens, horses, mules, hogs, etc." In short, all biological studies would be irreparably crippled. The faculty statement concluded with the charge that "the fact of evolution" was disputed only by a few churchmen intent upon rejecting all interpretations of God's methods other than their own. In the name of religion these churchmen were now seeking to prevent men from using their God-given intelligence to contemplate "God's own Realities." [46]

By the time the counter-blast from State College became public, Massee had been replaced at the Bible conference by Riley. It was clear, however, that Riley would not allow the faculty statement to be the last word on the matter. On May 15, 1922, the day of his arrival, he declared from the pulpit of the Baptist Tabernacle that there was "not one scintilla of evidence" to prove evolution; quite to the contrary, evolution had been discredited in all "advanced scientific circles." Following Massee's lead, he claimed that when a Christian embraced the "monstrous" theory, he forfeited his right to the title of Christian. Having stated his position, he then challenged the State College scientists to defend theirs in a public debate with him. The professors accepted the challenge. But in accepting it, they disclaimed any intention of "fighting the Bible" and again emphasized "that there are no more theories explaining how evolution goes on than there are theories and interpretations of the Bible as expressed in the different creeds." Their argument was that the existence of various theories attempting to explain evolution did not detract from the demonstrated fact of evolution any more than different interpretations of the Scripture lessened the validity of its

46. *News and Observer,* May 14, 1922; *Greensboro Daily News,* May 15, 1922.

fundamental truths. In their second public pronouncement, the faculty group designed Professor Zeno P. Metcalf, a well-known entomologist, as its spokesman in the debate.[47]

Riley suggested as the query: "Resolved, that the evolution hypothesis is neither scientific nor spiritual." Metcalf immediately raised objections on the grounds that evolution, not a particular hypothesis to explain its operation, was the issue. By mutual agreement the query was changed to read: "Resolved, that evolution is a demonstrated fact." Metcalf was to take the affirmative, and Riley the negative. By accepting the challenge, the professors had the privilege of selecting the time, place, and moderator of the debate. They chose R. I. McMillan of Pullen Memorial Baptist Church as moderator and scheduled the affair for the afternoon of May 17, 1922, in Pullen Hall on the college campus. After expressing his delight at the prospect of "taking on" an "avowed" evolutionist in public, Riley hastened to explain the great disadvantage under which he would have to perform. He claimed that the professors had scheduled the debate on his last day in Raleigh in a setting hostile to him, had selected a moderator with whom he was unacquainted, and had rigged the query so that they took the affirmative side, which was "commonly regarded as advantageous." Riley also complained that the scientists were unwilling to debate the "dual proposition" expounded in their reply to Massee whereby they claimed that man could be an evolutionist and a Christian at the same time. "When I challenged them to defend that proposition," he asserted, "they straightway cut off the latter half. I don't wonder. It is a difficult position to defend." But Metcalf's "natural advantages" were not sufficient to deter Riley from engaging in a debate for the sake of arriving at "truth." [48]

At four o'clock on the afternoon of May 17, 1922, the appointed hour for the debate, a crowd of two thousand jammed Pullen Hall. The first of the protagonists to arrive was Riley, a tall, rather handsome man with flashing brown eyes. The applause that greeted him was dwarfed by the deafening roar that erupted with the appearance of Metcalf, a small bespectacled man "leaning to the in-

47. *News and Observer*, May 15, 16, 17, 1922.
48. *Greensboro Daily News*, May 17, 1922; *News and Observer*, May 17, 1922.

conspicuous." After the protagonists shook hands and heard the rules under which they would operate, Metcalf opened the debate that lasted for an hour and a half. The biology professor, reading from a carefully prepared text, marshalled the evidence for evolution with scientific precision. "By evolution," he said, "we mean the demonstrated fact that living things have changed in geological times and are changing now from simple to complex forms." After utilizing a wealth of geological and biological data to support his position, Metcalf concluded with the simple statement: "I am a Christian. I have accepted in its entirety the fact of evolution, and I have never found anything in evolution to shake my fundamental Christian religion." [49]

In his turn, Riley attempted to refute the validity of evolution. A facile orator and an evangelist experienced in the manipulation of audiences, he spoke with passion and conviction. Always smiling, he shifted the attack with bewildering rapidity; at one moment he was reciting an anecdote that brought outbursts of laughter and the next he was delivering a cryptic indictment in solemn, incisive phrases. He maintained that matter and energy were at a standstill in the universe, that nothing new had been "created" since God formed man out of dust, and that Darwin had been discredited for years. He attempted to show that the Bible was not only scientifically accurate but also contained knowledge of scientific phenomena which modern thinkers claimed to have discovered. For example, he insisted that Moses, rather than Harvey, discovered the circulation of the blood. Riley was master of many oratorical devices, but in the debate he proved himself to be particularly skilled in the use of ridicule. At one point he picked up a volume on evolution, smirked at its pictures of prehistoric men, and made much ado about the pronunciation of their names. After deriding the whole idea of "the survival of the fittest," he told the audience: "Come on up here after the debate and look at these pictures, and I am sure you will see somebody who looks like them when you get downtown. I am glad that the weak don't die. Some of you folks may develop into something yet if you stick around for 500,000,000 years." [50]

49. *News and Observer*, May 18, 1922.

50. *News and Observer*, May 18, 21, 1922; *Greensboro Daily News*, May 18, 1922; Maynard Shipley, *The War on Modern Science: A Short History of the Fundamentalist Attacks on Evolution and Modernism* (New York, 1927), pp. 87–88.

Perhaps nothing pointed up the difference in the treatment of the issues by the two protagonists so poignantly as Riley's answers to four questions asked by Metcalf:

"METCALF: 'Why do living organisms present themselves in such marvelous graded series, protozoan to man, bacterium to dandelion?'

RILEY: 'That is the order of God's creation. He began with grass and ended with man.'

METCALF: 'Why do the higher organisms develop the non-useful structures known as vestiges?'

RILEY: 'Who said they were non-useful? God may have a function for them that you have not found out. I still have my appendix and I'm going to keep it. Those 186 I never did have.'

METCALF: 'Why should individual organisms in their development go through the wasteful process of forming ancestral structure, merely to have them disappear before the organism is full grown?'

RILEY: [Answering this question Dr. Riley applied the same reasoning developed in his answer to the second question, elaborating it with incident and sarcastic comment.]

METCALF: 'Why among the vast array of simple animals and simple plants known to have lived in the coal age not one flowering plant nor one mammal has been found?'

RILEY: 'That is down where God began.' "[51]

This interchange not only pointed up the widely divergent contexts from which the protagonists spoke but also demonstrated the difficulties in communication between the laboratory and the pulpit. Nevertheless, it was generally agreed that the debate was "quite without parallel in the annals of polemics hereabouts."[52]

The affair received widespread publicity throughout the state. But editorialists generally refrained from choosing sides. The Raleigh *News and Observer* treated the whole affair humorously in an editorial entitled, "The Old Codger and Evolution," in which the writer pleaded his ignorance of biological science.[53] The *Greensboro Daily News*, on the other hand, considered the whole performance as

51. *News and Observer*, May 18, 1922.
52. *News and Observer*, May 21, 1922.
53. *News and Observer*, May 17, 18, 1922.

potentially dangerous because it provided the "Minneapolis whirling dervish" an opportunity for creating additional excitement by his "pulpit demogoguery." [54] The *Goldsboro News* described the Riley-Metcalf encounter as one by which "nobody was edified" or "converted" but "everyone was highly interested not to say amused." [55] Certainly, the debate sparked discussion of religion and science in general and aroused an interest in evolution in particular. During the next four years, in fact, theological affairs and disturbances became newsworthy enough to vie with murder and politics for layout space in North Carolina newspapers.

At the same time that North Carolinians were listening to sermons and debates on evolution, they were also reading literature and seeing movies that enhanced their interest in the controversy over evolution. In the summer of 1922 theaters in the state attracted unprecedented crowds to view a movie entitled "Creation," which depicted the creation of the world according to the Genesis account. God appeared as "an old man with a long beard"; the animal and vegetable kingdoms were shown to have been complete in the beginning without the aid of any evolutionary process. Although few spectators questioned the source of the movie, Nell Battle Lewis was convinced, on the basis of certain evidence in her possession, that it was merely a piece of propaganda concocted as "a part of the fundamentalist campaign against evolution." [56]

Perhaps even more instrumental in quickening public interest in the evolution issue were the syndicated columns by William Jennings Bryan published in many of the larger newspapers in North Carolina. His "Weekly Bible Talks" was a regular Sunday feature that provided a weekly sampling of Bryan theology. His occasional column, "What Commoner Bryan Is Saying," gave the reader his opinions on a wide variety of current issues. Bryan utilized both as a platform for battling evolution, the last and "greatest" reform to which he dedicated himself. North Carolinians in general revered the Commoner as the hero of rural America who was still engaged in a mighty struggle to preserve rural virtues, especially the old-time religion. By 1921 they were reading Bryan's indictments of Darwinian

54. *Greensboro Daily News*, May 17, 18, 1922.
55. Quoted in *News and Observer*, May 21, 1922.
56. *News and Observer*, August 17, 1922.

evolution and his plea for Christian taxpayers to assert their "legal rights" by banning evolution from all tax-supported classrooms.[57] In his column of September 4, 1921, Bryan declared:

> Evolutionists are leading their followers away from the Creator, away from the Word of God, and away from the Son of God. They teach that man is a lineal descendent of the lower animals—that he has in him, not the breath of the Almighty, but the blood of the brute. They tear out of the Old Testament, the first chapter of Genesis, and then having discarded the miracle, they tear out the first chapter of Matthew and deny the Virgin Birth. They would, in effect, dethrone Jehovah, strip the Bible of its claim to inspiration, and libel the Master by branding him as the illegitimate son of an immoral woman. This creed denudes life of its spiritual elements and makes man the brother of the beast.[58]

In short, Bryan held evolution responsible for "the destruction of faith" and for the modern sin of "mind worship." To challenge Bryan's interpretation in North Carolina, one ran the risk of incurring the wrath of his followers who contemptuously dismissed critics as "little two by fours," "non-entities," and "rat terriers barking at the mastiff." [59]

Bryan's fight to preserve the virtues of rural America received support and endorsement from a frequent visitor to North Carolina, John Roach Straton, the flamboyant minister of New York's Calvary Baptist Church. His commencement speeches and revival sermons during 1920 and 1921 depicted in graphic detail the sins emanating from vice-ridden urban America where paganism, fed by the evolutionary infidelity, flourished among the "teeming millions" of foreign-born inhabitants. The hundreds of North Carolinians who heard his frequently delivered sermon entitled "Fighting the Devil in Modern Babylon" undoubtedly had their prejudices against the city confirmed and also got the notion that evolution was an "alien" philosophy nurtured in the wicked atmosphere of urban America. Confronted with population statistics showing the rise in urban population in their own state, North Carolinians were increasingly

57. See the files of *Greensboro Daily News, News and Observer,* and *Charlotte Observer* beginning in 1921.
58. *News and Observer,* September 4, 1921.
59. *Mount Olive Tribune,* quoted in *News and Observer,* July 2, 1922.

anxious to protect the righteousness of their rural way of life by excluding the heresies of the city.[60]

The various external forces that operated in North Carolina during the first three years of the postwar decade intensified and magnified the evolution issue. Under the circumstances it was unlikely that questions about the orthodoxy of William Louis Poteat and Wake Forest College, raised by T. T. Martin in 1920, would be settled without a controversy of significant proportions. The *Charlotte Observer* characterized the Riley-Metcalf debate as the culmination of a series of events which reopened the discussion of Poteat's views.[61] The free-lance evangelists, Bible Conferences, movies, and newspaper columns by Bryan raised the specter of evolution, convinced many that most modern evils were products of this "imported theory," and produced a climate in which polemics and controversy would thrive. Since modern evils had been traced to a single cause, salvation obviously required the elimination of that cause. The first move, however, was to eliminate the chief advocate of the dreaded theory, namely William Louis Poteat. By May, 1922, "threats of ousting the Wake Forest president" were being "openly made."

60. *News and Observer*, May 2, 1920, May 21, 23, April 15, August 16, September 4, 1921, December 19, 1923; see also Stanley Walker, "The Fundamentalist Pope," *The American Mercury*, VIII (July, 1926), 257–65.

61. See *Charlotte Observer*, May 31, 1922; Linder, "William Louis Poteat and the Evolution Controversy," pp. 139–41.

3 ∽ CLERICS IN COMBAT

"In a sense hypocrisy is the inevitable by-product of every religion. Men are never as good as their ideals and never as conscious as the impartial observer of the divergence from them. Every religious person commits the error of solipsism in some form or other, the sin of claiming for himself what he will not grant to his brothers."

—REINHOLD NIEBUHR

In spite of the rising clamor over evolution, William Louis Poteat refused to be silenced or to be pressured into retracting his former statements on the subject. In a series of highly publicized lectures on "Heredity and Eugenics" at the North Carolina State College summer school in 1921, he explained how the individual repeated "in his evolution from the single fertilized cell all the stages in the evolution of the race." After discussing why acquired characteristics were not inherited, he observed that "wooden legs are not inherited, but wooden heads sometimes are." As if to confound those Baptist brethren so persistently critical of his "evolution talks," he wound up his stay in Raleigh by preaching at the Baptist Tabernacle. The fact that his pulpit address at the Tabernacle was received with enthusiasm equal to that which greeted his scientific lectures at the college was a commentary on his remarkably diverse talents. Small wonder then that such a man should hold the unique distinction of being the only person in the history of the state to serve as president both of the Baptist State Convention and the North Carolina Academy of Science.[1]

In the following year, on November 20 and 21, 1922, Poteat was again in the capital city to deliver another series of lectures on the general subject of heredity. This time his host was Meredith College, a Baptist institution for women. During each of the lectures the college auditorium was filled to capacity by students and "a large number of outsiders." His treatment of such technical subjects as the chemical property and nature of protoplasm was delivered "with the fineness of expression that delighted the most non-scientific mind." "Whether you like it or not," he boldly proclaimed, "you are all akin to all that lives, not merely the humble members of the animal kingdom, but the humbler of the vegetable kingdom as well." In his other discourses Poteat asserted that "heredity was a greater force than either environment or training" and attempted to demonstrate how the science of eugenics might be employed to improve the race.[2]

On many occasions Poteat publicly defended Wake Forest College against charges of departing from "the fundamentals of the faith." At the meeting of the Baptist State Convention, held in Rocky Mount on November 15 through 17, 1921, the college president insisted that the institution was loyal "to the truth of Christ as interpreted by Baptists." "Christ is the light of the world," he said, "and Wake Forest College is an agency for its denomination." But never did Poteat apologize for the fact that evolution was taught in the college. His candid answer to a query by the *Religious Herald*, then investigating charges made against Baptist schools, was characteristic. When asked whether there were any teachings at Wake Forest which ignored God or discredited commonly accepted tenets of the Christian religion, Poteat replied: "I am happy to say that there is no such teaching. The doctrine of evolution as the divine method of creation has been taught here frankly for years, and that proclaims God and supports the fundamental tenets of our holy religion." He repeatedly maintained that Wake Forest was a Baptist "lighthouse" and that

1. *News and Observer*, July 13, 14, 15, 17, 1921.

2. Mary Lynch Johnson, *A History of Meredith College* (Raleigh, 1956), p. 163; *News and Observer*, November 21, 22, 1922.

its faculty and students were children and ministers of light who welcomed rays from every quarter. In order to remain true to its mission, the college had to welcome "light from the laboratories . . . where men pick their painful way through the mysteries of nature as God beckons them to follow in His footsteps." He also reminded his brethren that Christianity arose in "the best culture of its time" and that when Christians had not abused and misrepresented their religion, it had "been the nourishing mother of the best culture ever since." [3]

The Wake Forest president not only proclaimed his views on evolution from the speaker's rostrum but he also explained and defended them in various types of publications. His main publication outlet in North Carolina was the *Biblical Recorder*, the organ of the Baptist State Convention, whose editor solicited articles from him directly and reprinted his works that appeared in other journals. In one of his articles in the *Recorder* in March, 1922, Poteat suggested that Saint Paul might have been a theistic evolutionist in view of passages in Acts and Ephesians which proclaimed a common ancestry for all races. Other Pauline writings seemed to him to indicate that biological "variation occurred through isolation." This article in which Poteat attempted to utilize the Bible to verify his scientific view in the same manner that fundamentalists used it to falsify that view triggered a storm in Baptist circles. The article brought into the open the mounting criticism of his teachings.[4] During the spring of 1922, the *Biblical Recorder* devoted its columns almost exclusively to polemics related to evolution. The crucial question was whether Poteat's views and the teachings of evolution at Wake Forest constituted a breach of the Baptist faith.

Many Baptists were convinced that their college should be purged of the doctrine without delay. A few offered cogent replies to Poteat's articles; some admitted that they were "puzzled" and confused by the whole discussion; and still others, whose reaction was more emotional than rational, simply demanded a law against the evolution heresy. J. J. Taylor, a Leaksville minister and a leading critic of Poteat, admitted that evolution had become an "acute" issue

3. *Biblical Recorder*, LXXXVII (January 4, 1922), 4; *ibid.*, LXXXVII (February 22, 1922), pp. 6–7.

4. *Biblical Recorder*, LXXXVII (March 8, 1922), 1; see also *Greensboro Daily News*, May 12, 1922.

with the Baptist laity in North Carolina primarily because of the Seventy-Five Million Campaign, which was designed to "give our schools better equipment and to make them distinctly Christian." Rejecting Poteat's suggestion that Saint Paul was an evolutionist as a bit of foolish speculation, Taylor severely criticized the college president for attempting to lend respectability to the "godless" theory by adding the word "theistic." "A theistic evolutionist," Taylor declared, "is a person who believes in God and at the same time accepts a theory which denies His existence." Even more specific in his criticism was Robert H. Spiro, an Asheville clergyman who also denied that an evolutionist could be a Christian. He argued that evolution's guarantee of mankind's upward course was incompatible with the Christian concept of the fall of man. The Resurrection was likewise incompatible with a theory that held that life arose only from life. Both Taylor and Spiro challenged Poteat to define his so-called "theistic evolution" in such a manner that would clearly demonstrate its consistency with the basic tenets of the Christian religion.[5]

Throughout April and May, 1922, critics of Poteat who were far less sophisticated in their views than either Taylor or Spiro bombarded the *Biblical Recorder* with articles. One of these, W. J. Berryman, objected to evolution because it made "the Bible a fable and Christianity a myth." In his critique of Poteat's essay regarding the evolutionary views of St. Paul, Berryman wrote: "The whole evolution theory seems to be something like this: One day or one aeon or one something, a clod or some such lifeless thing that had evolved from nowhere or some such place, and from nothing or some such being, suddenly said to itself, 'Look here, you are not evolved to lie here. Get busy and evolute.' It was done as the clod said, and our most ancient granddaddy, the single life germ, or Mr. Protoplasm, came into being."[6] Another correspondent of the *Recorder*, Grover C. Phillips, who was delighted that evolution had not undermined Poteat's faith "in a living God," nevertheless offered Baptists a choice between Moses and Darwin. He argued that Moses, the author of the

5. *Biblical Recorder*, LXXXVII (April 5, 1922), 1; *ibid.*, LXXXVII (May 10, 1922), 1, 4; Suzanne C. Linder, "William Louis Poteat and the Evolution Controversy," *The North Carolina Historical Review*, XL (April, 1963), 140.

6. *Biblical Recorder*, LXXXVII (April 5, 1922), 1.

first five books of the Bible, was "steeped in the best Egyptian learning of the day" and had as much opportunity "to accept or reject the theory of evolution as we have in our later day." Therefore, if God had not made man by a special act, Moses would have said so rather than stating emphatically that God created man in His own image. To counter Poteat's suggestion that Paul was an evolutionist, Phillips quoted from the apostle's letter to the Corinthians which stated that "there is one kind of flesh of men, another flesh of beasts, another of fishes. . . ." Other critics in essential agreement with Berryman and Phillips pointed out that neither science in general nor a belief in evolution in particular were "necessary for salvation" and indicated that the true Christian could survive "hardships and afflictions" better without either.[7]

One of Poteat's most persistent adversaries, D. F. King, renewed his efforts to cleanse Wake Forest of the Darwinian heresy amid this atmosphere of intense controversy. By the spring of 1922 he was again suggesting that Poteat was unfit for the college presidency and that his attempts to clothe evolution in a religious garb was in itself an act of dishonesty. "No statement that Dr. Poteat could make," he declared, "would be worth the paper on which it is written so long as he believes, teaches, upholds, or defends evolution." King implored Baptists to settle the matter by taking a vote in the Baptist State Convention. Voicing similar sentiments, an anonymous writer in the *Biblical Recorder* who labeled himself "One of the Crowd" maintained that the exposure of the evolution "infidelity" at Wake Forest had convinced the average Baptist that the Seventy-Five Million Campaign was all in vain. Pointing to democracy as a Baptist fundamental, the writer advised his brothers to invoke their right to have a voice in what their schools taught. The idea of submitting the views of Poteat and of the Wake Forest faculty to a vote in the state convention was championed by an increasing number of Baptists during the spring of 1922.[8]

The friends of Poteat did not remain idle while he was under attack. They testified to his catholicity, defended his right to hold views different from those of the majority, and lauded his services to the college and the denomination. Some of Poteat's followers,

7. *Biblical Recorder*, LXXXVII (May 24, 1922), 4.
8. *Biblical Recorder*, LXXXVII (May 17, 1922), 3.

especially among the clergy, answered charges against him in lengthy articles and letters in the *Biblical Recorder*.[9] Bernard W. Spilman, a well-known Baptist minister who had lived in Poteat's home while he was a student at Wake Forest, declared: "If there is a devout, humble servant of Jesus Christ who believes in the Bible from lid to lid . . . that man is William Louis Poteat."[10] Among the stalwart friends of Poteat and Wake Forest were Archibald and Livingston Johnson, whose orthodoxy was complemented by their respect for intellectual freedom. While they might disagree with Poteat on the question of evolution, they were willing to defend his right to hold such views and to remain at the head of the college so long as his views did not plainly contradict Christian tenets. Neither of the Johnson brothers was ever convinced that Poteat's embrace of evolution had altered his position regarding any essential Christian doctrine. Archibald Johnson, in *Charity and Children*, maintained that there was "such a thing as being too orthodox," and that the history of the church was filled with examples of "orthodox brethren who abused everybody who would not see a thing exactly as they did." Admitting that the champion of strict orthodoxy was usually honest and sincere, Johnson was also convinced that his honesty and sincerity were often negated by a zeal "so narrow, provincial and intolerant" that orthodoxy became bigotry. He urged North Carolina Baptists to move slowly and "considerately" in the matter of evolutionary teachings and, above all, to avoid appeals to popular prejudice and the use of intemperate rhetoric. In his opinion the failure of Baptists to pursue such a course had already created a great deal of noise about "troubles" which for the most part were purely imaginary. For him the haggling over theological minutiae which characterized so much of the debate over evolution generated far more heat than light among laymen who in reality were "babes in Christ." Lest his position be misunderstood, Johnson disclaimed any intention of handing over Baptist institutions to non-Christians. "There is no foundation," he said, "for the idea that because a man is a teacher he should be allowed to teach what he pleases in another

9. *Biblical Recorder*, LXXXVII (May 3, 1922), 1; *Greensboro Daily News*, May 12, 1922; *News and Observer*, May 26, 1922.

10. *Biblical Recorder*, LXXXVII (May 10, 1922), 1; see also C. Sylvester Green, *B. W. Spilman: The Sunday School Man* (Nashville, 1953), pp. 122–23.

man's school." He adhered to what he called the principle of "voluntariness" whereby a teacher possessed a freedom of choice either to abide by the general principles on which a denominational college rested or to exclude himself from its faculty by refusing to subscribe to its basic principles. The professor's right to believe what he desired was a matter of conscience and conviction over which a denominational organization had no control. But the denomination, like any other agency, was obligated to protect the integrity of its institutions and could therefore eliminate personnel who were clearly subversive.[11]

Livingston Johnson was also in a position to exert considerable influence in Poteat's behalf as editor of the *Biblical Recorder* and as a trustee of Wake Forest College. In both capacities he proved to be a friend of intellectual freedom. As editor of the denominational paper, he attempted to be fair to both sides in the evolution controversy and, at the same time, to plead for "unity and peace" among Baptists. "We trust," he declared, "that the *Biblical Recorder* will never degenerate into a forum for a denominational debating society." Johnson maintained that the relations between science and religion should be friendly rather than antagonistic and that harmony could be achieved "if each moves in its proper sphere." [12] In delineating these spheres, he declared:

> Science deals with facts, religion must accept things on faith; science endeavors to account for things according to natural laws; religion accepts the supernatural; religion should accept whatever science has demonstrated to be a fact; science should not deny the supernatural, upon which important religious doctrines are based. If science will stay in its own field and not assume a superior attitude in things religious, and if religion will remember that the Bible was not written as a scientific treatise, and expresses itself in natural rather than scientific terms, we believe that much of the supposed conflict between the two will be removed.[13]

Although Johnson did not specifically include evolution among the

11. *Charity and Children*, XXXVI (February 9, 1922), 4; *ibid.*, XXXVI (May 18, 1922), 4.
12. *Biblical Recorder*, LXXXVII (April 12, 1922), 6; see also *ibid.*, LXXXVII (November 30, 1921), 6.
13. *Biblical Recorder*, LXXXVII (April 12, 1922), 6.

demonstrated facts of science, he defended Poteat's right to believe that evolution was God's method. And on May 8, 1922, he wrote, "We have never doubted Dr. Poteat's Christianity." [14]

As the discussion of evolution in Baptist circles became increasingly acrimonious, Poteat decided to accept the challenge of his critics and spell out his understanding of theistic evolution. He felt that such an explanation might help to dissipate some of the emotionalism and return the debate to a more reasonable plane. Editor Johnson placed the columns of the *Biblical Recorder* at his disposal, and his series of articles on evolution again exhibited his rare talent for translating scientific technicalities into a language meaningful to laymen. He began by defining evolution as "the doctrine that present living things are descended with modification from earlier living things." Then he set about to validate his assertion that evolution was a demonstrated fact; after discriminating between evolution and the theories explaining evolution—between the fact of evolution and the factors of evolution—he traced the development of the evolutionary hypotheses from the ancient Greeks to Lamarck and Darwin, thence to Weismann, Mendel, and De Vries. The debate in scientific circles, he said, no longer concerned the fact of evolution; scientists had accepted evolution almost universally since the opening of the twentieth century. Poteat wondered whether his critics had been asleep when the "procession passed" and accused them at this late date of compromising before the intelligence of the world the very religion which they claimed to be defending. He further charged them with deception when they forced upon men such "false alternatives" as "Darwin or Moses" and "the Bible or science." One of his most effective blows against the anti-evolutionists was his analysis of their famous list of twenty-one "truly great scientists" who considered evolution "an unsupported guess." Of the twenty-one Poteat found that "two do not appear in biographical dictionaries, five are misrepresented, seven won reputations in other than biological fields, six have been in the graves for more than forty years, two of these having died long before Darwin's great book was published." Similarly he scrutinized the manner in which fundamentalists equated a scientific theory with a "fancy or guess" and concluded

14. *Biblical Recorder*, LXXXVII (May 8, 1922), 6.

that such tactics smacked of a deliberate attempt to confuse the lay mind. The obvious implication of Poteat's analyses was that fundamentalists, in seeking to protect the integrity of the Holy Scriptures, resorted to means neither holy nor scriptural. For such people to charge theistic evolutionists with "disloyalty to the Christian faith," with "clandestine efforts to undermine religion," was both ironic and ridiculous. The Wake Forest president called upon the fundamentalist zealots to stop their unfair and unchristian efforts to discredit Christian scientists.[15]

In another essay in the *Biblical Recorder*, Poteat attempted to explain how a Christian could embrace evolution without sacrificing his religious principles. His principal point was that most outstanding evolutionists gave God a central place in the creative and evolutionary scheme. He also argued that such Christian fundamentals as the deity of Christ, incarnation, atonement, and resurrection were in no way affected by one's belief in biological evolution. And whether his critics believed him or not, Poteat maintained that his Christian faith had been strengthened, rather than weakened, by his scientific investigations. With a candor and humility rarely displayed in the debate over evolution, the Wake Forest president stated publicly:

> I have been teaching here [Wake Forest College] for forty-three years, teaching biological sciences forty years. I have discredited neither the Genesis account of the origin of man nor the Gospel account of the origin of Jesus Christ. And there has been no concealment of my attitude. I have published two books on the relation of science and religion. Whenever I have referred to the creation account in Genesis I have taken pains to say two things—that the Bible is not a textbook in science and the affirmation there is of the divine agency in the process without a word about the method of creation. I frankly believe that God created all things and animals, man included, by the method of evolution. I find myself utterly unable to resist the considerations in support of that method. There I stand, and I cannot help it." [16]

Furthermore, Poteat found it difficult to believe that the anti-evolutionists could really be serious in their attempt to stamp out the theory of evolution, since it would be virtually impossible to

15. *Biblical Recorder*, LXXXVII (April 19, 1922), 3.
16. *Biblical Recorder*, LXXXVII (April 22, 1922), 3.

"disentangle and expurge" a conception so thoroughly embedded in the intellectual life of the day as evolution.[17]

Those who hoped that Poteat's exposition would soothe the troubled waters were to be sorely disappointed. No sooner had his articles been published than J. J. Taylor renewed his attack. The Leaksville minister described Poteat's definitions of theistic evolution as a "saddening disappointment" that rambled "off into irrelevant matters" without explaining "how and where God operates." Moreover, Taylor claimed that Poteat's definition, distinguished primarily by its "ambiguity and inconclusiveness," was stated in terms unintelligible to "the plain people." Even if the common folk had understood, Taylor said, they would have recognized that Poteat's theory of evolution was atheistic and that the president of the very college that depended upon their support had aligned himself with that group of "ungodly and destructive men" known for their arrogance and patronizing attitude.[18]

The persistence of such assaults not only brought the two Baptist papers to Poteat's rescue but also aroused the ire of the secular press. The *Raleigh Times* lauded Poteat's refusal to join "the excursion back to the Dark Ages," by retracting his scientific opinions in the face of the fundamentalists' cant.[19] Even more severe in its editorial criticism of the anti-evolutionists, the *Greensboro Daily News* challenged the Baptists of North Carolina to return to reason and to appreciate the greatness of William Louis Poteat as an educator, scientist, and Christian leader. "For the Baptists of North Carolina to reject a really great teacher," the *Daily News* declared, "because his years of patient investigation of truth have put him somewhat out of line with the views of some backwoods exhorter who doesn't know the derivation of the word 'evolution,' much less its meaning, would remove Wake Forest from serious consideration as an institution of collegiate standing." [20]

The clamor over the evolutionary teachings of Poteat finally forced the Wake Forest College board of trustees to consider the issue at its meeting late in May, 1922. A committee of trustees interviewed

17. *Ibid.*
18. *Biblical Recorder*, LXXXVII (May 10, 1922), 4.
19. *Raleigh Times*, April 25, 1922.
20. *Greensboro Daily News*, May 12, 1922.

Poteat in order to "ascertain his views on the great fundamental doctrines of our faith." The head of the committee was Richard T. Vann, former president of Meredith College and a Baptist leader whose influence in North Carolina was probably second only to that of Poteat himself. A man of broad learning with a strong commitment to the freedom of conscience, Vann had been closely associated with Poteat for many years and readily defended his right to hold his own particular views on evolution. Vann himself, in all probability, did not subscribe to the Darwinian theory; he refused to be classified either as a modernist or as a fundamentalist. On one occasion he admitted privately that the whole controversy was "utterly stupid" and, with a twinkle in his eye, added: "But I am inclined to think that the jackiest of the asses are the fundamentalists." [21] In short, Vann's influence was an important factor in the highly favorable report rendered by the committee to the full board of trustees. In the meantime, a host of alumni and former students of Poteat, many of whom were prominent Baptist ministers, had rallied to his defense and had made known their views to the trustees.[22] The college president was summoned before the board and informed of its vote of confidence by none other than the venerable Baptist spokesman, Dr. R. H. Marsh, a trustee of the institution for a half century. By a unanimous vote the trustees expressed their confidence in Poteat as a "Christian and as a teacher" and pledged him their wholehearted support. Shortly thereafter, Poteat reiterated the position that he had stated to the trustees in an address to the students entitled "Culture and Consecration." Livingston Johnson, one of Poteat's most loyal supporters among the trustees during the investigation, maintained that this "remarkable address," coupled with the findings of the board, ought to satisfy all who had ever questioned his fitness for the college presidency.[23] Convinced that further treatment of the evolution issue in the *Biblical Recorder* would serve no useful purpose, Johnson announced: "We think it best for the college and the cause in general that this discussion close. We have reason to believe that this agitation has shaken the faith of many who have read it, and if

21. Gerald W. Johnson to the author, April 21, 1963.
22. See *Biblical Recorder,* LXXXVII (May 3, 1922), 1.
23. *News and Observer,* May 31, 1922; *Biblical Recorder,* LXXXVII (May 31, 1922), 6–7.

the faith of any has been strengthened, we have not heard of it." This announcement brought an end to the discussion of evolution in the *Biblical Recorder* until 1925 when Editor Johnson, under pressure from the anti-evolutionists, temporarily reopened its columns for an airing of their views.[24]

The decision of the trustees and the termination of the evolution discussion in the *Recorder* did not deter those bent upon having the issues decided by a vote of the state convention. The peculiar organization of the Baptist denomination allowed those elements to fan the evolution fires in local congregations and associations. Try as they would, the Baptist leaders who desired to avoid a convention squabble found it increasingly difficult to soothe these local groups so agitated by the disturbances over evolution. One observer noted that, in North Carolina, Baptists of extraordinary distinction had "no more authority in matters of faith and doctrine than is possessed by some semiliterate pastor of some Little Bethel in the remote backwoods." [25] The lack of theological sophistication among some of the brethren was evident at the state convention in 1921 when a church official had to explain that "the authorized version" of the Bible was "not written in English by Saint James . . . a disciple and brother of our Lord." [26] In June, 1922, a Baptist layman who edited a weekly newspaper expressed a sentiment common among rural Baptists: "There was a time when I wanted to go to Wake Forest worse than anything but God had something better in store for me than a diploma from a Baptist college. It would have ruined me. I can see that very plainly now. . . . Wake Forest is having its troubles over the teaching of evolution. It is all right with the trustees and the big city preachers of the denomination. But some of the common folk out in the backwoods don't like the idea of being first cousin to the ape, and they are threatening to start something." [27]

No one was more acutely aware of this threat than those Baptist leaders anxious to preclude a convention fight over evolution. They were also aware of the peculiarities of the Baptist denominational organization which complicated their task. The Baptist structure

24. *Biblical Recorder*, LXXXVII (May 31, 1922), 6–7; see below p. 172.
25. Gerald W. Johnson, "Billy with the Red Necktie," *The Virginia Quarterly Review*, XXX (Autumn, 1943), 557.
26. *Biblical Recorder*, LXXXVII (November 23, 1921), p. 3.
27. *The Fool-Killer* (Boomer, N.C.), June, 1922.

contained three primary units: the local congregation that claimed autonomy; the association composed of "messengers" from congregations in a given district; and the state convention also made up of "messengers" from local congregations and theoretically possessing no connection with the associations. In actual practice, however, the association was the key link in the organization because its sessions played a critical role in molding opinion regarding denominational issues.[28] A decision by the association usually influenced the local churches and, in turn, their messengers to the state convention. The denominational spokesmen anxious to forestall a convention row over evolution in 1922 were therefore alarmed by the increasing tendency of associations to pass resolutions denouncing evolution and criticizing Wake Forest for teaching it.

These resolutions merely reflected the uneasiness which first spread among Baptists as a result of T. T. Martin's attack on Poteat's views in 1920. Since then, the Bible conferences and exhortations of traveling evangelists had strengthened their suspicions that all was not right in their denominational college. By mid-1921 the "evolution infidelity" had become a topic of discussion in association meetings. At the meeting of the Flat River Association in that year, one official, R. E. Peele, roundly denounced evolutionists for their "germ theory" of creation and for their assaults upon "the old Book." He believed that this infidelity was spreading with the aid of the secular press, which generally "worshipped at the shrine of Evolution." [29] The Pilot Mountain Association, meeting on August 2, 1921, passed a series of resolutions condemning schools which destroyed the faith of the young by substituting the doctrine of evolution for the scriptural record. The association also demanded that all teachers in Baptist colleges be required "to give a clear and complete statement of what they believed touching the fundamentals of faith, and no one ought to be employed or retained in any of our schools who departs from standards set forth in the Bible plainly interpreted." [30]

By 1922, when the Baptist tension was running high, denomina-

28. See W. W. Barnes, *The Southern Baptist Convention, 1845–1953* (Nashville, 1954), especially Chapters I and XVII.
29. *Biblical Recorder*, LXXXVII (November 2, 1921), 1.
30. *Biblical Recorder*, LXXXVII (August 24, 1921), 14.

tional leaders stepped up their efforts to ward off a grass roots war on Poteat and Wake Forest on the evolution issue. That the college trustees and the denominational papers had endorsed Poteat was not sufficient. The local associations had to be convinced. A battery of Baptist leaders, including the Johnson brothers, Wake Forest professors, and others anxious to avoid a convention row, descended upon the association meetings during the three months before the opening of the convention. Through moral suasion they attempted to win endorsement of Poteat and the college program; failing in this, they sought to prevent any action at all by the association. But when an association insisted upon passing resolutions hostile to Poteat and his views, they tried, sometimes in vain, to mollify the severity of such measures.[31] Few Baptist spokesmen were more active in this effort than Richard T. Vann, the Secretary of the Education Board of the State Convention. His persuasive eloquence and powerful influence in local Baptist circles all over the state undoubtedly played a significant role in the outcome of the controversy. But even Vann, "the wingless bird" who could "outsing all the rest," was unable to sway the Gaston County Association at its meeting on October 18, 1922. He pleaded with the delegates to shelve their resolution on evolution, but it passed by a vote of twenty-three to three. This strongly worded measure condemned Wake Forest for teaching that "man and monkeys . . . [have] the same ancestor" and "that man has been evoluted through processes running through ages of time." Such teaching dishonored God and sapped "the foundations of faith in the infallibility of His Word." While lauding Poteat's personal character and intellectual ability, the Gaston group nevertheless warned that the continuation of the evolutionary teachings at Wake Forest would result in the withdrawal of the association's support.[32]

By the time of the meeting of the Baptist State Convention in December, 1922, the general consensus was that evolution would dominate the proceedings. The press concluded that the action of the trustees had "not visibly" diminished the agitation within the denomination at large, and that delegates from the mountain districts in particular would attempt to bar the teaching of evolution in all Baptist schools. However, the balance of power in the

31. See *Biblical Recorder*, LXXXVIII (August-November, 1922).
32. *Biblical Recorder*, LXXXVIII (October 25, 1922), 6–7.

convention was expected to rest with a group whose chief concern was the maintenance of denominational harmony, rather than the success of either modernism or fundamentalism. According to predictions, this group would affect a compromise and prevent "a straightout movement to oust Dr. Poteat." At any rate, the moderates did control the convention's committee on resolutions, the body which considered all resolutions sent up by the associations and offered on the floor of the convention.[33]

The ninety-second annual convention of North Carolina Baptists opened at Salem Church in Winston-Salem on December 12, 1922, with 498 delegates in attendance. The presence of almost twice as many delegates as attended the convention in 1921 indicated, according to some observers, the imminence of an explosion over evolution. Certainly the issue had figured prominently in the discussions of the Baptist ministers who gathered in an evangelical conference on the eve of the convention. At a banquet on December 12, attended by 145 Wake Forest alumni on hand for the statewide meeting, Poteat boldly raised the question of evolution and frankly discussed the agitation that it had inspired. Although he described the criticism of the college as unfair, he nonetheless advised the alumni to consider the motives that prompted it. "But the brethren who have criticized us are sincere," he declared," and it is their interest in the college that causes them concern. If they knew us better I think they would understand. I hope none of you will be harsh in your judgment of these good brethren, for they have the good of Wake Forest at heart just as we have." Such charitable words were disarming to those critics who accused Poteat of teaching a pernicious doctrine conspicuously lacking in charity.[34]

The climactic point in the convention came on the second day when the discussion focused on the educational work of the denomination. Richard T. Vann presided; his opening remarks were a plea for the delegates to support the denominational colleges and to view them with "sympathy and understanding." After a leading fundamentalist had offered a prayer at Vann's request, Poteat was

33. *News and Observer*, December 11, 13, 14, 1922; *Biblical Recorder* LXXXVIII (December 20, 1922), 4–5, 7; Green, *B. W. Spilman*, pp. 122–23.
34. *News and Observer*, December 13, 1922; *Biblical Recorder*, LXXXVIII (December 20, 1922), 4–5.

asked to speak on Christian education. This was the long awaited moment. The auditorium, jammed to capacity, exuded an atmosphere of "tip-toe expectancy." On many occasions Poteat had been called upon to address Baptist groups on the same topic. His method then had been to use the topic as a springboard for discussing controversial issues before his adversaries openly launched their attack. Usually his addresses developed into gospel sermons "so charged with passion and conviction" that any attack thereafter would have appeared as a mere slanderous ranting. He employed the same technique in the convention of 1922. The only difference was the significance of the occasion.[35]

When Poteat mounted the rostrum, a hush fell over the tense audience. Some of his bitterest critics had taken seats immediately in front of the platform. As the beleaguered college president began to speak, a slight "trace of nervousness" appeared in his manner, but soon "his soul was on fire as he talked of the mission of the Christian school." Few who heard him failed to be impressed by the eloquence, simplicity, and sincere conviction of his remarks. He captivated his audience and confounded his critics. None dared to attack a man whose Christian faith appeared to be so completely above reproach. New Testament in hand, Poteat began: "I want to read you a passage from a little book. I have this little book. I commend it to you. It is our final authority for faith and practice." He made no effort to explain his views on evolution and did not, in fact, refer to evolution except by implication. Yielding nothing of his scientific beliefs, he discussed the essentials of his faith, described his own convictions, and "bared his heart" in a manner that for him was rare even with his intimate friends. The central theme of his address was the need for an enlightened faith spacious enough to accommodate all realms of culture. Piety, though essential, was not to be confused with intelligence; Christianity demanded a "marriage of goodness and enlightenment." Poteat assured his audience that only Christian education, defined as "Christianity operating in the field of enlightenment," provided the moral dynamic capable of regenerating mankind. Such education must acquire and utilize all the knowledge that science offered. To fear that science might discredit Christian

35. Johnson, "Billy with the Red Necktie," p. 558; *News and Observer*, December 13, 1922.

faith was to demonstrate two forms of infidelity: the lack of commitment to Truth as exemplified by Christ and the doubting of the ultimate triumph of God's purpose of redemption in Christ. Science only provided clues "to the invisible things of God," an important service to be sure; but before the central mysteries of life, the method and apparatus of science stood in "helpless impotence." Poteat concluded with a plea for denominational unity and harmony based on a fast commitment to Christ, for internecine squabbling posed a far more serious threat to Christianity than science.[36]

The impact of Poteat's remarks was immediate. Even W. C. Meadows, pastor of Pore's Knob Church in the mountains of Wilkes County and a bitter opponent of his evolutionary views, joined the throng that surged toward the platform to shake his hand and to assure him of their loyalty. A couple from a Baptist church in High Point who had terminated their pledge of twenty-five hundred dollars to Wake Forest as a result of the evolution agitation paid the full amount and renewed their pledge after hearing him. Meadows "gladly" sponsored a resolution that endorsed Poteat's administration of the college as well as the theological position stated in his address. Those who came to the convention to attack Poteat wound up supporting this resolution, which also authorized the publication of his speech. Printed as a pamphlet under the title of *Christianity and Enlightenment,* the address circulated widely as an authoritative statement of Wake Forest's position in the modernist-fundamentalist dispute.[37] The secular press hailed Poteat's performance as a singular victory for the forces of enlightenment which would undoubtedly discourage attempts to suppress the teaching of evolution. Rare indeed was the editorial voice that carried any hint of criticism of Poteat's address.[38] Among the exceptions was William O. Saunders, editor of the Elizabeth City *Independent,* who claimed that Poteat had won a "sorry victory," resorting as he had to the tactic of "chloroforming" his adversaries.[39] But regardless of the type of

36. Green, *B. W. Spilman,* pp. 122–23; *News and Observer,* December 14, 1922; *Biblical Recorder,* LXXXVIII (December 20, 1922), 4–5.
37. *News and Observer,* December 13, 14, 15, 1922; William Louis Poteat, *Christianity and Enlightenment* (n.d., n.p.), pp. 1–13.
38. *News and Observer,* December 15, 1922; *Greensboro Daily News,* December 14, 15, 1922.
39. *Independent* (Elizabeth City), December 19, 1922.

victory, evolution had been shelved, at least temporarily, by the annual convention of the state's largest denomination.

During the next two years the issue did not seriously threaten to erupt again within official Baptist ranks. However, opposition to Poteat continued to exist among local Baptist groups, and criticism from out-of-state sources helped to keep alive the controversy that focused upon him. Poteat himself, by publicizing his views on evolution, tended to rekindle animosities among those whose enthusiasm for his convention address in 1922 cooled rapidly. When the evolution disturbance had spread to other denominations and created a row in the state legislature of 1925, Poteat again found himself in the center of the agitation. Certainly, the series of lectures which he delivered at the state university that year contributed to the renewal of the controversy among Baptists. Thus, the convention in 1925 was again confronted with a situation similar to that of three years earlier.

The Baptists were by no means the only ecclesiastical body affected by the agitation over evolution. Although the other denominations had no focus for their anxieties comparable to Poteat, they nevertheless shared the Baptists' concern over the flourishing state of secularism and its chief handmaiden, evolution. The Methodist Episcopal Church, South, was the second largest denomination in North Carolina; and, like the Baptists, the Methodists were involved in a fund-raising campaign for their colleges which made them more acutely aware of their ownership and control of these educational institutions. The Methodist Church also resembled the Baptist in that it contained a considerable number of clergymen with a minimum of formal theological education. The majority of Methodist ministers who possessed collegiate training had acquired it at Trinity College in Durham. While many similarities existed between the Methodists and Baptists, the former possessed certain theological and institutional features that tended to prevent a serious intra-church cleavage over issues raised by the fundamentalist-modernist conflict. First, the episcopal organization of the Methodists, with its annual conferences headed by bishops, made it easier to control zealots within the church. The two annual conferences in North Carolina, known as the North Carolina Conference and the Western

North Carolina Conference, were dominated in the 1920's by bishops who were determined to keep the church from dissipating its energies in theological debate. The second factor that discouraged a Methodist fracas over evolution was the traditional lack of doctrinal consciousness within the church. The practical living of the Christian life had historically "meant more to Methodists than hair-splitting theological discussions." [40] In the 1920's questions of prohibition and organization—the unification of the northern and southern Methodism—absorbed so much of their time and energy that it left little of either for debates over evolution.[41]

But the same climate that nourished anti-evolutionist sentiment among Baptists and other groups had its effect upon Methodists. Conference leaders not only had to apply considerable pressure through the church's episcopal organization but also had to exert a great deal of moral suasion in order to forestall revolts by extremist elements. For the first several years after the signing of the Armistice, the Board of Lay Activities of the North Carolina Annual Conference manifested great concern about the orthodoxy of church-supported educational institutions. At the meeting of the conference in November, 1920, in Rocky Mount, the Board implored the church to "see that these institutions are distinctly Christian, and that only such men and women are admitted to their faculties as will uphold Christian fundamentals and 'contend earnestly for the faith which was once and for all delivered to the saints.' " [42] But the election of President William Preston Few of Trinity College as Conference Lay Leader in 1922 brought an end to the Board's efforts to prescribe theological qualifications for faculty members of church colleges.[43]

President Few and Trinity College occupied a place in Methodism somewhat comparable to that of Poteat and Wake Forest in Baptist circles. Poteat was perhaps a more eloquent and effective platform

40. Nolan B. Harmon, *Understanding the Methodist Church* (Nashville, 1955), p. 26; see also Paul N. Garber, *That Fighting Spirit of Methodism* (Greensboro, 1928), pp. 126–27; see also Emory S. Bucke, ed., *The History of American Methodism* (New York, 1964), III, 262–89.

41. Files of the *North Carolina Christian Advocate*, 1920–1927, offer abundant evidence of the Methodist concern about prohibition and unification.

42. *Journal of the North Carolina Annual Conference of the Methodist Episcopal Church*, 1920, p. 73; hereafter cited as *Journal of N.C. Annual Conference* with the appropriate year.

43. *Journal of the N.C. Annual Conference*, 1922, p. 49.

performer than his Trinity colleague, but Few was wise in the ways of Methodist politics and under his administration Trinity College exerted a liberalizing influence upon the church as a whole. He refused to become excited by the evolution agitation; in his numerous addresses to quarterly conferences and other Methodist groups, he always counseled moderation. "In times of unsettlement like the present," he declared in 1925, "men have too frequently taken up extreme positions in one direction or another and have run upon sudden and sharp disaster." Although a mild-mannered moderate, Few possessed a quality of toughness often displayed in his dogged defense of academic freedom at Trinity. According to one observer, he staunchly opposed the movement in the annual conference to require all teachers in Methodist schools to sign a statement proclaiming their belief in the Apostles' Creed. "I would not require a teacher in my institution," Few asserted, "to sign the statement that he believed the name he was signing was his own." [44] Not only would he oppose such a regulation but would disregard it if the conference passed it. The endowment provided by James B. Duke in 1924 further secured Few's independence; it largely precluded any serious intimidation of the institution on financial grounds. Such positive resistance on the part of one so influential in the denomination and so strongly backed by the church leadership tended to head off a war on Trinity College by the vocal anti-evolutionists.

Another factor that militated against a serious rupture within Methodist ranks during the 1920's was the existence of the Pastors' School held during the summers at Trinity College. Sponsored by the college and the two annual conferences, the school was a conspicuous success from its opening in 1918. The hundreds of ministers from rural and small-town churches who attended it received instruction in theology and modern biblical scholarship from sophisticated professors representing various schools of thought. This experience was especially significant for those clergymen without formal seminary training. The Pastors' School fulfilled the hope of President Few, one of its founders, who envisioned it as an agency for unifying and liberalizing the Methodist Church in North Carolina. It lessened the possibility of acrimonious debate within the church over such issues

44. *News and Observer*, November 16, 1925; see also Woody, *The Papers and Addresses of William Preston Few*, pp. 110–17, 304–9.

as evolution, because it exposed ministers to the newer trends in theology and allowed them to air theological differences in the classroom. Imbued with a new respect for their denominational college, the ministers who participated in these summer sessions showed little inclination to impose theological proscriptions upon the institution and indeed helped to avert such a movement among the laity.[45]

Nevertheless, the North Carolina Annual Conference continued to receive petitions regarding "unorthodox doctrines," and in 1921 it adopted a set of resolutions intended as a statement of its own doctrinal orthodoxy. These resolutions did not mention evolution by name but the implication was clear. A special committee report accepted by the conference in 1921 condemned "those views of the Holy Scriptures" which assailed "the miraculous elements of the Word of God" under "the guise of modern scholarship." The committee's resolutions affirmed Methodist belief in an inspired Bible as the only sufficient guide in life and urged the elimination "from all connectional places" of those who could not honestly subscribe to it. But even these resolutions left so much room for interpretation that they were unlikely to trigger any heresy hunts in Methodist schools.[46]

While the conference attempted to prescribe doctrine, its real concern was more distinctly Methodist, namely a passion for righteous and humane causes, fostered by the denominational emphasis upon the idea of Christian perfection. The Board of Temperance and Social Service insisted that "it is not enough to preach the gospel in the abstract"; the church must continually wage war on the social evils. Although alcohol was the prime target of the reformers among North Carolina Methodists during the 1920's, other evils such as movies, the Ku Klux Klan, divorce, lynching, war, and "fashions of dress" were roundly denounced.[47] The *North Carolina Christian Advocate* summed up the Methodist position in the postwar era

45. Hersey E. Spence, *"I Remember": Recollections and Reminiscences of Alma Mater* (Durham, 1954), pp. 80–81; H. E. Spence, *When Preachers Meet: The Story of the North Carolina Methodist Pastors' School* (Greensboro, 1962), pp. 25–31, 66–72.

46. *Journal of the N.C. Annual Conference, 1921*, pp. 11, 27, 75–76; see also *Journal of the N.C. Annual Conference, 1923*, pp. 29, 64–66.

47. *Journal of the N.C. Annual Conference*, 1920, pp. 51–54; *Journal of the N.C. Annual Conference, 1921*, p. 61.

when it declared: "Orthodoxy of opinion is secondary to the orthodoxy of life. Not what a man thinks about religion but a personal religious experience is primary." Herein lay one of the major reasons for the failure of Methodists to become deeply disturbed by the evolution controversy.[48]

The Western North Carolina Conference seemed to be more susceptible to the dispute between modernists and fundamentalists than its counterpart in the east. In 1921 the Western Conference memorialized the General Conference in an attempt to have certain doctrinal standards established "for all officers and teachers in educational institutions owned or controlled by the Methodist Episcopal Church, South." The memorial also demanded that faculty members be required to belong "to some evangelical Protestant church . . . and believe in the inspiration of the Holy Scriptures, the Virgin Birth, and the Deity of Our Lord Jesus Christ."[49] This memorial took its place alongside others presented to the General Conference in 1922. These various appeals throughout Southern Methodism had inspired the bishops' Episcopal Address that year.[50] Since the bishops' action fell far short of the desires of fundamentalists within the Western Conference, the latter body continued to receive "numerous resolutions and other papers" concerning the prohibition of "heretical teachings in Methodist Colleges." On several occasions rifts appeared to be imminent within the conference. At the session of 1925, for example, a band of fundamentalists led by J. A. Baldwin of Charlotte promised a showdown fight on the floor of the conference against "those modernists of the rankest sort" who occupied positions of prominence in the church. That the anticipated fight failed to materialize was generally credited to "the fine art of Methodist diplomacy" and to the restraining hand of Bishop Collins Denny.[51]

48. *The North Carolina Christian Advocate*, LXIX (March 20, 1924), 1.

49. *Minutes of the Thirty-Second Session of the Western North Carolina Annual Conference of the Methodist Episcopal Church, South, 1921*, p. 84; hereafter cited as *Minutes of the Western N.C. Annual Conference* with the appropriate year.

50. Norman F. Furniss, *The Fundamentalist Controversy, 1918–1931* (New Haven, 1954), pp. 159–60.

51. *N.C. Christian Advocate*, LXVIII (July 19, 1923), 1, 4–5; *ibid.*, LXVIII (August 16, 1923), 1; see also Edwin D. Mouzon, *Fundamentals of Methodism* (Richmond, 1923), 85 pp.; *Minutes of the Western N.C. Annual Conference, 1923*, p. 74; *News and Observer*, October 19, 1925.

The high point of agitation within Methodist circles in North Carolina came at the meetings of the two annual conferences in the autumn of 1923. The disturbance centered around the so-called "Junaluska incident." During the previous summer, Dr. S. G. Bland, a Canadian theologian, had addressed the Training School for Sunday School Workers at the Methodist assembly grounds located in the mountains on Lake Junaluska.[52] Bland's modernist theology had offended some influential church spokesmen, especially Bishop James Cannon, Jr., who strenuously objected to those portions of the address which questioned the inspiration and authenticity of certain biblical passages. Both the religious and secular press aired the incident; and those Methodists influenced by the sermons of the free-lance evangelists and aware of the fracas over evolution among the Baptists became convinced that infidelity had infiltrated their own ranks. Women's organizations and boards of stewards in some local churches quickly passed resolutions affirming their belief in divine creation. R. L. Foster, a minister in the Western Conference, published a widely read little pamphlet in 1923 entitled *Facts and Fiction About Evolution.* Other ministers and a few laymen expressed anti-evolutionist sentiments in the church paper. Shocked by the "heretical teachings" of Dr. Bland, these Methodists were determined to eliminate such "iniquitous" influences from their midst and indicated that they would force the issue in the conferences of 1923.[53]

Before and during the meeting of the conferences, church leaders strove mightily to avoid an open clash between fundamentalists and modernists. Speakers at the church's Social Service Convention during July, 1923, counseled laymen to concentrate upon the more important business of social justice rather than becoming embroiled in "small controversies over dogmas and creeds." One speaker, Marvin Underwood, suggested that his fellow Methodists might well become less concerned with whether they were "descended from apes" and consider whether they were developing "such charac-

52. *N.C. Christian Advocate,* LXVIII (August 9, 1923), 1; *ibid.,* LXVIII (September 20, 1923), p. 27; *ibid.,* LXVIII (November 22, 1923), 1, 4–5; *Journal of the N.C. Annual Conference, 1923,* p. 29.

53. Richard L. Watson, Jr., ed., *Bishop Cannon's Own Story: Life As I Have Seen It* (Durham, 1955), p. 236; E. C. Durham, *If Evolution Is True* (New Bern, 1922).

teristics that might cause a reversion to that species." Bishop Edwin D. Mouzon also urged North Carolina Methodists to adhere to their historic principles by emphasizing "the religion of the Christian experience." "The historic position of Methodism," he declared, "is not that you make men Christian by first making them orthodox, but that if you can succeed in getting people converted and can lead them on to deeper experience of divine grace, you will keep them sound in faith." Mouzon's position, however, was challenged by another cleric of great influence, Bishop Warren A. Candler, who maintained that dogma and doctrine were the very foundations of all spiritual life and morality. Such divergence of opinion between two church leaders was itself testimony to the breadth of Methodist faith.[54]

When the North Carolina Annual Conference convened on November 14, 1923, in Elizabeth City, it faced an array of petitions and resolutions regarding Bland's statements and other unorthodox utterances in Methodist institutions. The conference leaders managed to shelve all of these documents except those relating specifically to the Junaluska incident. A resolution, adopted by a "rising vote," condemned the statements made by Bland, ordered the responsible church agency to prevent the repetition of such "teachings," and reaffirmed the church's faith "in a whole Christ, the divinely conceived and virgin born son of God, and in a whole Word, divinely inspired, for the whole world." [55] The Western Conference also precluded a floor discussion of the numerous petitions on "reported unorthodoxies" by referring them to committees—where they died. But a report by the conference's Sunday School board, which was adopted unanimously, called for the exclusion of all "doubtful disputations," a renewal of the evangelical note in Methodism, and an offensive against "all forms of incendiary rationalism on the one hand and of fanaticism of ignorance on the other." These statements in 1923 constituted the last official pronouncement by the

54. *Evening Telegram* (Rocky Mount), July 5, 1923; *N.C. Christian Advocate*, LXVIII (August 16, 1923), 1; *ibid.*, LXVIII (July 26, 1923), 5; see also Alfred M. Pierce, *Giant Against the Sky: The Life of Bishop Warren Akin Candler* (Nashville, 1948), pp. 235–50.

55. *Journal of the N.C. Annual Conference, 1923*, p. 29; *Evening Telegram*, November 15, 1923; *N.C. Christian Advocate*, LXVIII (November 22, 1923), 1, 4–5.

two conferences regarding the fundamentalist-modernist dispute.[56] Certainly, the church membership in North Carolina was essentially fundamentalist, a fact that makes the moderation of official actions of the denomination all the more remarkable. While Methodists as individuals continued to be concerned about evolution and related issues, the conferences ignored the subject in order to concentrate upon "social evils" and the problem of reunifying the northern and southern branches of the church.

The moderation exemplified by the conference pronouncements was also apparent in the church paper, the *North Carolina Christian Advocate*, which undoubtedly tempered the laymen's proclivity to become excited over evolution and modernism. Although the *Advocate* was by no means a modernist sheet, one of its editors, Marion Timothy Plyler, who shared the post with his brother, was a product of the University of Chicago where he had studied under some of the most outspoken modernist theologians in America.[57] Plyler, like Livingston Johnson, refused to allow his paper to degenerate into a debating forum and repeatedly warned Methodists of the dire consequences of factional quibbling. "The Bible is not a textbook in science," he explained in one editorial, "and neither is it an almanac that runs out of date with the passing seasons. But it is the sufficient and infallible rule of faith and practice. It is God's word with Jesus Christ as its supreme interpretor." [58] The *Advocate* at the same time maintained that Christianity was a supernatural religion that could not be reduced to "the plane of naturalism," but hastened to remind Methodists that their essential task was "to spread scriptural holiness over the land and not to be emissaries of hate or to wage needless warfare." Such emissaries could scarcely be expected to fulfill the Methodist hope of being "perfect in love." Furthermore, according to the *Advocate*, orthodoxy by Methodist standards was an exceedingly broad term that included all who accepted the Scriptures as "containing all things necessary to salvation." An orthodox Method-

56. *Minutes of the Western N.C. Annual Conference, 1923*, p. 74; *N.C. Christian Advocate*, LXVIII (October 25, 1923), 3.

57. For a sketch of Plyler's career, see Marion Timothy Plyler, *Through Eight Decades As Minister, Editor and Author* (Durham, 1951), pp. 19, 32–34, 47–54, 61–68.

58. *N.C. Christian Advocate*, LXVIII (January 3, 1924), 1.

ist was allowed wide latitude in interpreting the Bible for himself; certainly he was not required to accept a particular theory of inspiration. "According to Methodist standards," Plyler wrote, "the Bible is primarily a book to tell men how to be saved from sin"; and he added, "Salvation is both personal and social in the fullest meaning of these terms." [59]

By 1924 considerable pressure was being exerted upon the *Advocate* to take a clear-cut stand in the evolution controversy. The fundamentalist wing of the denomination considered Plyler's editorial position less Methodist than mere fence-straddling, and certainly his willingness to reprint such material as articles by Harry Emerson Fosdick did little to endear him to this group.[60] Finally in May, 1924, Plyler answered his critics in editorials that purported to spell out his position in the matter: he refused to be classified as either a modernist or a fundamentalist, but characterized himself as an adherent "to the doctrines of the Bible taught by the Methodist Church." Such doctrines included the virgin birth, deity of Christ, resurrection, and atonement. "It would be a great blessing," he concluded, "if our people would ignore entirely the whole business of the evolution controversy." [61] For the next six months, the paper followed its own advice and focused its attention upon strictly denominational matters. The occasional references to the conflict over evolution which appeared in the *Advocate* during the next three years were generally of the same temperate and moderate character as those in the earlier period.

Another sizable group of Methodists in North Carolina in the 1920's outside of the Methodist Episcopal Church belonged to what was called the Methodist Protestant Church. These Methodists, having revolted against the episcopal organization during the Jacksonian era, boasted of their "democracy" in which a president rather than a bishop presided over their annual conferences. Like their brethren still under the episcopal system, the Methodist Protestants demonstrated keen interest in social questions and waged relentless war on the Ku Klux Klan, soft drinks, cigarettes, and "mixed bathing

59. *N.C. Christian Advocate,* LXIX (January 17, 1924), 1; *ibid.,* LXIX (March 20, 1924), 1; *ibid.,* LXIX (April 24, 1924), 1.

60. See *N.C. Christian Advocate,* LXVIII (October 11, 1923), 5.

61. *N.C. Christian Advocate,* LXIX (May 15, 1924), 3; *ibid.,* LXIX (May 22, 1924), 1.

in modern swimming pools." But, above all, they crusaded in behalf of the Volstead Act and its enforcement and seldom met in official sessions without resolving to assist in making the Noble Experiment a success.[62] By 1922 the conference, in session at Henderson, officially expressed its concern over the moral breakdown that had "followed in the wake of the Great War." The very foundation of society was being "undermined by leaks great and small." For many of the Methodist Protestants the most serious leak was modernism, a "superfluous theology," which accommodated itself to a science predicated upon the theory of evolution.[63] One of the most severe critics of modernism and evolution within the denomination was J. F. Dozier, a minister and a great admirer of William Jennings Bryan. Deploring the arrogance of the evolutionists, Dozier described their theory as "a series of guesses" used to sustain a "philosophy of atheism." Despite reliable documentary evidence of supernatural intervention in human affairs, evolutionists disregarded scriptural testimony in the name of science and rested their case upon an "unproved hypothesis." [64]

During the evolution controversy the *Methodist Protestant Herald*, the conference organ edited by J. M. McCulloch, was a significant force for moderation. Editor McCulloch's orthodoxy was never in question; he subscribed to all the basic tenets of the fundamentalist theology. Yet he was equally adamant in his belief in freedom of discussion and insisted that the *Herald* should present both sides of the controversy. His own critiques of the issues in 1922 and 1923 were among the most profound to appear in the religious press of the state. He warned in particular against tendencies to provide oversimplified answers to complicated theological questions and against substituting emotion for "clear reason" in analyzing the various schools of theological thought. He was convinced that fundamentalists were often "so eager for supernatural revelation"

62. *Journal of the Ninety-Fifth Session of the North Carolina Annual Conference of the Methodist Protestant Church, 1921*, pp. 39–47; hereafter cited as *Journal of the N.C. Conference of the Methodist Protestant Church* with appropriate year.

63. *Journal of the N.C. Conference of the Methodist Protestant Church, 1922*, pp. 33–34, 43; *Methodist Protestant Herald*, XXVIII (June 29, 1922), 3.

64. *Methodist Protestant Herald*, XXVIII (March 16, 1922), 2; *ibid.*, XXVIII (August 10, 1922), 3.

that they "see it where it does not exist" and that modernists were so inclined in the opposite direction that "they fail to see it when it does occur." Similarly, fundamentalists taught as "fundamental" those doctrines that were actually peripheral, while modernists offered in the name of modernity those doctrines "whose falsity was shown centuries ago." By criticizing the fundamentalists for clinging to an untenable theory of scriptural inspiration, Editor McCulloch incurred the ill will of some of the more zealous fundamentalists among his subscribers. When one of these challenged his position in 1923, the result was a prolonged discussion in the *Herald* concerning "the errors in the Bible." [65]

McCulloch, however, did not limit his criticism to the fundamentalists. His analysis of the modernist credo led him to conclude that it, too, suffered from serious defects. One of these was a faulty logic that McCulloch considered the most serious weakness of the modernist position. For him the modernist had disregarded the fact that "mere external similarities do not prove internal similarities." Another criticism concerned the modernists' tendency to accept without question the Darwinian hypothesis of evolution as a scientific law to which all else must conform. He felt that the theory of evolution lent itself "a little better to the purpose of the atheist" because it removed God farther away. "The God of the evolutionists is too slow for us impatient mortals," he admitted. "We want a God that can speak and it is done." The editor of the *Herald* sought diligently, through his own calm and judicious articles, to raise the level of the discussion in his denomination above that represented by the oversimplified "God-or-Gorilla" approach. His efforts undoubtedly had some effect as a counterbalance to the inflammatory utterances that the laymen were hearing elsewhere. Even so, many Methodist Protestants continued to concern themselves with such questions as "Where did the monkey from which we are descended come from?" [66]

65. *Methodist Protestant Herald,* XXVIII (April 6, 1922), 1; *ibid.,* XXVIII (July 6, 1922), 1; *ibid.,* XXVIII (September 28, 1922), 1; the debate between McCulloch and J. A. Burgess is found in *ibid.,* XXIX (February 22, 1923), 1; *ibid.,* XXIX (March 8, 1923), 15–16; *ibid.,* XXIX (March 22, 1923), 4, 14; *ibid.,* XXIX (March 29, 1923), 9; *ibid.,* XXIX (April 5, 1923), 2–3; *ibid.,* XXIX (April 12, 1923), 2–3; *ibid.,* XXIX (April 19, 1923), 2.

66. *Methodist Protestant Herald,* XXVIII (April 6, 1922), 1; *ibid.,* XXVIII (July 6, 1922), 1; *ibid.,* XXVIII (September 28, 1922), 1.

For all the agitation over evolution and modernism among Methodists and Baptists, it was left to the Presbyterian church, the third largest denomination in North Carolina, to provide the fundamentalists and anti-evolutionists with the most solidly unified support in the state. The position of the Presbyterians may be explained in part by their rigid doctrinal standards defined in elaborate Calvinistic creeds such as the Westminister Confession. A creedal church composed largely of rural, conservative communicants often hampered easy adjustment to new theological ideas and interpretations. Nor did the Presbyterian academic institution, Davidson College, take a forthright stand against the fundamentalist offensive within the denomination. The college possessed a distinguished history, to be sure; but during the evolution controversy, it failed to exert among the Presbyterians an influence comparable to that wielded by Wake Forest and Trinity among the Baptists and Methodists, respectively. Even Cyclone McLendon vouched for Davidson's orthodoxy.[67] But Davidson's role in the fundamentalist-modernist conflict becomes more understandable when viewed in the light of the legacy bequeathed by the controversy over evolution which rocked the southern Presbyterian church forty years earlier. The storm center of that dispute was James Woodrow, a professor in Columbia Seminary in South Carolina, who was ultimately dismissed for his unorthodox views in 1884. Geographical proximity between Columbia and Davidson as well as the existence of close ties between the Presbyterians of North and South Carolina caused the Woodrow affair to have a particularly significant impact upon North Carolina Presbyterians who ever after maintained a persistent vigilance over the orthodoxy of their own academic institutions.[68]

Another factor that may help to explain the position of North Carolina Presbyterians in the evolution controversy was the activities of two nationally prominent Presbyterians, Billy Sunday and William Jennings Bryan. Regardless of their interdenominational appeal,

67. Walter L. Lingle, *Presbyterians, Their History and Beliefs* (Richmond, 1961), pp. 117–28; Baxter F. McLendon, *Defending the Faith and Other Sermons* (Clinton, S.C.), p. 28; *Charlotte News* quoted in *News and Observer*, February 7, 1923.

68. See Clement Eaton, "Professor James Woodrow and the Freedom of Teaching in the South," *The Journal of Southern History*, XXVIII (February, 1962), 3–17.

these men still wore the Presbyterian label that in itself made their appeals particularly effective among their fellow Presbyterians in North Carolina. Although individual ministers in the state favored more doctrinal flexibility than was allowed by the Bryan-Sunday variety of theology, there was little unified effort within the official ranks of the denomination to achieve such ends. On the contrary, the appeal of Bryan and Sunday to their Presbyterian brethren was strengthened by what amounted to denominational endorsement of their theology. Bolstered by the activities of these famous sons of the church, local Presbyterian fundamentalists waged a persistent campaign against the Darwinian theory on the grounds that it was contrary to the historic creeds of their denomination. Among the most active fundamentalists in North Carolina were Presbyterians who occupied key posts in the church such as Synod moderators and evangelists and influential figures within the presbyteries. It was no accident, therefore, that the most concentrated fight on evolution emanated from Charlotte and Mecklenburg County, a stronghold of Presbyterianism "of the blue stocking variety," that a Presbyterian governor banned evolution books from the public schools, that Presbyterians dominated the most active anti-evolutionist organization in the state, and that a Presbyterian elder sponsored the bill to outlaw the teaching of evolution.

The *Presbyterian Standard*, the organ of the North Carolina Synod published in Charlotte, placed itself in the fundamentalist camp at the very beginning of the controversy. The editors, J. R. Bridges and R. C. Reed, characterized themselves as "mossback conservatives" and persisted throughout the 1920's in their efforts to hold their brethren to their doctrinal vows. What began as an enlightened and moderate editorial approach to the issues in dispute had assumed an acrimonious tone by the middle of the decade. In January, 1924, the *Standard* explained that the modernists and fundamentalists differed primarily in their "attitudes toward the Bible": the fundamentalists viewed the Bible as the divinely inspired, "virtually inerrant," Word of God and only "infallible rule of faith and practice"; the modernists, while believing that God revealed himself in the Bible, refused to believe that God spoke "throughout the whole Bible with an authoritative voice." For the *Standard*, the chief defect of modernism was its lack of a stable anchor; the modernists relied too much on human reason and placed too much emphasis on the evolutionary nature of biblical teachings. "They find that the moral and religious teachings [of the Bible] underwent a slow and gradual development; consequently we must correct the earlier religious teachings by the later." Such a position, the *Standard* noted with alarm, was so far removed from historic Christianity that modernists should remove themselves from the traditional denominations and establish their own churches. "Don't feed from our larder," it warned, "while undermining our foundations." [69]

As 1924 progressed, the *Standard* became increasingly harsh in its criticism of evolution and modernism. It claimed that evolutionists reduced the Old Testament to the plane of naturalism, discarded Pauline theology because it was based on the story of Eden and the fall of man, and skirted shyly around the figure of Christ, whom they hesitated to label as a product of evolution. But, said the *Standard,* if the modernists pursued a logical development of their own ideas, they would have to consider Christ a "descendent of the same Semian stock as the rest of us." Of course, such an interpretation would invalidate the Christian religion. The *Standard* saw no need to modify the Word of God to satisfy the whims of a "few intellectuals" by eliminating all of Christ's teachings which failed to harmonize with evolution. Moreover, the issues at stake left no room for neutrality; they demanded a candid stand, either positive or negative, on the part of every churchman. The *Standard* proclaimed its readiness to stand by the inerrant scriptures, including the Genesis account, and to banish scientific theories whenever "these theories in any way contradict the Bible." [70]

Although the *Standard* often resorted to the use of extravagant language in damning the evolutionists and modernists, it probably offered the most penetrating statement of the fundamentalist credo to be found in the religious press of North Carolina. In the summer and fall of 1924 the editors sought to define what they believed to be the most fundamental of the Christian fundamentals—the divine revelation of truth. They claimed that it was necessary "to have a

69. *Presbyterian Standard,* LXV (January 2, 1924), 1–2; *ibid.,* LXV (January 16, 1924), 1; *ibid.,* LXV (January 30, 1924), 1; *ibid.,* LXV (February 20, 1924), 1.

70. *Presbyterian Standard,* LXV (March 26, 1924), 2; *ibid.,* LXV (May 14, 1924), 1.

revelation free from any doubt, else we would not know how to separate the true from the false." A faulty human reason could scarcely be risked in making a decision upon which salvation hinged. Therefore, the *Standard* rejected the modernists' claim that the revelation of truth could be "subjectively apprehended or acquired by the experience of each man for himself." Instead, reliance must be placed upon the miraculous, supernatural element in Christianity as the means of comprehending the "things of the Spirit of God." Therefore, the crux of the matter lay in whether doctrine or experience was primary. The fundamentalist position of the *Standard* required that doctrine be emphasized as more basic than experience, for the source of doctrines was "special divine revelation." Thus, Christian doctrines were "objective realities" absolutely independent of experience; and "Christianity as a system of religion was finished some nineteen hundred years ago" when its "limits were unalterably fixed by the lids of the Bible." Whatever else evolution was able to accomplish, it could "never alter or improve the Christian religion." [71]

In order to demonstrate the logic of its position, the *Standard* contrasted it with the theological stance of modernism which made experience more basic than doctrine. If experience gave rise to doctrine, then doctrine was earthly in its origin and possessed only such authority as subjective experience gave it. Springing from a subjective source, doctrine lacked any external authority, and religion itself, stripped of its supernatural qualities, was in "a state of flux, undergoing a process of evolution," in which each generation had to formulate its own doctrines. The *Standard* warned Presbyterians to beware of modernists parading in Christian trappings, lest they fall prey to the perils inherent in the vague, evolutionary theology of modernism. Spiritual impoverishment was certain unless Presbyterians adhered to a belief in the "Old Time religion based on the Old Time Bible" which was "plenary verbally inspired" and "infallible from Genesis to Revelation." [72]

Deviating sharply from this approach, however, was that of D. Clay Lilly, a well-known Presbyterian preacher from Winston-Salem.

71. *Presbyterian Standard,* LXV (August 30, 1924), 2; *ibid.,* LXV (November 5, 1924), 1.

72. *Presbyterian Standard,* LXV (November 5, 1924), 1; *ibid.,* LXV (May 14, 1924), 1.

Lilly had been persuaded to accept the pulpit at the chapel located at "Reynolda," the estate of the R. J. Reynolds family near Winston. The generous financial assistance of the Reynolds family enabled him to undertake a variety of experiments, one of which was the "Reynolda Conference" to discuss "the current crisis in Christianity." First organized in 1924, these conferences became annual affairs, attracting widespread attention. Twenty-five scholars and theologians representing all shades of opinion gathered at Reynolda in 1924 to "attempt to state the defense of our common faith in terms of today." [73] Among those who accepted evolution as a part of the Christian's intellectual apparatus were William Louis Poteat of Wake Forest College, Collier Cobb of the University of North Carolina, William H. Wood and John M. Mecklin of Dartmouth College, and Melvin G. Kile of Xenia Theological Seminary. The most outspoken critics of evolution were Leander Keyser of Hamma Divinity School and W. H. McPheeters of Columbia Theological Seminary. The trend of thought at the conference was "distinctly conservative in reference to divine revelation," but the factual inerrancy of the Bible was "pretty completely disassociated from spiritual infallibility." One observer at Reynolda in 1924 insisted that "men at either extreme are beginning to react toward a center of moderation." While these annual gatherings at the Reynolda estate helped to temper the anti-evolutionist activities within the Presbyterian church, they were scarcely able to offset the impact of those determined to banish "the Darwinian heresy." [74]

The reverberations of the evolution controversy were by no means confined to the larger denominations. Virtually all churches felt its impact, but some, like the Disciples of Christ, purposefully omitted any official recognition of the disturbance for fear of encouraging a dissension which would distract the church from its essential tasks. Therefore, C. C. Ware, editor of the Disciples' paper, kept its columns closed to all discussions of the evolution question.[75] Similarly, the United Evangelical Lutheran Synod of North Carolina

73. *Winston-Salem Journal*, June 15, 1924.

74. "The Reynolda Conferences," Scrapbook, Presbyterian and Reformed Historical Center, Montreat, North Carolina.

75. Interview with C. C. Ware, March 10, 1962.

managed to maintain intra-church harmony, although an overt rupture appeared imminent on several occasions. Dr. Ernest R. McCauley of the Holy Trinity Church in Raleigh was the chief spokesman for those Lutherans who refused to accept the idea that evolution and Christianity were incompatible. In all probability, however, the majority of the thirty thousand Lutherans in the state agreed with the staunchly anti-evolutionist views of the Reverend A. R. Beck, editor of the *North Carolina Lutheran*. Although this official synodical mouthpiece rarely included original editorials, most of those that it published during the first five years after its establishment in 1923 concerned various facets of the evolution controversy. The contents of these editorials placed the *Lutheran* second only to the *Presbyterian Standard*, among the church papers in the state, in its hostility to the teaching of organic evolution—"that rehash of old Grecian philosophy" being substituted "for the Old Book." [76]

Despite its comparatively small membership, the Protestant Episcopal Church was one of the most powerful denominations in North Carolina. Its constituency probably represented the most sophisticated elements in the state; and although the church did not escape the agitation over evolution altogether, it suffered little internal dissension as a result and probably contained fewer anti-evolution extremists than any other major ecclesiastical body in the state. The church papers that represented the two dioceses in North Carolina reflected the attitudes most prevalent among Episcopalians. On the one hand, the *Carolina Churchman*, organ of the Diocese of North Carolina, disregarded the evolution issue altogether. On the other, the *Mission Herald*, the organ of the Diocese of East Carolina edited by Theodore Partrick of Scotland Neck, took a forthright stand against all efforts to eliminate from the academic curricula everything that failed to fit a peculiar theological mold. In fact, the *Herald* was the only religious paper in the state whose editorial policy might be considered an expression of the modernist viewpoint. Partrick, however, sought to avoid flying in the face of orthodoxy; he pleaded for a "sane view of the live issues" and for a clear distinction between the essential and nonessential elements in religion. Disturbed by the

76. *North Carolina Lutheran*, I (September, 1923), 4; *ibid.*, III (March, 1925), 1, 7; *ibid.*, V (February, 1927), 6.

Methodist agitation over Bland's lectures at Junaluska, he warned his own people to steer clear of all attempts to curb modern scholarship and to avoid "unnecessary panic when facing the march of scientific study." [77]

The *Mission Herald* often discussed the relationship between science and religion and in skillfully executed editorials sought to dispel the notion that the two were incompatible. In one editorial in 1924 entitled, "Miracles of Faith and the Limitations of Science," [78] editor Partrick maintained that *great* scientists always realized the limitations of their methods and study and that religion was an aspect of reality beyond the reach of scientific inquiry. Among the great mysteries of faith "that illumine all life yet which cannot be explained in scientific terms" was the personality of Jesus, the study of which would forever lead to the conclusion that "He is Very God and Very Man." Partrick explained, too, that "much about our religious beliefs will change" with new discoveries and observations; yet the essence of faith belonged to the supernatural sphere, and admission to that sphere "is by faith and spiritual insight." Science, he declared, had "overturned many accepted ideas, not because she is a heretic, but in the interest of truth." The spirit of scientific inquiry should not therefore be met with the spirit of the Inquisition. Nor should people fear the "spirit of inquiry" as an onslaught upon faith in the Bible. "It seems to us," the *Herald* observed, "that it is the worst sort of scepticism to believe that our faith cannot be subjected to the clear light of advancing knowledge." If, in all discussions of science and evolution, churchmen would remember Saint Paul's dictum that spiritual realities could only be spiritually discerned, they would have little cause to fear the impairment of their faith at the hands of scientific inquiry.[79] The *Herald*'s crusade for "a sane view" of the evolution issue later received the official endorsement of the Diocese of East Carolina, when in 1926 it lodged a vigorous protest against any attempt to infringe upon academic freedom in the name of any particular brand of theology. This action was the only official statement by a major religious body in North Carolina directed specifically against the activities of the anti-evolutionists.

77. *Mission Herald*, XXXVII (February, 1923), 8–9; *ibid.*, XXXVII (December, 1923), 8; *ibid.*, XL (May, 1926), p. 8.
78. *Mission Herald*, XXXVIII (February, 1924), 11.
79. *Mission Herald*, XXXVIII (February, 1924), 11–12.

4 ~ THE FIRST SKIRMISHES

"If teachers of science use geology, biology and other sciences to unsettle the religious faith of our children, the Christian people of our country are not going to stand for it, and they ought not to stand for it."

—GOVERNOR CAMERON MORRISON OF NORTH CAROLINA

Regardless of the official stands taken by the various religious denominations, individuals from all communions continued to be disturbed by the "evolution question." To corroborate their views on the malign influences of evolution they did not have to rely upon the testimony of "foreign" evangelists. A native son who had achieved world fame as a fundamentalist theologian provided all the authority they needed to denounce and deride evolution. He was Amazi Clarence Dixon, who returned to North Carolina in 1922 to spend the Christmas holidays with his family. During his visit he delivered a highly publicized sermon in the First Baptist Church in Raleigh which attracted particular attention among Baptists in North Carolina where the name Dixon had long occupied a distinguished place in the history of the denomination. His sermon was probably the most comprehensive indictment of evolution uttered by a fundamentalist minister during the entire controversy in North Carolina.

The famous preacher began by explaining that his studies in both science and theology qualified him to speak with authority on the compatibility of evolution and Christianity. Then, turning to the scientific authenticity of evolution, he dismissed the Darwinian hypothesis as a "biological absurdity" contrived by the use of "unscientific procedures." Darwin's theory, resting on false assumptions, had produced a succession of equally false conclusions and other by-products that paraded as "science." Dixon denied that there was "a struggle for existence even among carnivorous animals," because God "provided a kinder method of preventing a dangerous increase." He also dismissed the so-called geological evidences of evolution because "rocks and fossils on this continent have been found to be in reverse order from those in Europe, rendering it impossible to determine the age of either by its relative position." Thus, he accused evolutionists of foisting off a "pernicious doctrine" as scientific truth upon a gullible public inclined to accept uncritically all pronouncements made in the name of science.

Moving to the theological implications of evolution, Dixon pointed to three major areas in which Darwinism made frontal assaults on Christianity: it disputed the whole Christian concept of the nature of man; it made Christ a mere man like all the rest who were products of "the jungle beasts"; and it reduced the Bible to "a mere record of human experience as men have struggled up from their jungle origins." "If man came down from God, created in His Own Image and has been wrecked by sin," Dixon declared, "then sin is . . . an enemy that ought to be expelled, but if man came up from the beast through the jungle, sin is an 'embryonic goodness' . . . [which] has no guilt and may be condoned, if not coddled." By rationalizing sin out of existence, the evolutionists encouraged all forms of immorality. And, according to Dixon, the prime example of the evil by-products of Darwinism was the recent history of Germany where Nietzsche and the higher critics had fostered a Darwinian philosophy that produced the spiritual bankruptcy responsible for World War I. But the world did not eliminate the evil by defeating Germany, for Bolshevism was merely another expression of the Darwinian heresy. "If Darwin was right and the evolutionists . . . are right," Dixon concluded, "Germany was right and Lenin and Trotsky are right." His association of evolution with Germany's "demoniac struggle for power" and Bolshevik Russia's "rule by bayonet" made Darwinism appear all the more menacing to

North Carolinians who at the time were under the spell of the wartime hysteria against "Prussianism" and the postwar Red Scare. Many were inclined to believe Dixon's conclusion that evolution was "the most infernal doctrine that ever came from the pits of hell." [1]

Local clergymen hostile to the teaching of evolution echoed the sentiments expressed by this famous native son. A Baptist minister in Zebulon, C. A. Jenkins, told his congregation on April 16, 1923, that "the hour has struck to lance this putrid ulcer [evolution] that has fastened itself on the body of our civilization threatening to destroy the Bible itself." Jenkins claimed that evolution had "pulled off its first stunt in the Garden of Eden and the Devil was the first evolutionist." To prove that the Darwinian hypothesis was little more than a bad guess he pointed to its "failure" to explain the soul, sex, or the origin of life, quoted nineteenth-century scientists hostile to the theory, and derided evolutionists for predicating a so-called scientific truth upon nonexistent "missing links." At the conclusion of his sermon the Zebulon Baptist Church passed resolutions requesting the dismissal of all faculty members in Baptist schools who taught or held "the theory of evolution in any of its forms." [2] Throughout North Carolina in 1923 and 1924 similar sermons on the "God-or-Gorilla" theme emanated from numerous pulpits. Preaching in Gastonia on February 17, 1924, Bishop Warren A. Candler of the Methodist Church castigated modernists and evolutionists for "spreading doubt and heresy." Early in the following year, Albert Sydney Johnson, a prominent Presbyterian minister of Charlotte, claimed the teaching of evolution led to "carnality, sensuality, bolshevism, and the Red Flag." His indictments of evolution soon gained him a place on the program of the annual meeting of the World's Christian Fundamentals Association.[3] All the while, J. Frank Norris, the peripatetic Baptist parson from Fort Worth,

1. *News and Observer*, December 27, 1922; the complete text of the sermon was printed in the *News and Observer*, December 31, 1922; for an account of Dixon's career, see Helen C. A. Dixon, *A. C. Dixon: A Romance of Preaching* (New York, 1931).

2. *News and Observer*, April 17, 1923.

3. *Gastonia Gazette*, February 18, 1924; *Charlotte Observer*, February 24, 1925; *Union Republican* (Winston-Salem), March 5, 1925; the "God-or-Gorilla" theme was apparently popularized by the publication of Alfred W. McCann's *God—or Gorilla* (New York, 1922).

Texas, was waging war on Poteat and Wake Forest in the columns of his fundamentalist paper called the *Searchlight*.[4]

Like the clergy, laymen were manifesting a growing interest in the disturbance over evolution. At civic clubs as well as in the church sanctuaries, laymen heard evolution discussed by protagonists of varying talents. Conversations at the bridge table, the country store, and the barber shop almost invariably turned to the subject that was being so widely discussed in the newspapers. Those who owned radios could listen to station WBT in Charlotte which carried the anti-evolutionist sermons of Luther Little, an influential Baptist minister.[5] Among the few documents that recorded the individual opinions of the laity were the letters-to-the-editor which began to appear in profusion in the major dailies by 1922. Rarely was there a letter from anyone who might be called an evolutionist or modernist. For the most part the correspondents were little more sophisticated in their views than the Goldsboro physician who wrote: "O, well, let the scientists evolve all they want to, but it will be a cold day in August before they convince many of us that there was ever a time in the history of the human race when man chattered among the coconut trees, and basked in the sunlight extended from a limb by his narrative." [6]

The arguments against evolution advanced during the opening years of the 1920's remained essentially the same throughout the decade. Critics contended that evolution was "unproved and unprovable," hence it was "unscientific" and ought not to be taught as science. But in the minds of many North Carolinians evolution was not a scientific question at all—it was a theological matter. Thus their chief objections to it were of a religious nature. Evolution appeared to deny the basic propositions of their Christian faith. It "contradicted" the biblical account of man's origins and substituted a belief in man's ascent from primitive conditions to a fuller life for the Christian concept of the fall of man. This substitution, in their

4. *Searchlight* (Fort Worth, Texas), August 3, 1923, February 29, 1924.

5. *Mooresville Enterprise*, January 20, 1927; H. W. Chase to Luther Little, February 16, 1925, The University of North Carolina Papers, Southern Historical Collection (University of North Carolina Library, Chapel Hill); hereafter cited as University Papers.

6. *News and Observer*, May 23, 1922.

opinion, invalidated the whole basis of the doctrine of sin. Moreover, the Darwinian heresy "cut the heart" from the New Testament's hope of salvation by making Jesus "a Jewish bastard." In short, evolution had fractured the foundations of the moral order and shaken faith in the eternal verities.

Equally disturbing to a people so conscious of race and ancestry was the assault that evolution appeared to make upon their traditional view of man. It "robbed him of his dignity" by reducing him to the level of a mere animal—the "first cousin of the ape." Such degradation distressed North Carolinians for two reasons in particular: first, it disturbed their notions of white supremacy which assumed a biological and intellectual superiority for their Anglo-Saxon ancestry; second, it seemed to jeopardize such basic institutions of human civilization as marriage, the home, and the family. "If the home is to be preserved as a sacred institution," one anti-evolutionist declared, "the Bible, which teaches that marriage came down from God and not up from the beast, must be preserved." Having denied that man was a moral being, the "jungle theory" spread abroad the notion that he was "a brute" with the attributes of a lower animal rather than those of a creature "made in God's own image." The acceptance of such ideas had resulted in secularism, heresy, sexual immorality, "busy divorce courts," the collapse of parental authority, adultery, juvenile delinquency, and the disintegration of the family. The fight against evolution was in large part an effort to save the children—the future generation—from being plunged "into the pits of darkness" by the teachings of "a dirty theory." It was essentially a struggle for power over the mind and the educational institutions in which the "tender minds" were being molded.[7]

The appearance of William Jennings Bryan in North Carolina in 1923 considerably enhanced the anti-evolutionist cause, because Bryan was still a hero of many North Carolinians who revered him as the political champion of rural America. They were enthusiastic in their support of his current efforts to defend the "old-time religion," itself a rural virtue, from the menaces of a secularism that emanated

7. *News and Observer*, February 29, March 28, 1924; *Goldsboro News*, August 4, 5, 6, 1926; Charles F. Bluske to William Louis Poteat, September 17, 1925, Poteat Papers; Sylvester Hassell, *Evolution* (n.p., 1925).

primarily from cities. Following World War I, Bryan energetically joined the movement to outlaw the teaching of evolution as a means of protecting orthodox Christianity. He publicly proclaimed the anti-evolution crusade as the greatest moral reform movement with which he had ever been associated. North Carolinians had maintained great interest in his latest crusade, especially his efforts to secure an anti-evolution law in Kentucky.[8] They had read his assaults on evolution which appeared in his syndicated newspaper articles. Many undoubtedly believed that a brief campaign by the Great Commoner in North Carolina would spell doom for the Darwinian menace. For these his first visit to the state was thoroughly disappointing because Bryan's speech in Tarboro on February 22, 1923, in behalf of the Kiwanis Education Fund contained no reference to evolution or Darwin.[9]

Bryan returned to North Carolina, again under the auspices of the Kiwanis Club, in the spring of the same year for a round of speech-making in Raleigh. This time he did not disappoint those who wished to hear in person his views on evolution. Over two thousand people from all parts of the state gathered in the Raleigh city auditorium to hear his address on April 28, 1923, which was delivered with the same eloquence and conviction "that stung Tar Heel Democracy into a frenzy of loyalty in days past." His address was entitled, "The World's Greatest Need," a topic that lent itself to a full scale indictment of evolution. Beginning with the assertion that the world's greatest need was the love of God, Bryan quickly moved to the real subject of his speech, evolution, which he described as the greatest single deterrent to the fulfillment of that need. The theory of evolution, he said, was "the only menace to religion that has appeared in the last 1900 years." He denounced as agnostics the scientists and pedagogues who ridiculed his fundamentalist theology and accused them of failing to understand the theory in which they placed so much faith. Clearly smarting under the criticism by academicians, the Great Commoner pointed to his honorary degrees as adequate evidence of his intellectual qualifications and challenged

8. See Frank L. McVey, *The Gates Open Slowly: A History of Education in Kentucky* (Lexington, 1949), pp. 221–36; Lawrence Levine, *Defender of the Faith: William Jennings Bryan, The Last Decade* (New York, 1965), pp. 277–78.

9. *News and Observer*, February 23, 1923.

any "son of an ape to match cards" with him. He boasted that the last so-called "scholar" to challenge his intelligence was a professor in Kentucky who ever since had been unemployed. Bryan dismissed as ridiculous "the spectacle of learned scientists trying to construct the missing links out of pieces of bone found in various excavations." There was nothing scientific about the theory of evolution; on the contrary, it was a ridiculous and dangerous "guess" that destroyed "men's faith in God, Christ, and the Bible." To demonstrate the insidious influence of evolution, he pointed to Darwin's own life which, wrecked by the theory, ended in the atheist's grave. The teaching of evolution in public schools would doom American children to the same terrible fate. When men believe they are descended from animals, Bryan argued, they lose their identity as men and glorify the brutish traits of their ancestors rather than seeking to attain the noble qualities of the human spirit. He refused to believe that "brute blood" flowed in man's veins or that the monkey was the ancestor of humanity. More than once the Great Commoner had his two-hour address interrupted by "deafening applause," but none of his remarks produced such obviously wholehearted approval as his concluding plea for the Christian taxpayers of North Carolina to drive the evolutionists from their public schools in order to preserve true Christianity and public morality.[10]

Neither of Bryan's visits to North Carolina during 1923 seem to have been the work of anti-evolutionists with any specific aim in mind. If he had been brought to the state to accomplish what he almost succeeded in doing in Kentucky, he undoubtedly would have appeared before the state legislature, which was in session during his first visit. No evidence suggests that such an appearance was even discussed by the legislators or anyone else. But regardless of the intentions of those who arranged his visits, his presence and speeches elicited widespread interest in the discussion of evolution and, for some, undoubtedly heralded the beginning of serious efforts to eliminate the Darwinian heresy from state-supported schools and colleges. On the other hand, Bryan's sojourns in the state created ideological difficulties for those who respected his past politics but disagreed with his current theology. Among those bedeviled by such divided loyalties was Josephus Daniels, personal friend of Bryan and

10. *News and Observer*, April 27, 28, 29, 1923.

editor of the influential Raleigh *News and Observer*. One observer noted that the Raleigh paper remained "silent in several languages." Actually Daniels grudgingly cast his lot against the anti-evolutionists but continued to laud Bryan and to insist that "half baked professors" had started the whole unfortunate controversy.[11]

The anxiety and alarm created by the discussion of evolution and its destructive influences soon aroused interest in means for safeguarding Christianity in North Carolina. By the summer of 1921 sentiment seemed to favor the teaching of Bible courses in public schools and colleges as the best way to counteract the spread of paganism. A proposed constitutional amendment to require Bible reading in all public schools had failed in 1913 largely due to the efforts of Judge Walter Clark and various Baptist leaders. The State Sunday School Association spearheaded the new movement to introduce Bible teaching in the public schools. Its spokesman, J. M. Broughton of Raleigh, presented a proposal to the North Carolina Teachers' Assembly, the statewide teachers' association, at its meeting in November, 1922. The Broughton plan provided for Bible instruction "directed by denominations working closely with public schools." Students would receive public school credit for such courses. The Teachers' Assembly was about to accept this proposal when Eugene C. Brooks, State Superintendent of Public Instruction, intervened to have the matter buried in a "study committee." Like others, Brooks feared that such a procedure would violate the principle of separation of church and state.[12]

During the next four years, the question of Bible instruction for public school credit was debated throughout North Carolina. Although the issue was permanently shelved by the Teachers' Assem-

11. *News and Observer*, April 28, 1923, February 20, 1925; Robert W. Winston, *Horace Williams: Gadfly of Chapel Hill* (Chapel Hill, 1942), p. 212; Gerald Johnson described the *News and Observer*'s position as follows: "It rolls a soft-boiled eye at the Ku Klux Klan and the Fundamentalists. It professes high respect for Thomas Jefferson, but obviously doubts that he intended the Bill of Rights to apply to Republicans, bootleggers, college professors and Socialists." Gerald W. Johnson, "Journalism Below the Potomac," *The American Mercury*, IX (September, 1926), 81.

12. *Biblical Recorder*, LXXXVII (July 27, 1921), 6; *ibid.*, LXXXVII (December 7, 1921), 7; *ibid.*, LXXXVII (January 4, 1922), 6; *ibid.*, LXXXVII (January 25, 1922), 4, 6; *News and Observer*, November 26, 1921; *The Papers of Walter Clark*, ed. Hugh T. Lefler and Audrey L. Brooks (Chapel Hill, 1950), II, 191, 208–20.

bly, other groups on the local level took up the cause.[13] By 1925 five cities in the state had authorized the establishment of Bible courses, and Charlotte's "Bible-in-the-Public-Schools-Central-Committee" was seeking to incorporate a required course in Bible study in the high school curriculum.[14] Dr. W. A. Harper, president of church-related Elon College, strongly favored "legal" recognition for Bible instruction so that credit might "be given for it toward high school graduation." State Superintendent of Public Instruction Arch T. Allen, who succeeded Brooks in June, 1923, opposed Harper's plan and suggested that gaining a "comprehensive meaning of the Christian religion" rather than high school credits would be a more appropriate aim for such instruction.[15] Allen was adamant in his opposition to public school credit for Bible instruction; his position became eminently clear when the Lexington city board of education presented its plan for handling Bible instruction. Under this proposal the school board would employ a full-time Bible teacher in the city high school to offer instruction in Bible "for no less time than history or English." The course and its instructor would be under the jurisdiction of a Bible Study Board of three members, two from the city's ministerial association and one from the city board of education. Allen considered the arrangement wholly unsatisfactory, and although he could not actually veto the scheme, his powers were sufficient to force the local authorities to amend and adjust the Bible study proposal so that the course was entirely elective and completely under the supervision of the board of education.[16]

At the same time various denominational groups were attempting to devise Bible courses in state-supported colleges. Although a prominent Baptist suggested a Bible curriculum for the state univer-

13. *The Presbyterian Standard* was one of the most avid champions of Bible study in the public schools. See the *Presbyterian Standard,* LXII (December 15, 1920), 3; *ibid.,* LXII (April 21, 1920), 3; *ibid.,* LXIII (January 25, 1922), 2.

14. A. T. Allen to Mrs. H. J. Spencer, October 28, 1925, Correspondence of the State Superintendent of Public Instruction, Department of Archives and History, Raleigh; hereafter cited as State Superintendent's Correspondence; *Biblical Recorder,* XC (October 8, 1924), 1.

15. W. A. Harper to A. T. Allen, February 4, 1925, A. T. Allen to W. A. Harper, February 5, 1925, W. A. Harper to A. T. Allen, February 6, 1925, A. T. Allen to W. A. Harper, February 13, 1925, State Superintendent's Correspondence.

16. J. H. Cowles to A. T. Allen, May 30, 1925, A. T. Allen to J. H. Cowles, June 2, 1925, State Superintendent's Correspondence.

sity in 1921, the Presbyterians soon assumed the leadership of the movement and in October, 1923, the Synod appointed a "Committee on Bible in State Schools of Higher Learning." This committee was instructed to contact other Protestant bodies in North Carolina about the possibility of interdenominational support of Bible professors in state colleges. Such teachers were to be paid by church funds and employed by the college trustees. On January 8, 1924, the Presbyterians convened a special meeting in Greensboro where twenty-four ministers representing eight denominations organized the Conference on Religious Education in Our State Institutions of Higher Learning. This group concentrated upon establishing Bible instruction at the University of North Carolina and created a subcommittee to work toward this specific goal. On February 5, 1924, representatives of the University and of the Conference met in the office of President Harry W. Chase in Chapel Hill and agreed in principle that Bible should be offered in some manner to University students. But no definite steps toward its implementation were taken. Although the Presbyterians continued to champion the cause, their enthusiasm for the project had diminished appreciably by the fall of 1924. Some credited this change of heart to their fear of losing control of the "chair in Bible." At any rate, the Synod instructed its representatives to the Conference late in 1924 to avoid any agreement whereby "control of the Bible teaching in the state institutions may be lodged in other than church hands." Negotiations between the University and the churches dragged on for several years without tangible results regarding the Bible courses. In the final analysis, an interdenominational School of Religion was established in Chapel Hill in 1926.[17]

The opposition to Bible instruction for credit in state-supported schools and colleges came primarily from those hostile to any measure likely to jeopardize the separation of church and state

17. Louis R. Wilson, *The University of North Carolina, 1900–1930: The Making of a Modern University* (Chapel Hill, 1957), pp. 539–41; *Evening Telegram* (Rocky Mount), January 11, February 6, 1924, May 30, 1925; *Gastonia Gazette*, January 12, 1924; Minutes of Special Meeting with Representatives of the Conferences on Religious Education in Our State Institutions of Higher Learning, February 5, 1924, University Papers; *Minutes of the One Hundred and Tenth Annual Session of the Synod of North Carolina, 1923*, p. 187; see below, pp. 180–81.

principle. Since the Baptist denomination had historically considered this principle to be one of its hallowed precepts it is not surprising to find a considerable number of Baptist leaders aligned against the movement to incorporate Bible study in the public school curriculum. The *Biblical Recorder*, probably the most outspoken opponent of the movement, maintained that any attempt by the state to teach religion would not only be contrary to the basic principles of American government but would also force upon the state a duty that it was not equipped to perform. However, the *Recorder* was equally adamant in its opposition to any attempt by the state to teach anti-Christian doctrines. "That things are being taught in some of our state schools which are contrary to important doctrines held by all evangelical denominations," the Baptist paper asserted, "is too well known to be denied." In brief, teachers in state-supported institutions had no more right to attack Christianity than they had to teach it.[18]

Much of the agitation about Bible instruction in tax-supported institutions focused upon the University of North Carolina, a storm center of denominational hostilities in the nineteenth century. Although the basis of the antagonism differed from time to time, the University was usually accused of atheism, irreligion, or infidelity before the demise of these sporadic outbursts. By the twentieth century its most persistent critics, the Methodists and Baptists, had reached a *modus vivendi* with the institution. But the Presbyterians who historically had been closely identified with the University assumed the role once played by the Methodists and Baptists. So many Presbyterians occupied positions of influence within the University during the nineteenth century that it was sometimes described as an agency of the Presbyterian church. However, the church's warm relationship with the University appeared to cool in somewhat the same degree that the number and influence of Presbyterian membership decreased.[19] This factor, coupled with the decline in outward piety on the Chapel Hill campus during the

18. *Biblical Recorder*, LXXXVII (July 27, 1921), 6; *ibid.*, LXXXVII (January 25, 1922), 6; *ibid.*, LXXXVIII (January 17, 1923), 6–7; *ibid.*, XC (April 8, 1925), 11.

19. Luther Gobbel, *Church-State Relationships in Education in North Carolina Since 1776* (Durham, 1938), pp. 58–59, 65–66, 159; Kemp Battle, *History of the University of North Carolina* (Raleigh, 1907), II, 478–93.

immediate post-World War I period, aroused anxiety among Presbyterians over the spiritual condition of the college. Like other denominational bodies, they viewed certain specific events as evidence of the institution's increasing disregard for the moral aspects of education. Required attendance at chapel services had been dropped just before World War I. Then, early in the 1920's, President Harry Chase discontinued the custom of presenting Bibles to all graduates at commencement, and finally the University offered no courses in Bible for credit.[20] All major denominations frowned on these omissions, but the Presbyterians led a spirited attack on "the godless education" provided by state schools. The *Presbyterian Standard* utilized the findings of Professor James H. Leuba of Bryn Mawr to support the charge that such institutions were manned by modernists and infidels who were producing spiritual aridity among the new generation. The obvious implication with which many North Carolinians agreed was that Leuba's description aptly fitted their own state university.[21]

When efforts to include Bible courses in the curricula of tax-supported schools failed to win immediate approval, many North Carolinians concluded that the only alternative was to outlaw those "teachings" that contradicted the Bible. A citizen of La Grange expressed a common sentiment when he declared: "If we forbid the teaching of the Bible, let us forbid the teaching of evolution." For some, the unwillingness of the state schools to offer Bible instruction for credit merely confirmed their suspicions that such schools were hotbeds of agnosticism. "When one forbids the Bible to be taught," a Goldsboro citizen declared, "it seems to be bordering on being anti-Christian." [22] Moreover, the discussion of Bible instruction in public institutions coupled with Poteat's triumph in the Baptist State Convention in 1922 helped to shift the focus of the evolution controversy from the church-related schools to the state colleges and public schools. This shift was all the more understandable in view of the background of hostility between denominational and state

20. Julian S. Carr to H. W. Chase, February 2, 1924, University Papers.
21. *Presbyterian Standard,* LXI (December 15, 1920), 3; *ibid.,* LXV (January 2, 1924), 1–2, 4.
22. *News and Observer,* March 5, 8, 1922.

schools in North Carolina. Since vestiges of this antagonism continued to exist, it was easy for churchmen to discover that state educational institutions were the real culprits and to blame them for "the rampant secularism" that engulfed the state. Whatever the reasons for the shift, the evolution controversy in North Carolina by late 1923 concentrated upon publicly supported schools rather than upon denominational colleges.

Evidence of this change became apparent in January, 1924, when the sub-textbook commission, composed of professional educators, made its biennial recommendation regarding state-adopted textbooks to the State Board of Education. At this juncture, Governor Cameron Morrison, ex-officio chairman of the Board, intervened to suggest that two of the six recommended biology books, Gruenberg's *Elementary Biology* and Trafton's *Biology of Home and Community,* be rejected on the grounds that their references to evolution disqualified them for use in public schools. "One of these books teaches that man is descended from a monkey," the Governor declared, "and the other that he is a cousin to the monkey. I don't believe either of them." An illustration in Trafton's book which showed the gibbon, orangutan, chimpanzee, gorilla, and man sketched across the same page moved Morrison to remark: "I don't want my daughter or anybody's daughter to have to study a book that prints pictures of a monkey and a man on the same page." In accordance with Morrison's suggestion, the two biology textbooks were stricken from the list of adoptions, although some questioned the legality of the rejection.[23] Later, State Superintendent of Public Instruction Arch T. Allen, who apparently acquiesced in the Board's decision, confessed that he did not know what effect, if any, the action had upon the teaching of evolution in public schools.[24]

The intervention by the Governor was not surprising in view of his own orthodox Presbyterianism and warm endorsement of the fundamentalist revivalists then engaged in crusades in North Carolina. The

23. Director of Publication to George Thorpe, August 13, 1924, State Superintendent's Correspondence; *News and Observer,* January 24, 1924; Edgar W. Knight, "Monkey or Mud in North Carolina," *The Independent,* CXVIII (May 14, 1927), 515–16; Maynard Shipley, *The War on Modern Science: A Short History of the Fundamentalist Attacks on Evolution and Modernism* (New York, 1927), p. 88; *Gastonia Gazette,* January 24, 25, 1924; *New York Times,* January 24, 1924.

24. S. A. Ashe to A. T. Allen, July 15, 1925, A. T. Allen to S. A. Ashe, July 23, 1925, State Superintendent's Correspondence.

Governor was a regular attendant at the revival services of Mordecai F. Ham early in 1924. At one service in which Ham sought to "connect the teaching of evolution to the sin of adultery," Morrison led the applause and contributed fifty dollars to the "free-will offering." Later, in March, 1924, the Governor invited the evangelist to hold prayer services in the Executive Mansion for a selected group of 150 guests. Ham, in his turn, publicly acknowledged Morrison's friendship. "There isn't any man in the state who has made my work any easier," he declared on one occasion. On another, he described the rejection of the two biology textbooks as "the greatest act that any governor of any state ever did. . . ." He reveled in the thought that the Governor's action would halt the teaching of evolution in all public schools in North Carolina and reminded teachers that any further discussion of the subject in the classroom would make them guilty of "bootlegging an outlawed theory." [25] Billy Sunday, who was in the midst of his evangelistic crusade in Charlotte, also hastened to congratulate Governor Morrison for his elimination "of the evolutionary books" and to assure him that the Lord would continue to bless the Old North State so long as "she has chief executives who acknowledge Him as fearlessly and confidently as you have done." [26]

Other responses to the Governor's action were considerably less complimentary. While much of the press simply recorded the deed without editorial comment, a few journals expressed alarm at what they considered the Governor's presumptuousness. The *Greensboro Daily News* was plainly outraged; the *Mission Herald,* the Episcopal church paper, questioned the "governor's ability to judge either the scientific accuracy of the book or the reality of its contradiction of any spiritual truth." Although the *News and Observer* omitted editorial comment, Nell Battle Lewis facetiously described Morrison's action as "that executive decree extraordinaire by which science has been put in its place in North Carolina." [27] The *New York Times*

25. *News and Observer,* February 25, March 24, 27, 30, 1924; Shipley, *The War on Modern Science,* p. 89; S. A. Ashe, *Should Evolution Be Taught in Public Schools?* (n.p., 1925), 2 pp.

26. *News and Observer,* January 29, 1924.

27. *Greensboro Daily News,* January 24, 25, 26, 1924; *Mission Herald,* XXXVIII (February, 1924), 12; *News and Observer,* February 3, 1924; W. O. Saunders' Elizabeth City *Independent* ridiculed the Governor's attempt to eliminate "evolution textbooks." Saunders entitled his newspaper story "Refuses to Stand up Alongside Monkey—Governor Morrison Isn't Going to Invite

devoted an editorial to what it considered the "ridiculous" and "humiliating" decision regarding evolution books in North Carolina. "It is no disgrace to recognize the animals and even the monkeys as poor relations," the *Times* observed, "but it is a disgrace to deny an enormous congeries of facts indisputable by any reasoning being." [28] Against this barrage of criticism, the *Charlotte Observer,* alone among the major dailies, defended the Governor as a true "guardian of the schools" who was fighting to have children taught "the things their fathers were taught, and by which teachings the best lives have been lived." [29]

Governor Morrison not only continued to revile evolutionists until the end of his term early in 1925 but for several years after his retirement. Addressing an Elks Convention in December, 1924, he declared that North Carolina was an "old-fashioned, Christian state" which had "no room for so-called educators who are preaching and teaching the kind of evolution that holds that the human race sprang from a tadpole, developed into a frog, thence into a monkey." The state had no money to waste upon such "highbrow ignoramuses." [30] As time passed, Morrison became even more extravagant in his denunciation of evolutionists. In a speech at a Presbyterian church in Charlotte in July, 1926, he called evolution "a fool theory" without the slightest hint of scientific data to support it. "We are forbidden by the constitution to teach the Bible in our public schools," he declared, "but any little infidel can teach irreligion there." No scientist, he said, had ever learned anything about the religious world except Louis Pasteur who "proved that there was nothing to Darwin's theory." Pasteur was a religious man far different from "these peanut-headed professors who, having nothing to do but read Huxley, Tom Paine, the Devil, and the rest of them, try to teach us that man is descended from a monkey." Reflecting on his own actions, Morrison stated: "When I was governor, I looked over the textbooks and found this theory of Darwin's. You know Darwin's theory of the descent of man is just a sideshow to this evolution

---

Chance of Somebody Seeing a Resemblance." Keith Saunders, *The Independent Man* (Washington, 1962), pp. 91–92.

28. *New York Times,* January 25, 1924.

29. *Charlotte Observer,* January 25, 1924; see also *Presbyterian Standard,* LXV (January 30, 1924), 1.

30. *Gastonia Gazette,* December 8, 1924.

question, and I found that these books had monkeys and men all mixed up there together. This fool theory, I told the State Board of Education, must be thrown out." The former governor concluded with the warning that those "little college professors who teach this monkey business . . . will soon compose an army of little highbrows hunting jobs." [31]

Morrison's exclusion of the "evolution books" naturally inspired much enthusiasm among the anti-evolutionists and encouraged them to seek a more complete victory by marshalling the coercive powers of the state against the teaching of Darwinism. In the long run, however, the governor's action was perhaps more of a detriment than an asset to the anti-evolutionists because thereafter they tended to overestimate their strength or at least their ability to win legislative approval for their goals. Unfortunately for their cause, Morrison's term expired before the showdown in the legislature; and his successor, Angus W. McLean, another Presbyterian, avoided any involvement in the controversy. By mid-1924, however, the possibility of an anti-evolution law had already begun to receive serious consideration, and public concern about evolution was manifesting itself in various ways. Local school boards were hesitant to employ teachers suspected of the Darwinian heresy; candidates for public office announced their stand in the controversy; newspapers aired every incident related to evolution and aligned themselves on the issue. The war against Poteat flared into the open again. Leading the anti-Poteat chorus was the Texas parson J. Frank Norris who had declared that Poteat's brand of evolution made "the chinch that eats you for midnight lunch and the louse that crawls down your back" close relatives of man. This distant crusader was assisted by local foes of the Wake Forest President who distributed unsigned, derogatory sheets calling for his dismissal.[32]

As the evolution controversy gained momentum, the anti-evolutionists increasingly identified the spread of Darwinism with the "godless education" of the state colleges. As usual, the University of

31. *Charlotte Observer,* July 5, 1926; see also Knight, "Monkey or Mud in North Carolina," pp. 515–16; "Warning from a Former Governor," *Crusaders' Champion,* I (January 15, 1926), 23.

32. *Searchlight,* April 18, 1924.

North Carolina bore the burden of their criticism. Paganism, they argued, had replaced Christian piety as the dominant force at Chapel Hill.[33] The rapid changes at the University after World War I, just as the champions of orthodoxy launched their offensive against the new order, helped to revive old suspicions and to reopen old wounds. For some of the conservatives, the University had become the habitat of "foreigners," meaning non-North Carolinians in general and "Northerners" in particular. At least it was the source from which "foreign" doctrines such as evolution emanated. Moreover, individual faculty members were brazenly voicing views and opinions that were alien and disturbing to "the old conservative commonwealth." But even more shocking was the pronouncement of these "foreign" notions by native sons. For example, Collier Cobb, a professor of geology, was a persistent defender of evolution who maintained that nothing in the theory contradicted Christianity. "Evolution," he declared, "is God's method of operation in the realm of nature," while "Christianity is God's plan of operation in the spiritual world." Robert W. Winston, another North Carolinian and well-known University figure, published a widely acclaimed article in 1924 in which he attempted to demonstrate that the biological investigations of Darwin had strengthened, rather than weakened, the position of thoughtful Christians. "We . . . [ought] to go a step further," he concluded, "and thank God for Charles Darwin and for a theory of life which has broadened and humanized knowledge and dignified the concept of God." Winston warned against confusing biological evolution with evolutionary philosophy and reminded his readers to avoid the error of assuming that Darwin dealt with the origin of life. Despite the cautious tone of his article, his conclusions incensed the fundamentalists who by 1924 were willing to credit Darwin with little other than the most malevolent influences.[34]

Far more disturbing to the anti-evolutionists were the McNair Lectures delivered at the University during the postwar period. This lectureship had been established by John Calvin McNair, a conserva-

33. *North Carolina Lutheran*, IV (February, 1926), 6.

34. Collier Cobb, *Evolution and Christianity* (n.p., 1920); Robert W. Winston, "The Noose of Darwin and the Neck of Orthodoxy," *The Journal of Social Forces*, III (November, 1924), 111–17; *Gastonia Gazette*, November 19, 1924; Stephen Gardner to Robert W. Winston, December 5, 1924, Winston Papers.

tive Presbyterian and graduate of the University in 1840, for the purpose of showing "the mutual bearing of science and theology upon each other." The McNair indenture specified that the lectures were to be delivered by a member of an evangelical denomination and published in book form within twelve months after delivery.[35] An impressive array of scholars including John Dewey, Shailer Matthews, and Roscoe Pound had held the lectureship since 1915. Led by the Presbyterians who claimed a special interest in the McNair indenture and acted as its extra-legal guardians, fundamentalists viewed with mounting alarm the types of lecturers being selected by the faculty committee. They were convinced that the lectureship was becoming a platform for "foreigners" to disseminate modernistic teachings contrary to the evangelical Christianity specified by McNair.[36]

The opposition first appeared publicly in response to the lectures delivered in the spring of 1922 by Charles Allen Dinsmore, professor of religion in the Yale Divinity School. Dinsmore discussed the general subject, "Religious Certitude in an Age of Science," in three lectures entitled: "The Influence of Science on Modern Religious Thought"; "The Nature and Truth of Religion"; and "What We Know and What We Believe." Anti-evolutionists found a great deal in these lectures to confirm their fears concerning the orthodoxy of the University community. Dinsmore sought to distinguish between scientific and religious knowledge, criticized dogmatism in both spheres, and urged religionists to respect the contributions of science. He frankly embraced the studies of higher critics and the principle of evolution. "The Creator has left a record of his activities in the rocks," the Yale professor declared, "which compels all informed minds to relinquish the venerable chronology which asserts that only six thousand years have elapsed since Creation." He alienated fundamentalists still further by suggesting that some churchmen had confused the temporary form of their faith with its eternal substance and had replaced the gospel of love by a fierce zeal for dogma.[37]

The *Presbyterian Standard* loudly objected to these views and claimed that there was nothing in the lectures to inspire "certitude"

35. See the Preface in William Louis Poteat, *Can a Man Be Christian Today?* (Chapel Hill, 1925).
36. *Charlotte Observer*, January 6, 1925.
37. Charles Allen Dinsmore, *Religious Certitude in an Age of Science* (Chapel Hill, 1924), 102 pp.

in the sphere of religion. On the contrary, the *Standard* found Dinsmore guilty of holding virtually all "modern ideas" that tended to undermine religious "certitude" and of expressing his own radical views of revelation with a dogmatism far more rigid than that of the fundamentalists whom he so severely criticized. The Dinsmore lectures, according to the Presbyterian paper, constituted a blatant perversion of the McNair indenture and provided a classic example of why "church people oppose state institutions." [38]

The criticism that greeted Dinsmore's performance in 1922 reached far more serious proportions three years later when the University invited William Louis Poteat to deliver the McNair Lectures. Poteat's selection may have been intended to overcome the prevalent criticism that Southerners had been conspicuously absent among the lecturers. But if Poteat was a native, critics were quick to point out that his ideas were "foreign." For some, the selection of Poteat was tantamount to University endorsement of his views on evolution, an interpretation that fitted their claim that state institutions had fallen prey to the pagan spirit. Even more significant, however, was the timing of the announcement of Poteat's selection: it took place just on the eve of the legislative struggle over an anti-evolution bill and therefore furnished the advocates of such a measure an important propaganda weapon.[39]

Although the focus of the anti-evolutionist attack had shifted from church colleges to state schools, few men in North Carolina understood so intimately the nature and meaning of the controversy as William Louis Poteat. Before unusually large audiences this Baptist biologist delivered his three lectures on the Chapel Hill campus in May, 1925.[40] Collectively entitled "Can A Man Be a Christian To-Day?" the lectures were delivered with the same eloquent simplicity that characterized Poteat's other utterances on similar subjects. He attempted to explain the complex nature of the contemporary era, to disentangle the substance of Christianity from the impedimenta accumulated over the centuries, and to suggest means whereby men in a scientific age might still achieve the rewards

38. *Presbyterian Standard,* LXV (October 8, 1924), 1; see also *Biblical Recorder,* XC (November 12, 1924), 5.
39. W. L. Poteat to H. W. Chase, January 22, 1925, University Papers.
40. *Chapel Hill Weekly,* May 7, 1925.

of the Christian faith. Moderate in tone, these lectures nevertheless expressed his conviction that scientific evolution, viewed correctly, posed no threat to scriptural integrity. But, according to Poteat, the current controversy, generated by extremists, had forced upon men false alternatives. Extreme fundamentalists were compromising Christianity before the intelligence of the world, while zealous modernists were committing an error just as grave by denying the worth of the Scriptures. He pleaded for a return to the path of the wise which recognized that science and religion occupied two distinct spheres of reality, each possessing authority in its own sphere. The failure to make this distinction had produced a confusion in men's minds conducive to the view that science, and indeed all modern education, was antagonistic to religion. Regardless of the continuing tempest within his own church, Poteat clearly indicated that fundamentalist zealots were obstructing efforts to keep Christianity vital for modern men by their insistence upon biblical literalism and doctrinal inflexibility.[41]

Acclaimed nationally as profound and mature, these lectures were considered all the more remarkable for having emanated from the South. When they were published by the University Press, the *Greensboro Daily News* declared that the lectures constituted "the most significant volume that has come out of North Carolina in years. . . ."[42] All was not praise, however; the fundamentalists, especially those within Poteat's own denomination, were outraged. Hostile critics seized upon his McNair lectures as another lever by which to pry him from the presidency of Wake Forest College. Sylvester J. Betts, a Baptist minister of Raleigh who had long engaged in anti-evolutionist warfare, published a pamphlet in which he presented a page-by-page critique of Poteat's utterances in Chapel Hill. Betts accused him of a long list of theological heresies which included: the substitution of the "protoplasmic, amoebic theory" for the Genesis record of creation; the rejection of "the verbal plenary inspiration of the whole Bible"; the relegation of divine revelation to the realm of "mere literature"; and the outright denial of the Christian concept of the fall of Man. The Baptist minister not only

41. Poteat, *Can a Man Be a Christian Today?*, 110 pp.
42. Suzanne C. Linder, "William Louis Poteat and the Evolution Controversy," *The North Carolina Historical Review*, XL (April, 1963), 147–49.

called for the elimination of Poteat and his heresies from Wake Forest but also for the banishing of evolution from all tax-supported schools by the enactment of a legislative statute.[43] All the while, the Presbyterian Synod busied itself with resolutions and other actions designed to exert enough pressure on the University to insure the elimination of all modernists and evolutionists from the McNair lectureship in the future.[44]

The agitation triggered by the announcement of Poteat's lectures was dwarfed by the furor that erupted over another University sponsored project, the *Journal of Social Forces*. In its issue of January, 1925, *Social Forces*, a scholarly sociological magazine edited by Professor Howard W. Odum and published under the imprimatur of the University, included two articles that elicited loud protests. One of these articles, entitled "The Development of the Concept of Progress," by Professor L. L. Bernard of Cornell University, sought to explain the origins of various types of divinities. In so doing it described the gods as "products of the folk imagination," the concept of the fall of man as a myth, and the theological notion of progress as a relatively primitive concept that became secularized through the teachings of the prophets.[45] The second article, by Harry Elmer Barnes of Smith College, entitled "Sociology and Ethics: A Genetic View of the Theory of Conduct," was largely devoted to the primitive morality of American society as expressed in its views toward sex. Barnes placed much of the responsibility for the "unhealthy" attitudes toward sex upon the Christian church. Rather than fostering a "scientifically valid system of ethics," the church derived its ethics from "an alleged sacred book" which in reality was "a product of the folkways and mores of the primitive Hebrews." Thus, "the monstrous theological desire to create more souls" had thwarted all efforts to deal scientifically with a vast population increase among "the least capable classes" which was "progressively degrading the race." Barnes concluded that two thousand years of

43. S. J. Betts, *Criticism of Dr. Poteat's Book Recently Published* (Raleigh, 1925).

44. *Presbyterian Standard*, LXVI (May 13, 1925), 9; *ibid.*, LXVI (October 28, 1925), 1.

45. L. L. Bernard, "The Development of the Concept of Progress," *The Journal of Social Forces*, III (January, 1925), 207–12.

religion had failed to produce "a reliable and definitive body of rules for conduct, either personal or social." [46]

The January issue of *Social Forces* which contained these articles had scarcely been mailed from the University Press when the protests began, at first a few relatively mild dissents, then increasing in both number and severity until the two sociological pieces became statewide issues. Later in the year William Jennings Bryan even referred to them in his last, undelivered address at Dayton.[47] Editor Odum soon found it futile to suggest that they were "highly technical treatments" intended for the specialist or that each article, constituting a minor portion of a larger work, could only be understood in this broader context.[48] That the storm continued to gain momentum was due to several factors peculiar to the socio-intellectual climate of North Carolina at that time. Not only did the articles appear to constitute a blatant attack on certain precepts of Christianity but they were written by "foreigners" who took "the evolutionary philosophy" for granted. For a university supported by the money of Christian taxpayers to allow one of its publications to become the mouthpiece of such "rank infidelity" was merely a confirmation of charges made by the evangelists, Governor Morrison, and other anti-evolutionist crusaders.

Those sympathetic to the views represented by these forces soon transformed the *Social Forces* articles into something of a *cause célèbre*. Odum was swamped with orders for the January issue of *Social Forces*, and most of the orders were from those who read few technical journals in their own field, much less in sociology. Several Baptist associations vehemently protested the views expressed in the articles. The Gaston County Association, led by the Reverend W. C. Barrett of Gastonia who figured prominently in denominational squabbles over Poteat, petitioned the new governor, Angus W. McLean, to cut off all state funds used for the publication of the

46. Harry Elmer Barnes, "Sociology and Ethics: A Genetic View of the Theory of Conduct," *The Journal of Social Forces*, III (January, 1925), 212–31.

47. *Bryan and Darrow at Dayton: The Record and Documents of the "Bible-Evolution Trial,"* ed. Leslie H. Allen (New York, 1925), pp. 194–95.

48. Howard W. Odum to the Editor, February 20, 1925, Howard W. Odum Papers (University of North Carolina Library, Chapel Hill).

Journal of Social Forces. The petition also protested against the employment of instructors in any state institution who were known to "hold" or teach views contrary to Christian fundamentals. Various ministerial groups—but none more loudly than the ministerial association of Charlotte—voiced their criticisms of the articles and placed the responsibility for their publication squarely upon Odum and Chase.[49] Ultimately civic groups and even the Mooresville Chapter of the Ku Klux Klan joined the ministers in censuring the University for "this serious offense against the faith and feelings and life work of the Christian people of our state." [50] The editor of the *Hickory Record* described Odum's "explanations" as unconvincing efforts to evade responsibility for destroying "the faith of young men and women in things held sacred by their fathers." Another critic suggested that Odum might feel more at home in Soviet Russia.[51]

The fiercest criticism of the articles by Barnes and Bernard emanated from the same Presbyterian quarters so disturbed by the McNair lectures. The Presbyterian ministers of Charlotte and Burlington, the Orange presbytery, and several individual clergymen of prominence publicly denounced the University for allowing the publication of material so obviously "unsound, irreligious, and hurtful to the cause of Christianity." Albert Sydney Johnson, pastor of the First Presbyterian Church of Charlotte, wrote Odum that the articles constituted "an insidious attack upon the whole realm of supernatural revelation." Rather than scholarly analyses, the two essays were "vicious assaults" without the slightest attempt at objectivity.[52] The *Presbyterian Standard,* taking up editorial cudgels against the *Journal of Social Forces* for printing articles that "struck at the very heart of true religion," placed all responsibility for this travesty upon Chase and Odum.[53] Undoubtedly, the most active

49. *Presbyterian Standard,* LXVI (February 25, 1925), 1; Petition to Governor A. W. McLean and the Honorable Members of the Legislature, March 2, 1925, Report of Charlotte Ministerial Association, March 2, 1925, Odum Papers; *News and Observer,* March 4, 1925.

50. *Mooresville Enterprise,* March 12, April 9, 1925; *Commonwealth* (Scotland Neck), February 19, 1925.

51. Johnson Avery to Howard W. Odum, March 2, 1925, Odum Papers.

52. A. S. Johnson to Howard W. Odum, February 28, 1925, Odum Papers; *Presbyterian Standard,* LXVI (February 25, 1925), 1; *Greensboro Daily News,* April 13, 1925; *News and Observer,* October 13, 1925.

53. *Presbyterian Standard,* LXVI (March 4, 1925), 2.

Presbyterian in this affair was William P. McCorkle, an elderly pastor-at-large of the Orange presbytery whose ancestors had figured prominently in the early history of the University. When the *Journal of Social Forces* appeared, McCorkle was already deeply disturbed by what he believed to be a perversion of the McNair indenture, but for the moment his attention was diverted to the sociological articles which he severely criticized in a widely distributed pamphlet. His primary complaint was that "Northern" heretics had been permitted to conduct "an infidel propaganda campaign" in a University sponsored publication.[54]

The incident involving the *Journal of Social Forces* obviously included a number of elements which heightened the fundamentalists' suspicions of the University. Nothing, however, aroused the ire of the religious community more than the "supercilious tone" with which Barnes treated the whole subject of Christian ethics. The usually moderate Methodist paper, the *North Carolina Christian Advocate,* objected strenuously to such "impractical and absurd" discourses gaining immunity in the name of "academic freedom" in an institution "that a Christian civilization has built." Its advice was to "bring all atheists into the open." [55] The *News and Observer* and the Baptist *Biblical Recorder* agreed that *Social Forces* should be reprimanded and singled out Barnes's article for special rebuke. "If two thousand years of religion has failed to provide reliable rules for conduct," the Raleigh newspaper was convinced that a hundred years of sociology "had done little better." [56]

Perhaps the criticism which was the most painful for Odum was that by Theodore Partrick, Jr., a liberal spokesman for the Episcopal church who as editor of the *Mission Herald* had long been a staunch defender of academic freedom. Partrick admitted that Barnes's

54. William P. McCorkle to Howard Odum, September 19, 1925, Howard W. Odum to William P. McCorkle, September 25, 1925, William P. McCorkle to Louis Graves, September 26, 1925, Odum Papers; William P. McCorkle, "The Creed and Program of Modern Sociology," *Biblical Recorder,* XC (March 18, 1925), 1; see *ibid.,* XC (March 25, 1925), 4.

55. *North Carolina Christian Advocate,* LXX (February 26, 1925), 2; see also Howard W. Odum to M. T. Plyler, February 12, 1925, Odum Papers.

56. *News and Observer,* February 21, 1925; Howard W. Odum to Josephus Daniels, February 12, 1925, Odum Papers; *Biblical Recorder,* XC (March 4, 1925), 6; *ibid.,* XC (March 25, 1925), 4; *Biblical Recorder* declared that its opposition to the union of church and state did not mean approval of a "union of the devil and the state." *Ibid.*

interpretation of the history of ethics gave a much needed jolt to the intellectually lethargic clergy whose "ignorance" of sociological research was "profound"; and he exonerated Chase and Odum of responsibility for the views expressed in either article. But he agreed that the protests were "not altogether unjust" because Barnes had indulged "in too many sneers." Sneering at orthodoxy and convention "*a la* Mencken" was in Partrick's opinion the most dangerous and least effective way to fight extreme fundamentalism.[57]

Odum labored mightily to combat the various charges leveled at him and his publication. He was fully aware that the very survival of the journal was at stake. Only three years old, the periodical lacked the financial solvency necessary to disregard a protest so likely to affect its income. Cognizant of the precarious position of the magazine, Barnes authorized Odum to repudiate his article if it would ease the situation, but Odum rejected this suggestion on the grounds that criticism had to be confronted sooner or later and that he was unwilling to surrender in the first skirmish without a real fight.[58] Therefore, he plunged into the fray in an effort to combat the protests against the articles by Barnes and Bernard. When confronting his critics, Odum always assumed full responsibility for the contents of the journal. He explained his own religious views in correspondence and public addresses and invited his harshest critics to visit the University in order to determine for themselves whether the institution was really a sinister place. He urged Barrett, McCorkle, and Johnson to spend a weekend at his home in Chapel Hill to "talk over" their differences. He also requested these fundamentalist leaders to submit articles for publication in *Social Forces*. Only McCorkle responded favorably to Odum's suggestion; he did visit the University campus and he later promised to write two articles for the journal, "not for money but simply for the love of truth." One of those tentatively entitled "Christianity and Social Progress," which was to refute "the Barnes thesis," had induced the minister "to start reading sociology." Neither article, however, was

57. Theodore Partrick to Howard W. Odum, March 2, 1925, Howard W. Odum to Theodore Partrick, March 4, 1925, Theodore Partrick to Howard Odum, March 11, 1925, Odum Papers; *Mission Herald*, XXXIX (March, 1925), 8.

58. Harry Elmer Barnes to Howard W. Odum, February (?), 1925; Howard W. Odum to Harry Elmer Barnes, February 28, 1925, Odum Papers.

ever completed. But McCorkle continued his energetic efforts to establish means of restraining those activities within the University that undermined "the conservative Christianity of the Old Commonwealth." [59]

Throughout the incident over the *Social Forces* articles, Odum refused to be bullied into submission. Describing himself as a product of rural, fundamentalist Methodism that spawned "Ku Kluxers" and anti-evolutionists, he maintained that his fight for the *Journal of Social Forces* was in reality a fight to protect North Carolina from "the effects of enthusiastic, mass-minded and dogmatic intolerance so much in evidence elsewhere in the South." He also argued that "such a startling attack" on *Social Forces* was ridiculous in view of the fact that it was a "super-technical journal" without a single subscriber among the undergraduates at the University whom it was supposed to be "ruining." At one point he asserted that his Christian faith had survived the training for two Ph.D.'s in two supposed "infidel institutions" only to be severely shaken now by the scurrilous and unfair tactics used by churchmen to muzzle scholarly discussion which they interpreted as inimical to Christianity.[60] "It sometimes seems a little hard," he declared, "to produce what in the universities is generally conceded to be the most comprehensive journal of its kind in the English language and for the same effort to be proclaimed at home an enemy of the common good." [61] Though occasionally displaying such signs of despair, Odum persisted in his struggle to

59. Howard W. Odum to M. T. Plyler, February 12, 1925, Howard W. Odum to Governor A. W. McLean, March 6, 1925, Howard W. Odum to W. C. Barrett, March 5, 1925, Howard Odum to Walter West, February 23, 1925, William P. McCorkle to Howard W. Odum, September 19, 1925, William P. McCorkle to Howard W. Odum, September 30, 1925, Odum Papers.

60. Howard W. Odum to Josephus Daniels, February 12, 1925, Howard W. Odum to M. T. Plyler, February 12, 1925, Odum Papers. One sardonic North Carolinian remarked, "What I have long feared at last has happened. Somebody has read the *Journal of Social Forces*." Gerald W. Johnson, "Chase of North Carolina," *The American Mercury*, XVII (July, 1930), 187.

61. Howard W. Odum to Theodore Partrick, March 4, 1925, Odum Papers; see also George B. Tindall, "The Significance of Howard W. Odum to Southern History," *The Journal of Southern History*, XXIV (August, 1958), 290–91; Howard W. Odum, *An American Epoch: Southern Portraiture in the National Picture* (New York, 1930), pp. 158–59, 169–70; Gerald W. Johnson, a professor of journalism at the University, reported that Odum offered to resign in order to spare the University further embarrassment and that President Chase refused even to consider such a move. See Johnson, "Chase of North Carolina," pp. 187–188.

maintain the *Journal of Social Forces* as a forum for the unimpeded discussion of social issues. The outcome remained in doubt for more than a year, and only after the prolonged crisis over evolution had begun to subside did it become apparent that Odum's concept of *Social Forces* would prevail.

At the same time that the state was astir with the agitation over the McNair lectures and the articles in the *Journal of Social Forces,* another incident occurred that provided additional grist for the anti-evolutionist mill. This time, however, the heresy emanated from a state college other than the University and thereby confirmed the widely held view that "infidelity" had permeated all state educational institutions. The culprit was Albert S. Keister, a professor of sociology at North Carolina College for Women in Greensboro, whose offense was committed in a class that he was conducting in Charlotte for public school teachers. At a meeting of the class on January 5, 1925, a brief, impromptu discussion of evolution had been opened when a student asked Keister "what a belief in evolution did to one who believed in the Bible." He replied that evolution forced such a person to discard literal interpretations of portions of the Genesis account of creation and to view the account as an attempt by a people in a prescientific age to explain the origin of life. Hence, Genesis or at least portions of it constituted "a form of mythology." Later a distorted version of this statement made it appear that Keister had flatly pronounced the whole Bible as "a bit of Israelitish mythology," a phrase actually used by one of the members of the class to describe the professor's view of the opening chapters of Genesis. Unfortunately for Keister, the teacher in the class whom he noticed taking notes on his extemporaneous comments was the wife of a prominent Presbyterian minister of Charlotte. She promptly delivered her notes to her husband who, armed with evidence of such heresy, laid the matter before the local ministerial association. Upon a motion by the Reverend S. F. Conrad, the association passed a "scorching resolution" on January 12, 1925, rebuking Professor Keister for "teachings" which destroyed faith in the Bible and "sapped the very foundations of Christianity." [62]

62. *Charlotte Observer,* January 11, 14, 15, 16, 18, 21, 1925, February 10, 1925; Albert S. Keister to the author, April 28, 1963; *Greensboro Daily News,* January 13, 1925.

Within a few days the "Keister incident" had become newsworthy enough for front-page coverage in the press. Embellishments soon transformed a few brief remarks uttered by a professor in response to a direct question by a student into a lengthy lecture devoted to derogatory remarks about the Scriptures. S. F. Conrad concluded that Keister was an atheist. A "listener-in" on Keister's classes claimed that the sociologist not only expounded "infidel ideas about the Bible, but about the racial question likewise." Several parent-teacher associations, chambers of commerce, and chapters of the Ku Klux Klan denounced such evolution-inspired infidelity and demanded the immediate dismissal of Professor Keister from the faculty of a tax-supported school. Al Fairbrother, a Greensboro resident who was as hostile to the ideas of Einstein as to those of Darwin, characterized Keister as "an imported highbrow" trained at the very seat of infidelity, the University of Chicago, and sent to the South to proclaim that Christianity was "a lie." [63] Numerous citizens wrote letters to newspapers demanding the expulsion of so obvious an atheist from the staff of a state college. Some even suggested that the legislature withhold all appropriations from North Carolina College for Women until Keister "had been fired." In an editorial extremely critical of the Greensboro professor, the *Charlotte Observer* concluded that the incident pointed up the acute need for legislative restrictions on the teaching of evolution in publicly financed schools.[64]

Within official denominational circles the Presbyterians displayed the greatest concern over the affair. The Presbyterian Ministers' Association of Charlotte voiced its complaints against Keister in a strongly worded resolution dispatched directly to the Governor. Their statement referred to Keister's views as "repugnant to the Anglo-Saxon people that compose the State." It objected therefore not only to his unorthodox theology but also to his "infidel ideas" about racial problems.[65] The *Presbyterian Standard* wondered whether North Carolinians were "willing to sit at the feet of this

63. *Charlotte Observer*, January 14, 15, 18, 1925.

64. *Charlotte Observer*, January 21, 1925; *Greensboro Daily News*, January 11, 13 ,14, 20, 21, 22, 1925.

65. Resolution of the Presbyterian Ministers' Association, Charlotte, February 16, 1925, Papers of the Governors of North Carolina (Department of Archives and History, Raleigh).

disciple of Modernism in its rankest form, who judges our faith by that of Chicago." The paper charged that Keister, having "made short work of inspiration and reduced the Bible stories to mere legend," was only one example of many in state institutions who were instilling "their subtle poison into the minds of our young women, and thus touching the coming mothers of the future." The *Standard* also joined those demanding financial reprisals against state-supported colleges that continued "to bow to Baal." [66]

Throughout the agitation Keister himself refused to be drawn into a debate by attempting to answer his critics. He simply stated that the whole affair had been grossly distorted by an accumulation of rumors based on hearsay. Despite the storm raging about him, he retained his position both as a professor in the state college and as a teacher of the extension class in Charlotte. As he stepped from the train in Charlotte two weeks after his fateful utterance, he was greeted by Harry Harding, the city superintendent of public schools, who diplomatically suggested that discussions of evolution should be avoided altogether in the extension class since Charlotte was such a "blue stocking Presbyterian town." Keister readily accepted the advice and continued to hold his classes. More serious, however, was the pressure upon President Julius I. Foust of North Carolina College for Women to dismiss Keister from the faculty at the end of the academic year. Some of the college trustees, heeding the advice of their local friends, were determined to rid the institution of such a controversial figure. President Foust exerted every effort to prevent what he considered a breach of academic freedom. He "sat up all night" with one trustee in an attempt to prevail upon him to vote for Keister's retention. Foust's labors resulted in the decision of the trustees to re-elect Keister to the faculty.[67] Such action merely strengthened the conviction of anti-evolutionists that the elimination of atheists and infidels could not be entrusted to the governing boards of state institutions. Nothing short of a legislative statute to cover all tax-supported schools would suffice.

The Keister incident, the announcement of Poteat's selection as McNair lecturer for 1925, and the publication of the ill-fated articles

66. *Presbyterian Standard*, LXVI (January 21, 1925), 2; see also *Biblical Recorder*, XC (January 28, 1925), 6; *ibid.*, XC (February 4, 1925), 1, 6.
67. Albert S. Keister to the author, April 28, 1963.

in the *Journal of Social Forces* occurred at approximately the same time that the state legislature of 1925 convened in its biennial session. All three events seemed to corroborate vague rumors and public exhortations regarding the existence of sinister forces within public educational institutions. Such forces were usually identified in the public mind with evolution, "foreigners," unorthodoxy in religion, and other phenomena considered threats to the established order. Many of these threats appeared to be manifested in one way or another in the trio of events in January, 1925, so that it was no accident that the legislature then in session was called upon to enact a statute to prohibit the teaching of evolution, the menace that was considered the parent of all the others.

5 ∽ THE LEGISLATIVE BATTLE

"The Monkey has replaced the Donkey in Tar Heel Democracy."

—THE GREENSBORO DAILY NEWS

The attack on the evolutionary views of William Louis Poteat in 1920 by a Mississippi evangelist had precipitated far more than merely a disturbance among Baptists. It unleashed a controversy that involved numerous groups and affected vital areas of the socio-intellectual life of the state. Newspaper discussions, public debates, Bible conferences, revivals by itinerant evangelists, denominational squabbles, and pronouncements by academicians had continually broadened the scope of the ferment during the first half of the 1920's. Movements to eliminate "infidel" evolutionists from the church-related colleges and to incorporate Bible study into the public school curriculum certainly had not achieved a success that would guarantee the safety of orthodox Christianity. Fundamentalists could see no effective check upon the advance of secularism, modernism, or evolution. The decisive moment had arrived in 1925: North Carolina must either remain a Christian Commonwealth or succumb to the forces of the anti-Christ. Encouraged by Governor Morrison's banning of two "evolution books" and the success of anti-evolutionist efforts in Oklahoma and Florida, the fundamentalists decided to attempt a more complete victory by marshalling behind the cause the coercive powers of the state. Their legislative crusade against Darwinism in 1925 coincided with a similar movement in Tennessee which ultimately succeeded.

On January 8, 1925, the second day of the legislative session, Representative David Scott Poole of Raeford introduced House Resolution Number Ten, known generally as the "Monkey Bill." This spare, tight-lipped country editor, son of a Confederate veteran, had for twenty years been a school teacher during the "winter months." While teaching, he learned the printer's trade and thereafter combined the two jobs. His editorial career began with the *Scotch Scion*, which he established at Red Springs. From 1915 until his death Poole edited the *Hoke County Journal* in Raeford, where he also served as mayor and as justice of the peace. The Poole family has long been identified with the Presbyterian church in North Carolina in both lay and clerical capacities. D. Scott Poole himself was active in the Presbyterian circles as a ruling elder, clerk of the synod, and teacher of a Sunday School Bible class. He was unquestionably a man with strong and sincere religious convictions rooted in orthodox theology that had no place for the Darwinian theory of evolution. A careful reading of the *Origin of Species*, a copy of which he owned, convinced him that biological evolution was totally incompatible with the divinely inspired Scriptures, especially those describing man's creation. Believing "every word in the Bible," he concluded that any deviation from the Genesis account of creation cast doubt upon "all the Bible." So disturbed was he by the menacing implications of the Darwinian theory that he decided, at the age of sixty-three, to carry the battle to the state legislature. The basic issue in his campaign for the House of Representatives during the elections of 1924 was to save North Carolina from the nefarious influences of Darwinism.[1]

True to his promise after a successful campaign, Representative

1. *Journal of the House of Representatives of the General Assembly of North Carolina, Session of 1925*, p. 18; Robert Lawrence, *Here in Carolina* (Lumberton, N.C., 1939), p. 97; R. D. W. Connor, *Rebuilding an Ancient Commonwealth* (New York, 1928–1929), III, 146–47; Nell Battle Lewis, "North Carolina," *The American Mercury*, VIII (May, 1926), 42; Memorandum by William L. Poole, January 13, 1962; *The North Carolina Manual, 1927*, ed. A. R. Newsome, (Raleigh, 1927), pp. 547–48; Edgar W. Knight, "Monkey or Mud in North Carolina," *The Independent*, CXVIII (May 14, 1927), 516.

Poole introduced the following anti-evolution resolution in the legislature:

Resolved by the House of Representatives, the Senate concurring, that it is the sense of the General Assembly of the State of North Carolina that it is injurious to the welfare of the people of the State of North Carolina for any official or teacher in the State, paid wholly or in part by taxation, to teach or permit to be taught, as a fact either Darwinism or any other evolutionary hypothesis that links man in blood relationship with any lower form of life.[2]

The immediate reactions to this bill ranged from warm endorsement to belligerent opposition. But one of the most prevalent was to regard it as a ghastly specter which, if ignored, might pass quietly from the legislative scene. Others, like the editor of the *Hendersonville Times*, ridiculed the measure as "pure poppycock" and "assinine non-sense" that would die in the Committee on Education without serious discussion. More often than not, however, such bluster merely served as a façade to conceal the real alarm of those whose worst fears regarding the evolution controversy had suddenly become an actuality.[3] At any rate, the introduction of Poole's resolution alerted the protagonists to amass their front-line political forces. Both camps had to adjust to changes in leadership personnel: the anti-evolutionists no longer possessed the strong arm of the governor since Cameron Morrison had been replaced in the Executive Mansion by Angus W. McLean, who steered clear of the controversy; the opponents of Poole's bill, on the other hand, could no longer look for guidance to Poteat because he viewed the impending struggle as one in which spokesmen of state-supported, rather than denominational, schools must assume the leadership.[4]

Within the General Assembly the anti-evolutionists could count upon strong support from a battery of legislators. Among these were

2. *News and Observer* (Raleigh), February 16, 1925; *Commonwealth* (Scotland Neck), February 17, 1925; *Courier* (Asheboro), February 19, 1925; the original copy of the Poole anti-evolution bill and the minority report on it is found in the Legislative Papers of 1925, Records Center, State Department of Archives and History, Raleigh.

3. *Hendersonville Times*, February 13, 17, 1925.

4. Harry W. Chase to W. L. Poteat, February 16, 1925, University Papers; W. L. Poteat to Howard W. Odum, February 16, 1925, Odum Papers.

several prominent political figures: Zebulon Vance Turlington of Iredell County, a Presbyterian elder and graduate of the University of North Carolina Law School, who was a veteran legislative champion of prohibition; the flamboyant Thomas C. Bowie, an Episcopalian and graduate of both Yale and the state University, who bore scars of many political fracases as the representative from Ashe County; and Miss Julia Alexander of Mecklenburg County, a state University educated attorney and the lone female member of the General Assembly, whose forebears were Presbyterians of the bluestocking variety. Others, perhaps less well-known but occupying key committee posts, joined the anti-evolution chorus.

The opposition to the Poole Bill in the General Assembly included equally influential members whose talents, influence, and official capacities figured decisively in the destiny of the legislation. The hostility of Henry Groves Connor, Jr., an Episcopalian from Wilson and chairman of the House Committee on Education, proved to be a crucial factor. From a family distinguished for its public service, Connor embodied the best in the ancestral tradition. Repeatedly, during the discussions of the Poole Bill, he displayed the calm judgment and deep commitment to fairness which had gained him universal respect. Equally effective in the opposition to the measure was Walter Murphy of Rowan County, also an Episcopalian and chairman of the powerful Committee on Appropriations. A hard-headed realist known for his persuasive eloquence and mental agility, Murphy wielded considerable power in state Democratic circles as a member of the party's executive committee and as elector-at-large. But "the institution nearest his heart" was his alma mater, the University of North Carolina, which he had served for many years as a member of its board of trustees and as an official of its alumni association. A third important critic of the Poole Bill, Representative Sam Ervin, Jr., of Morganton, was another University alumnus and Episcopalian who feared any such restrictive legislation as the Poole Bill. Since neither Murphy nor Ervin were members of the Education Committee, their roles during the hearings on the bill, if any, probably took the form of influencing uncommitted members against it. Their impact only became evident when the measure reached the floor of the House. In the meantime, the organization of the opposition to the Poole Bill fell to Connor, whose position as committee chairman forced him to assume, at least overtly, an impartial attitude.[5]

The legislative leadership on both sides of the struggle came primarily from the ranks of the University of North Carolina alumni. This fact possessed particular significance in view of the peculiar position that the University occupied in the minds of North Carolinians and especially legislators. The belief that the University-trained lawyers dominated the General Assembly was not without validity. Some of them rather blindly followed the lead of their alma mater regarding the Poole Bill; others arrived at their decisions in such matters by processes identical to those of the University spokesmen who in some instances had formerly been their mentors. At any rate, the outcome of the anti-evolution legislation depended to a large extent upon the ultimate stand adopted by the "University lawyers" in the General Assembly.[6]

Apparently, officials of the University as well as the administrators of other state colleges at first underestimated the seriousness of the impending struggle. Representative Connor advised the leading educators of the critical implications of the situation and requested President Eugene C. Brooks of North Carolina State College to coordinate the strategy of the state institutions regarding the Poole Bill. Already under attack for what some called his attempt to transform the state's agricultural and engineering college into a liberal arts institution, Brooks was unwilling to jeopardize further the sizable appropriations he had requested from the legislature by assuming a prominent role in the evolution controversy. Such circumstances help to explain his absence from Raleigh during the height of the legislative fight. Similarly, President Julius I. Foust of the state college for women and the chief executives of the state institutions at Boone and Greenville failed to respond publicly to the Poole resolution. Poteat of Wake Forest promised only to attend the

5. *The North Carolina Manual, 1927*, p. 557; *Commonwealth*, February 19, 1925; *Catawba News-Enterprise* (Newton), February 24, 1925; *Daily Advance* (Elizabeth City), February 19, 1925; *The North Carolina Manual, 1925*, p. 570; Lawrence, *Here in Carolina*, p. 82; Memorandum by Senator Sam Ervin, Jr., May 23, 1961.

6. The House of Representatives in 1925 contained thirty "lawyers" trained at the University.

committee hearings but indicated that he would avoid any direct involvement.[7]

Four days before the hearings, Chairman Connor, alarmed by the lack of organized opposition to a measure that so vitally affected the institutions of higher learning, wrote his brother, R. D. W. Connor, professor of history at the University:

I don't think that it should be assumed that the Poole Bill may be taken lightly. I am quite sure that our academic friends do not realize the fact that there is throughout North Carolina a very strong undercurrent of feeling that the doctrine of Darwinism or Evolution, or whatever it may be called, is an invention of the Devil. This feeling is fed by many ministers of the Gospel. How strongly Mr. Poole will be able to have this feeling presented at the hearing, I do not know. In looking over the committee, I am a bit anxious to avoid, if possible, having the bill go upon the floor. Of course, if Poole is in earnest he can get up a minority report.[8]

Since arrangements with President Brooks had obviously gone askew, Connor urged the University officials to act immediately. His aim was to defeat the bill so decisively in the committee that its supporters would surrender without a floor fight.

Connor's alert brought the University machinery into action at once. President Harry W. Chase now assumed command of the opposition to the anti-evolution bill, and from this point on, the fundamentalists concentrated the burden of their fire upon him rather than Poteat. "You have fought our battles long enough," Chase remarked to Poteat, "and now we are going to do some fighting ourselves."[9] The University president assumed Poteat's mantle at a critical moment. The three widely publicized incidents that occurred in January, 1925 (which were discussed in the preceding chapter), had appreciably complicated the situation: the "heretical doctrines" accredited to Professor Albert S. Keister of North Carolina College for Women while teaching an extension class in sociology at

7. H. G. Connor, Jr., to R. D. W. Connor, February 6, 1925, University Papers; Lewis, "North Carolina," pp. 36–44; *Durham Morning Herald*, February 20, 1925; Willard B. Gatewood, Jr., *Eugene Clyde Brooks: Educator and Public Servant* (Durham, 1960), p. 247.

8. H. G. Connor, Jr., to R. D. W. Connor, February 6, 1925, University Papers.

9. *Goldsboro News*, August 4, 1926; see also Harry W. Chase to W. L. Poteat, February 16, 1925, University Papers.

Charlotte; the publication of "irreligious" articles in the *Journal of Social Forces;* and the appointment of Poteat to the University's McNair lectureship.[10] Chase realized that for him to lead the opposition to the Poole Bill might well jeopardize the financial status of the University, which, of course, depended upon legislative appropriations. On the other hand, for him to remain silent in the face of what he considered an entering wedge likely to destroy academic freedom would induce the most distinguished members of the faculty to accept the tempting offers that had recently been made to them by The Johns Hopkins University, The University of Wisconsin, and other institutions. Chase believed that the situation left him no alternative—he must exert every effort to defeat a measure that, in his opinion, compromised the basic principles of any academic community.[11]

The hearings on the Poole bill opened on February 10, 1925. The unusually large crowd in attendance forced the committee to transfer its proceedings from a small room in the Agriculture Building to the Hall of the House of Representatives. With the understanding that each side would have an hour to present its case, the proponents of the measure initiated the proceedings. As manager of the bill, Poole himself began by explaining the gravity of the situation in which nothing less than "the religion of the Lord Jesus is on trial." He utilized the standard argument that since the State was forbidden to teach theology, it naturally had no right to teach that the Bible was a myth and Christianity a mere superstition. He pointed out that such practices were not only unconstitutional but clear violations of the will of a majority of North Carolinians.[12]

10. W. L. Poteat to H. W. Chase, January 22, 1925, University Papers; Howard Odum to Josephus Daniels, February 12, 1925, Howard Odum to M. T. Plyler, February 12, 1925, Odum Papers; *News and Observer*, February 13, 1925; *Greensboro Daily News*, January 11, 14, 20, 1925; memorandum by Albert S. Keister, April 28, 1963; Edwin Mims, *The Advancing South: Stories of Progress and Reaction* (Garden City, 1926), pp. 15–16, 305.

11. H. W. Chase to A. W. McLean, February 16, 1925, H. W. Chase to Edgar Pharr, February 16, 1925, University Papers.

12. *Greensboro Daily News*, February 11, 1925; *News and Observer*, February 11, 1925; *Durham Morning Herald*, February 11, 1925; *Charlotte Observer*, February 11, 1925; William A. Crow, "Religion and the Recent Evolution Controversy with Special Reference to the Issues in the Scopes Trial" (Bachelor of Divinity thesis, Duke University, 1936), pp. 57–58.

The first speaker introduced by Poole was James R. Pentuff, a Baptist minister from Concord, whose elaborate academic pedigree was, according to some observers, as dubious as his recent involvement in a fertilizer manufacturing enterprise. Nevertheless, as the star performer in the anti-evolution cast, he appeared in the role of an expert on biological evolution. The Darwinian theory was, according to him, a "mere figment of imagination without any basis in fact and hence should not be foisted upon school children as science." He pointed out that Darwin was an agnostic whose infidel theory had long been "exploded," but publishers and teachers continued to spread the heresy because they were unwilling to "dig in and keep up" with the newer scientific developments. In conclusion he related what his niece had told him about being forced to study Darwin at the University. The *Raleigh Times* described Pentuff's discourse as a prime demonstration of the "crass ignorance" characteristic of clerical pseudo-scientists who sought "to clear the right of way for the divine plan." The Concord minister retaliated by suing the *Times* for slander.[13]

Following Pentuff's address to the Committee on Education several committee members who favored the Poole Bill assumed the floor. Julia Alexander proclaimed her belief in "the Bible from cover to cover" because it was a supernatural book. She explained that if she believed otherwise, she would be "afraid to go back to Mecklenburg." [14] Two other committeemen, Ralph Hunter, a minister of the Associate Reformed Presbyterian Church, and Robert Madison, a professor of languages at the Cullowhee Normal School and a Methodist steward, endorsed the position of Pentuff and expressed their intentions to fight the "insidious doctrine of evolution." Other

13. *News and Observer*, February 11, 1925; *Raleigh Times*, February 11, 1925. Pentuff was one of the most vitriolic critics of Poteat and his evolutionary views. Since Pentuff claimed such a formidable academic pedigree, Poteat investigated his past and found, among other things, that he had earned an A. B. from Furman College, attended the Southern Baptist Theological Seminary, and acquired a "dubious" doctoral degree from Shurtleff College. J. S. Pate to William Louis Poteat, September 10, 1925, J. G. Davis to W. L. Poteat, October 5, 1925, W. J. McGlophlin to W. L. Poteat, October 12, 1925, William Louis Poteat Papers (Wake Forest College Library, Winston-Salem); see also James R. Pentuff, *Christian Evolutionists Answered and President W. L. Poteat's Utterances Reviewed* (n.p., 1925).

14. *Raleigh Times*, February 11, 1925.

members of the Education Committee who favored the anti-evolution bill reserved their comments until they had heard the other side.[15]

At this juncture, the opponents of the Poole resolution within the committee actually lacked any organization or advanced preparation with which to counter the arguments of the Poole forces. In the absence of anyone else, Harrison Yelverton of Wayne County, a Harvard-educated Episcopalian, was temporarily acting as leader of the opposition. But the pause that followed the anti-evolutionists' arguments pointed up the lack of co-ordination in the opposition camp. The momentary silence ended, however, when Chase rose to address the audience. A thunderous applause greeted the University president, who had chosen to represent his institution rather than send members of the science faculty.[16] His advice to Collier Cobb, a well-known University scientist and outspoken defender of evolution, indicated that Chase had no intention of allowing faculty members to risk their academic reputations in the legislative arena. "I am planning to go down [to Raleigh] myself," Chase said, "and I believe it would be better for me to be the goat . . . than for a man who is known to be teaching evolution to be put in a position where he might have to defend himself." [17]

A hush fell over the applauding crowd as the slight, white-haired Chase began his address. Describing himself as a representative of an institution long respected for its intellectual honesty, he stated that he was "not here to discuss evolution as a biologist but to speak in behalf of human liberty." Both church and state, he continued, were primarily interested in the moral welfare of the individuals entrusted to their care, yet the church was attempting to deny teachers a privilege that its ministers exercised without restraint. The Poole Bill would prohibit the teaching of evolution in the classroom without interfering with the preaching of evolution from the pulpit. Chase further declared that the implications of the Poole Bill were to him the cause of far more concern than the mere matter of teaching evolution, because the measure in effect was an "abridgement of the

15. *News and Observer*, February 11, 1925; the career of Robert L. Madison is sketched in William E. Bird, *The History of Western Carolina College: The Progress of an Idea* (Chapel Hill, 1963), pp. 9, 17–20, 70–72.

16. *News and Observer*, February 11, 1925.

17. H. W. Chase to Collier Cobb, February 7, 1925, University Papers.

freedom of speech guaranteed by the Constitution." "Shall we," he asked, "write into that article of the Constitution *except* to school teachers?" He concluded with the declaration: "Mr. Chairman, . . . if it be treason to oppose the bill offered in the name of tyranny over the mind for the purpose of abridging the liberty of one class of our people, I wish to stand here in the name of progress and make my protest." [18] A little later, when Chase was reminded that the University appropriations had not yet cleared the Legislature, he snapped: "If this University doesn't stand for anything but appropriations, I, for one, don't care to be connected with it." Representative Thomas L. Neal of Caswell County, a member of the Education Committee and a Presbyterian elder, accused the University president of trying "to sidetrack the main question by raising the issue of free speech" and promised to send his sons to Davidson College in order to insure their safety from the Darwinian heresy.[19]

Two members of the North Carolina State College science faculty continued the argument against the anti-evolution bill in the absence of President Brooks. Bertram W. Wells, a botanist, and Zeno P. Metcalf, an entomologist and an old hand at fighting anti-evolutionists, sought to demonstrate the compatibility of Christianity and the evolution theory. "I am here," Wells declared, "as a living exponent of the Christian religion in all its essentials and also of evolution *as a fact*." He then offered a brief explanation of the scientific method in an attempt to refute Pentuff's charge that evolution was a mere "figment of the imagination." Representative Neal interrupted to ask when, in the process of evolution, man acquired a soul. The professor, joined by Chase, replied that such a question was "unanswerable" and "quite beside the point" since scientists generally recognized the existence of a soul. Representative Madison then put the question in a slightly modified form: "May I ask the gentlemen from State College at what stage of transformation of man from an amoeba that he parted with his tail and acquired a conscience?" Before anyone else could answer, Chase quipped: "Does the gentle-

18. Memorandum by Gerald W. Johnson, April 21, 1963; Archibald Henderson, *North Carolina: The Old State and the New* (Chicago, 1949), II, 575; Virginius Dabney, *Liberalism in the South* (Chapel Hill, 1932), p. 295.

19. *News and Observer*, February 11, 1925; Crow, "Evolution and Religion," pp. 57–58, Louis R. Wilson; *The University of North Carolina, 1900–1930: The Making of a Modern University* (Chapel Hill, 1957), pp. 512–13.

man mean that they occurred at the same time?" Only after vigorous raps of the gavel did the Chairman quiet the roar of laughter provoked by Chase's retort. Madison's query caused William Louis Poteat to stir restlessly in his seat in the crowded gallery. Turning to a friend, the Wake Forest president whispered: "Biologically he [man] has never lost his tail and here is some evidence that he has never acquired a conscience." [20]

During the three hours of committee hearings, various individuals spoke on the issue. Committee members, Neal Lucas, a Johnston County Republican, and J. C. Braswell, a Nash County physician, joined a minister from High Point who posed as a spokesman for the Junior Order of Mechanics in supporting the Poole Bill as a necessary defense against "this monkey business." A student from State College claimed that his Christian faith had been strengthened, rather than weakened, by the evolutionary teachings of Metcalf and Wells. Claiming her feminine prerogative to have the "last word," Julia Alexander closed the hearings by a reiteration of her biblical literalism and advocacy of the Poole measure. During her speech the crowd began to disperse, leaving the committee to deliberate and return its report. Already taut, the atmosphere reached a new level of tension when the committee's vote resulted in a tie and threw the fate of Poole's bill into the lap of Chairman Connor. Without the slightest hesitation, Connor announced: "I break the tie by voting for an unfavorable report on the bill." As he had anticipated, however, the proponents of the resolution drew up a minority report which was designated as special order of the House for 8:00 P.M., February 17, 1925.[21]

A feeling of despair had gripped Chase as he emerged from the committee hearings. After a "most careful nose-counting" of the 120 members of the House, he calculated that only 55 votes could be mustered against the Poole Bill. Outside the chamber he met Tom Bost, the correspondent for the *Greensboro Daily News,* who inquired about his despondent attitude. When Chase explained his anxiety about the outcome of the legislation, Bost replied: "But what

20. *Greensboro Daily News,* February 11, 1925; *News and Observer,* February 11, 1925; Suzanne C. Linder, "William Louis Poteat and the Evolution Controversy," *North Carolina Historical Review,* XL (April, 1963), 144.

21. Crow, "Evolution and Religion," p. 59; *News and Observer,* February 11, 1925; *Greensboro Daily News,* February 11, 1925.

are you worrying about? If you have 55 men of your own in the House, you are all right, because Poteat has 20 alumni there." Although Chase found it difficult to believe that the Baptists would support his cause, Bost was confident that the Wake Forest-educated legislators would remain loyal to what they had learned at the feet of Poteat. Obviously, the traditional Baptist emphasis upon the separation of church and state and Poteat's long-standing defense of intellectual freedom were not lost upon the Wake Forest alumni in the General Assembly when they came to grips with Poole's measure. The final outcome of the legislation, which revealed the essential accuracy of Bost's prediction, was, in effect, a personal triumph for Poteat, whose "boys" furnished a virtual phalanx of opposition.[22]

The week between the committee hearings and the floor debate was a period of frantic activity on the part of the protagonists in the legislative fight.[23] As usual, the daily newspapers of the larger cities joined the ranks of the opposition. The influential Raleigh *News and Observer*, whose editor, Josephus Daniels, had been "surprised" by the intensity of feeling displayed at the committee hearings, finally took a clear-cut stand in the controversy. Daniels echoed the editorial position of the Winston-Salem *Sentinel* which claimed that the real danger in the bill was the establishment of a precedent "to direct what men should think or teach." "Truth will prevail in the long run in every conflict," the *News and Observer* declared. But it must win by faith and reason and cannot be helped by legislation." [24] Other journals characterized the bill as "something out of the Middle Ages," and joined the *Durham Morning Herald* in calling upon "the college men in the Legislature" to protect "the good name of this enlightened State." [25] The *Fayetteville Observer* and the *Asheville Times* took their editorial cues from Chase. The *Times* declared: "It is not a question of the truth or falsity of the evolution theory. This is a problem which each man is free to settle for himself. . . . It is a question, however, of academic freedom and in the last analysis religious freedom. It involves the whole issue of freedom of speech

22. Memorandum by Gerald W. Johnson, April 26, 1963.
23. H. W. Chase to Haywood Parker, February 23, 1925, University Papers.
24. *News and Observer*, February 12, 16, 17, 1925.
25. *Greensboro Record*, February 11, 1925; *Durham Morning Herald*, February 15, 1925.

and conscience. Shall our teachers be free to follow truth wherever it leads them or submit to political censorship?" The *Times* implored the General Assembly to save North Carolina from disgrace in the eyes of the nation.[26] The *Greensboro Record,* in a similar vein, observed that the Poole Bill presented a "fitting example of the dangers that politicians encounter when they seek to enter the field of religion and education." It expressed the hope that the legislature would leave "the question of school curriculum to school authorities." [27] Decrying the "monkeyshines" of the General Assembly, the Wilmington *Morning Star* further suggested that the legislators "prove by a more dignified and Christian demeanor that man is made in the image of God." Other editorialists, notably in the *Concord Daily Tribune* and the *Fayetteville Observer,* pointed out that already the "unregenerate" were laughing "in their sleeves at the manner in which the believers appeal to the law of the land to make people good and to prevent them from lapsing into unbelief." [28]

Undoubtedly, the *Greensboro Daily News* was the most persistent journalistic critic of militant fundamentalism in the State. Leading the editorial chorus against the Poole Bill, the Greensboro paper viewed the situation as a war upon the state colleges prompted by politicians and religious bigots who believed that "foreigners" now infested these institutions and spread their "foreign" scientific theories at the expense of the Christian populace of North Carolina. The term "foreigner," of course, referred to non-Southerners, especially those of Republican persuasion. President Chase, a Massachusetts-born Republican, fitted this damning label to perfection. Some of the "pious patriots" dubbed him "a homeless liberal" and "damn Yankee who's ruinin' our boys." So strongly was Representative Turlington convinced of the presence of "sinister influences" at Chapel Hill that he promised to fight University appropriations, presumably on the grounds that a threat of financial strangulation would force Chase into line. The *Daily News* lampooned Turlington as "the Iredell Apostle swearing by the Epistle of Poole," who typified the parochialism and bigotry of the anti-evolution

26. *Fayetteville Observer,* February 17, 1925; *Asheville Times,* February 16, 1925.

27. *Greensboro Record,* February 17, 1925.

28. *Morning Star* (Wilmington), February 17, 1925; *Fayetteville Observer,* February 17, 1925; *Concord Daily Tribune,* February 17, 1925.

campaign. Equally adamant in its defense of Chase, the *Daily News* described him as an extraordinarily courageous man unwilling to remain idle while Poole tried to turn the University "over to political and pious hoodlums who resent the breadth of thought it encourages." Throughout its discussions of the issues, however, the Greensboro paper repeatedly professed its own Christian convictions and characterized the anti-evolutionists as unworthy standard bearers of Christ. "The Christ in whose name this proceeding is invoked," one editorial declared, "stands so clear and serene above these petty bickerings that the very fact that followers of Him seek thus to bolster His position becomes in itself an act . . . very close to sacrilege. . . ."[29]

President Chase, all the while, busied himself with speeches, conferences, and correspondence to galvanize public sentiment against the Poole bill. Three days after the committee hearings, he explained in an address to the Chapel Hill student body the University's position regarding anti-evolution legislation. He began by saying:

> . . . with this institution I feel this matter is entirely removed from the realm of expediency. It is intimated to the University that opposition to the measure might injure the University's support, that it might alienate some of the University's friends. That is unfortunate. But the real University, gentlemen, is more than the campus, it is more than the buildings, it is more than any particular group or generation of faculty or students. The real University is an ideal. It is a spiritual thing . . . and those of us to whom the preservation and perpetuation of that ideal are . . . entrusted . . . are obliged to feel that it lives in the realm of principle, where consideration of expediency cannot enter.[30]

Chase then outlined the specific reasons for the University's determined opposition to the Poole bill: (1) the vague and ambiguous nature of the measure placed every teacher of natural science in jeopardy and exposed him to humiliation for any statement that he might make regarding evolution; (2) the measure infringed upon the

29. *Greensboro Daily News*, February 12, 15, 16, 1925.

30. *Chapel Hill Weekly*, February 19, 1925; *Greensboro Daily News*, February 14, 1925; H. W. Chase, "Address to the Student Body," February, 1925, University Papers.

teacher's freedom of speech and upon the *state* college students' liberty to learn, since it placed restrictions only upon the study of biology in state-supported schools; (3) the bill was designed to silence teachers only, leaving preachers free to expound evolution without restraint; and (4) the free competition of ideas was essential in the search for truth, for which the passage of a law was no substitute.[31] Chase's statement reached a wide audience through the elaborate coverage it received in the press and undoubtedly prodded some of the more timid University alumni to take a definite stand against the legislation.

In addition to public statements, Chase sought support for his position through direct contacts with influential citizens. He remained in close touch with Connor and Murphy, who advised him on matters of strategy. He in turn furnished these legislators ammunition to use against the anti-evolution arguments.[32] On February 14, 1925, he suggested that Murphy might use as "a talking point" the fact that passage of the bill would in effect "dismantle" the University, since "it would be impossible to retain the services of many of its best men who feel that their self respect is impaired if they have to work under such restrictions." [33] Typical of much of the correspondence that emanated from the University president's office was a letter to Edgar W. Pharr, Speaker of the House of Representatives, in which Chase candidly outlined the effects of the Poole Bill upon the University. He wrote:

> The question is not whether people are teaching evolution as a fact. It is the easiest thing in the world to read into utterances what was never intended. It is simple to accuse a man of things he cannot disprove in this controversial region. The passage of the Poole Resolution would virtually set up a tribunal before which every teacher of science and related subjects could be badgered, worried, and disgraced. Good men will simply not teach in an environment of

31. Chase, "Address to the Student Body," February, 1925, University Papers.

32. H. W. Chase to Charles G. Rose, February 13, 1925, H. W. Chase to Francis Winslow, February 13, 1925, H. W. Chase to Graham Woodard, February 13, 1925, H. W. Chase to Nat A. Townsend, February 13, 1925, University Papers.

33. H. W. Chase to H. G. Connor, February 13, 1925, H. W. Chase to Walter Murphy, February 13, 1925, H. W. Chase to Walter Murphy, February 14, 1925, University Papers.

that sort. While the bill in itself provides no penalty, the actual penalty is clear. It is the putting of genuine and earnest men, devoted to truth, in the position of criminals in the eyes of the State anytime that an utterance of one of these men may appear questionable under the act to any hearer. This is an intolerable position for men to find themselves in. It is an abridgement of the freedom of discussion and of thought which would go a very long way toward ruining the University because it deals with the vital educational process itself, of which the appropriations and buildings are simply the means to create.[34]

Chase also telegraphed Governor McLean that the Poole measure would create an "intolerable" situation and set the "University back 25 years." Similar messages went out to ministers, prominent University alumni, and other influential persons. He advised his cohort at State College, Professor Bertram Wells, that in the event the Poole Bill passed the House, "we should be ready to turn loose on the Senate." [35]

Chase's activity produced immediate results. Petitions opposing the anti-evolution bill which had been circulated by University alumni appeared on the legislators' desks. Twelve University scientists drew up a statement in which they argued that the theory of evolution was indispensible to the teaching of science and frankly declared that "the evidence in favor of the theory is now overwhelming." This statement was handed to Connor for "use at his discretion." Telegrams to legislators and state government officials came from various parts of North Carolina.[36] Rather typical was the message to the Governor from S. J. Ervin, Sr., of Morganton: "The Poole Resolution threatens incalculable injury to our schools and colleges. Prejudice against our churches on the part of the young people who will attribute this intolerance to the influence of the

34. H. W. Chase to Edgar Pharr, February 16, 1925, University Papers.
35. H. W. Chase to Angus W. McLean, February 16, 1925, H. W. Chase to B. W. Wells, February 13, 1925, University Papers.
36. H. W. Chase to R. W. Winston, February 15, 1925, Robert W. Winston Papers (Southern Historical Collection, University of North Carolina Library, Chapel Hill); Gerald W. Johnson to Archibald Johnson, February 16, 1925, William B. McNider *et al.* to the General Assembly, February 17, 1925, University Papers; Gerald Johnson wrote his father: "Can't you file a protest against the Poole Bill before tomorrow night? It means all our heads including Poteat's." See Gerald Johnson to Archibald Johnson, February 16, 1925, University Papers.

churches and thereby to the cause of religion. May we beg your influence against it." [37] Although Governor McLean avoided involvement in the controversy, Sam Ervin, Jr., heeded his father's advice by joining the crusade against the measure.

The advocates of the Poole bill did not remain idle while its opponents girded themselves for the showdown in the House. But the former already had their front-line forces marshalled and merely had to hold fast. The "infidel" articles in the *Journal of Social Forces* and the Keister incident in Charlotte provided these forces timely and capital ammunition that they exploited fully. Many civic and ministerial organizations bombarded the legislators with petitions calling their attention to these evidences of the acute need of some law to ban evolution.[38] The anti-evolutionist's cause received warm endorsement in a few small, rural weekly newspapers such as the *Stanly News Herald* of Albemarle and the *Nashville Graphic.* Virtually alone among the major city dailies, the *Charlotte Observer* cast its lot with the advocates of the Poole Bill and laid the blame for the critical situation upon "high brow professors" who chose "to stick by the monkey" rather than "live by the Bible." [39]

Similar sentiments emanated from various religious quarters, notably the *Presbyterian Standard.* The *Standard* argued that the Christian taxpayers had a right to say "what should and should not be taught" in the schools financed by their tax money. "When a teacher accepts a position in our schools," the Presbyterian paper declared, "he tacitly agrees to give up some of his rights to freedom of speech." The anti-evolutionists in general complained that Chase's references to "free speech" and academic freedom were mere gimmicks to sidetrack the main issue and "create confusion in the minds of his hearers." [40] In a sermon on "The Poole Bill and the

37. S. J. Ervin, Sr., to Angus W. McLean, February 16, 1925, Governors' Papers (Department of Archives and History, Raleigh).

38. *Commonwealth,* February 13, 1925; *Raleigh Times,* February 14, 1925; *Charlotte Observer,* January 6, February 10, 1925; Presbyterian Ministers' Association of Charlotte to Angus W. McLean, February 16, 1925, Governor's Papers; *Mooresville Enterprise,* March 12, April 9, 1925.

39. *Union Republican* (Winston-Salem), March 5, 1925; *Charlotte Observer,* January 18, February 19, 1925; other small papers which opposed the Poole Bill included *Hendersonville Times,* February 17, 1925; *Messenger and Intelligencer* (Wadesboro), February 19, 1925; *Jackson County Journal* (Sylva), January 16, 1925; *Beaufort County News,* February 19, 1927.

40. *Presbyterian Standard,* LXVI (February 18, 1925), 1.

Bible," broadcast over radio, Dr. Luther Little, pastor of the First Baptist Church in Charlotte, joined his Presbyterian brethren in maintaining that freedom of speech was "always a qualified proposition." For him, federal legislation during World War I provided sufficient precedent for legal restrictions upon such civil rights. He utilized the familiar argument that the separation of church and state not only forbade the teaching of religion in public schools but likewise prohibited the teaching of irreligion.[41]

By the date designated for House consideration of the education committee's minority report on the Poole Bill, the opponents and advocates of the measure, respectively, had closed ranks and girded themselves for the showdown. On February 17, 1925, at eight o'clock in the evening, Speaker Pharr brought down the gavel amid a tumultous confusion in the House. The "surging crowd" that thronged the chamber refused to heed the Speaker, even when he ordered the sergeant-at-arms to clear the aisles "of the jam." The "vast popular showing" moved the *Greensboro Daily News* to remark that "holiness had never hobnobbed in such impressive array." Amid the confusion, Connor pleaded with the crowd to allow the legislators to proceed with their deliberations in an orderly fashion, otherwise police protection would have to be requested from the city of Raleigh. Such pleas were futile, and after a quick conference with Poole, he moved to adjourn the proceedings. The passage of the motion meant the cancellation of "the big show" many had trekked to Raleigh to witness.[42]

The following day, February 18, the House resumed its deliberation of the anti-evolution measure under relatively peaceful circumstances. The next two days brought forth a virtual plethora of parliamentary manuevers. One of these was a bill sponsored by two prominent legislators, R. O. Everett of Durham and I. G. Greer of Watauga County. Called "an act to renew religious liberty in North Carolina," the Everett-Greer proposal provided that any state official or employee who reflected upon, or in any way discredited, the religion of another was to be liable to conviction for a misdemeanor

41. H. W. Chase to Luther Little, February 16, 1925, University Papers; *Greensboro Daily News*, February 16, 1925.

42. *News and Observer*, February 18, 1925; *Charlotte Observer*, February 18, 1925, *Greensboro Daily News*, February 18, 1925; *House Journal*, p. 265.

and loss of his state job. On February 18, Representative Everett sought to head off a prolonged debate on the Poole Bill by a motion to table the minority report from the committee. But the bill survived its "first ordeal by fire" when three legislators changed their votes before the tabulation of the final vote on Everett's motion. The defeat of the motion was the signal for the proponents of the Poole Bill to launch their marathon debate.[43]

Zebulon V. Turlington opened the defense of the measure with an impassioned appeal for its passage as the means of saving the Bible and its teachings from the onslaught of heretics. He particularly emphasized that the resolution merely prohibited the teaching of evolution as a fact, and therefore it in no way curbed freedom of speech. According to him, North Carolina had fallen into a sad plight in which "professors are lined up against the folks." He also charged that Chase had said that the teaching of atheism at the University was merely "a matter of conscience." Despite Chase's vehement denial of any such statement, it continued to be quoted by his critics. Turlington concluded with the observation that the real opposition to the Poole bill came from the textbook lobbyists who feared a decline in the sales of their evolution-oriented textbooks. Then, the Iredell solon relinquished the floor to Robert L. Madison, the Cullowhee Normal School instructor who represented Jackson County. Madison berated the measure as "merely a warning, an admonition" and pointed out, with obvious reference to Chase, that "liberty should not be confused with license." "All freedom that society knows," he explained, "is freedom under the law, and as society grows more complex, freedom of its members becomes more circumscribed." The normal-school professor earnestly pleaded for the passage of the legislation on the grounds that biological evolution was simply "a tissue of guesses and false inferences" which "highbrow professors" had substituted for facts.[44]

In the course of the debates most of the ardent anti-evolutionists had an opportunity to speak in behalf of their cause. The author of the controversial measure, Poole, pledged his confidence in the "integrity of our state institutions" and frankly admitted that he had

43. *Raleigh Times,* February 18, 1925; *Daily Advance,* (Elizabeth City), February 17, 1925; *Greensboro Daily News,* February 19, 1925; *News and Observer,* February 18, 19, 1925; *House Journal,* pp. 280, 290–91.

44. *Catawba News-Enterprise* (Newton), February 24, 1925; *Greensboro Daily News,* February 19, 1925; *Mooresville Enterprise,* August 20, 1925.

never intended to precipitate a "fuss over the question of separation of church and state." Ralph N. Hunter, a Presbyterian minister who represented Polk County, essentially agreed with Julia Alexander's conviction that the passage of the Poole Bill would set "the joy bells of heaven" ringing. In a thinly-veiled reference to Chase and his "imported" faculty, Representative James C. Braswell, a physician from Nash County, caustically characterized Chapel Hill as the habitat of "descendants of New England bull mastodons temporarily in the South to teach that the Bible is a myth and Christ a Santa Claus." [45]

In their turn, the opponents of the anti-evolution legislation fired a few salvos of their own. Representative Sam Ervin of Burke County, heeding his father's advice, heaped ridicule upon the Poole bill. "Such a resolution . . . ," he observed, "serves no good purpose except to absolve monkeys of their responsibility for the human race." Ervin argued that the legislation would, by implication, imperil freedom of speech and would "insult" the Bible and Christianity merely by its existence upon the statute books. For him, if the Christian religion required such a "weak-kneed" resolution to sustain it, "then that religion cannot claim to be powerful enough to save men's souls." [46] Another legislator observed that a vote for the Poole Bill was about as sensible as favoring a law that "would make it illegal for a tadpole to shed his tail within two miles of a public school." [47]

For the opponents of the Poole Bill, however, a new and disturbing element entered the debate on February 19, 1925, when Connor offered a substitute for the Poole resolution that had been prepared by Richard T. Vann, a highly influential Baptist leader and former president of Meredith College. Connor explained his move as a "compromise" that would avoid the dangers of the Poole measure and at the same time insure respect for the convictions of an orthodox constituency. Although opposed to any restrictions of civil liberties, Connor felt that his substitute was necessary lest he and other opponents of the bill fall prey to the same spirit of intolerance of which they accused the anti-evolutionists. Practically identical to

45. *News and Observer*, February 19, 20, 1925; *Greensboro Daily News*, February 20, 1925; *Catawba News-Enterprise*, February 24, 1925.
46. *Raleigh Times*, February 18, 1925; *News and Observer*, February 19, 1925; Memorandum by Sam J. Ervin, Jr., May 23, 1961.
47. *Durham Morning Herald*, March 9, 1925.

the Everett-Greer measure shorn of the penalty clauses, the Connor substitute provided:

> Section 1. It is the sense of the General Assembly . . . that whilst we assert for ourselves a freedom to embrace, profess, and observe the religion of our choice, each respectively, that we cannot in any civil capacity, deny an equal freedom to others. Section 2. That we do declare it as the settled policy of this State that all those who serve in a civil, military or any other official capacity, should do no act nor utter any word, tending to reflect upon or to discredit or otherwise affect anyone's religion, any book or books held by others to be sacred or of religious authority.[48]

Advised earlier about the possibility of such a substitute, Chase immediately raised objections on the grounds that it was "unwise and impracticable." He maintained that existing constitutional guarantees regarding religion were adequate without additional legislation. Furthermore, statutory regulation in the religious and intellectual sphere was highly treacherous. Chase was convinced that the Connor resolution and the Everett-Greer proposal, because of their vague, nebulous nature, contained potential dangers almost equal to those in the Poole Bill.[49]

The University president was not alone in his opposition. The *Greensboro Daily News* reminded the legislators that "no religion can be propped up by legislative action" and urged them to rise above the "mire" and "return to reason." The Wilmington *Morning Star* characterized the Connor proposal as implying "more religion in freedom, and less freedom in religion if it implies anything." The more adamant opponents of the anti-evolutionists who essentially agreed with these journalistic sentiments found themselves fighting two skirmishes simultaneously, for they were as unwilling to accept the substitutes as the original. Their idea of "compromise" was not watered down legislation to be enacted as a sop to the anti-evolutionists.[50]

48. *Catawba News-Enterprise,* February 24, 1925; *News and Observer,* February 20, 1925; *House Journal,* p. 290.

49. H. W. Chase to R. O. Everett, February 18, 1925, H. W. Chase to R. T. Vann, February 16, 1925, H. W. Chase to H. G. Connor, February 17, 1925, H. W. Chase to Walter Murphy, February 17, 1925, University Papers.

50. *Greensboro Daily News,* February 19, 1925; *Morning Star,* February 17, 1925; *Durham Morning Herald,* February 19, 1925.

On the other hand, many North Carolinians were convinced of the need for some type of restrictive legislation to check the corrosive influence of secularism. For them the Connor substitute had a special appeal: it appeared to guarantee religious freedom at the same time that it insulated evangelical Christianity from the assaults of the "non-believers." Forcefully defending this position, the Baptist *Biblical Recorder* argued that the Connor measure would accomplish the general aims of the Poole Bill without risking union of church and state, which was so "objectionable" in the latter. Undoubtedly many legislators could have relieved themselves of considerable pressure from their constituents by voting for Connor's resolution; by such action they could appear as defenders of religious freedom and as special friends of Christianity. The measure was defeated largely by two mutually hostile groups—those who objected to political-religious legislation and the anti-evolutionists unwilling to accept so little.[51]

At a critical moment in the House debates on February 19, 1925, silence fell over the chamber as the weary legislators turned their attention to the large, shambling figure who had gained the floor. Walter Murphy, the Rowan legislator and former University quarterback, had decided to speak his mind on the issues. And his address left no one in doubt regarding his position, for he denounced the Poole Bill and its substitutes as pernicious measures likely to create far more problems than they would ever solve. For Murphy, a man's religion was "strictly a matter between him and his God" which scarcely needed legislative supervision of the sort envisioned by the various bills; actually, he said, a statute attempting to regulate the relationship between theological and scientific beliefs would be the epitome of absurdity. "I am not so much interested," he concluded, "in what I am evolved from as in whither I am going. That which shall come to me in the future as far as good is concerned will come through the atoning blood of Jesus Christ." In short, he counseled the legislators to leave the problem of salvation to some other agency and concentrate upon those problems more likely to achieve solution through legislative action. According to many sources, Murphy's address "clinched" the death of the anti-evolution movement in the General Assembly of 1925. Since Chase was one of

51. *Biblical Recorder*, XC (February 25, 1925), 7.

those who considered the speech decisive, it was perhaps no coincidence that the University selected the commencement exercises of 1925 as the occasion to bestow an honorary degree upon Walter Murphy.[52]

Following Murphy's address on February 19, 1925, the House refused to consider the Connor substitute by a vote of 70 to 41. Then, turning to the original proposition, it killed the Poole Resolution by a vote of 67 to 46. An analysis of this vote reveals that the majority of the alumni of both the University and Wake Forest College in the House opposed the anti-evolution legislation. Approximately one half of those who endorsed the Poole measure claimed no collegiate training whatsoever, although all four medical doctors in the chamber favored its passage. The votes likewise seemed to reflect a correlation between the intensity of the evolution controversy within the various Protestant denominations and the religious affiliation of legislators; 52 per cent of the Baptists, 45 per cent of the Presbyterians, 40 per cent of the Methodists and 15 per cent of the Episcopalians in the House voted for Poole's measure. But in proportion to their total number in the House as well as the state as a whole, the Presbyterians contributed the greatest support for the bill. Moreover, a similar analysis of the vote on the basis of the sectional division of the state reveals that proportionately the mountain county legislators gave the anti-evolution bill its greatest support, followed in order by those from the Piedmont and the coastal plains.[53]

The death of the anti-evolution legislation in the General Assembly provoked a sigh of relief among the opponents of the measure. Shortly after the demise of the Poole Bill, President Chase confided to a friend: "Our legislature, Thank God, is within a few days of its expiring gasps. We will all draw a long breath when the brethren go home for good." [54] The *Winston-Salem Journal*, the *Durham Morning Herald*, and the *Greensboro Daily News* believed that the dispatch of the measure to its "timely grave" offered hope for the

52. *News and Observer*, February 20, 1925; Memorandum by Sam J. Ervin, Jr., May 23, 1961; Lewis, "North Carolina," pp. 42–44; *Raleigh Times*, February 20, 1925; *Franklin Times* (Louisburg), February 27, 1925.

53. *Raleigh Times*, February 19, 1925; *News and Observer*, February 20, 1925; *Charlotte Observer*, February 20, 1925; *House Journal, 1925*, pp. 280, 290–91.

54. H. W. Chase to Beardsley Ruml, March 3, 1925, University Papers.

future.[55] The Wilmington *Morning Star* considered the defeat of Poole's bill and kindred measures as "the most judicious act of the current General Assembly." The *Raleigh Times,* also basking in victory, thanked the legislators for allowing "elbow-room" for North Carolinians to use their God-given intelligence.[56]

Other newspapers that had opposed anti-evolution laws spent little space in editorial rejoicing. They turned their attention to the "situations that spawned the Poole bill." The *Smithfield Herald* and the *Greensboro Daily Record* agreed that the bill was "very properly killed," but warned the state schools, especially the University, that its defeat did "not allow a lot of little two-by-four professors to teach the sort of evolutionary doctrine that would undermine Christianity." [57] In reflecting upon the situation, the *News and Observer* held "the flippant, iconoclastic instructors" responsible for the crisis that produced the Poole Bill. Editor Daniels urged college faculties to consecrate themselves "to investigation, discussion and reverence for truth, faith in God, and a yearning to lead the student body into the Way, the Truth and the Light." [58] Reporting to his constituents, Representative Richard T. Fountain, of Rocky Mount, suggested that further controversy could be avoided if educators would "take care . . . as to what they say when they make addresses." [59] In short, the defeat of anti-evolution legislation was not to be regarded as license for radicalism, but rather as a cue for institutions of learning to take a critical view of themselves and to avoid flying in the face of orthodoxy.

Certainly the defeat did not signify a triumph for extreme modernism; in fact, the term "modernist" was inappropriate for virtually all opponents of the measure. For the most part, they were religious fundamentalists and moderates who preferred to have their faith compete in the free marketplace without the aid of a legislative "prop" rather than risk a violation of the principle of separation of church and state.

55. *Winston-Salem Journal,* March 8, 1925; *Greensboro Daily News,* February 23, 1925; *Durham Morning Herald,* February 20, 21, 1925.
56. *Morning Star,* February 20, 1925; *Raleigh Times,* February 20, 1925.
57. *Greensboro Record,* February 21, 1925; *Smithfield Herald,* February 24, 1925.
58. *News and Observer,* February 20, 1925.
59. *Evening Telegram* (Rocky Mount), March 24, 1925.

6 ∽ POST-POOLE STRUGGLES

"It is not a question of the truth or falsity of the evolution theory. This is a problem which each man is free to settle for himself. . . . It is a question, however, of academic freedom and in the last analysis of religious freedom. It involves the whole issue of freedom of speech and conscience. Shall our teachers be free to follow the truth wherever it leads them or submit to political censorship?"

—THE ASHEVILLE TIMES

Few people believed that the defeat of the Poole Bill had ended the evolution controversy. Those who thought otherwise grossly underestimated the tenacity of the anti-evolutionists. The suggestion by the Wilmington *Morning Star* that Darwin be allowed "to rest in peace and obscurity" held little promise of success.[1] That the anti-evolutionists had other notions was abundantly evident in sermons, tracts, letters-to-the-editors, and editorials that attended the death of the first attempt to ban "the Darwinian heresy." The *Presbyterian Standard* called upon all citizens who considered themselves Christians to select in the next general election only those legislators sympathetic with the moral traditions of "this Christian Commonwealth." [2] Perhaps the most ominous warning came from the *Biblical*

1. *Morning Star*, February 22, 1925.
2. *Presbyterian Standard*, LXVI (March 4, 1925), 2.

Recorder shortly after the demise of the Poole Resolution: "Those who have the management of the State institutions would just as well learn that this question is not settled and will not be, until freak and free-lance teachers, who disregard public sentiment, and trample the Constitution, are dismissed from the faculties. The masses of our people may be 'suspicious,' 'prejudiced,' and 'uninformed' but they are the sovereigns in this state and will not forever submit to evils against which they have thus far protested in vain." [3] Poole himself urged "all Christian school boards" to exert their full authority against the teaching of evolution until the next biennial session of the legislature when his statewide anti-evolution law would achieve success.[4]

Those who considered the defeat of the Poole Bill in 1925 as a major victory for academic freedom were well aware that the mere threat of such legislation had achieved many of the same results as an actual statute. A few local boards of education were quick to heed Poole's advice about eliminating the evolution menace within their jurisdictions. The Mecklenburg County Board of Education was the first to act. In March, 1925, it banned the teaching of evolution and "anything that brings into question . . . the inspiration of the Bible." Acting on the recommendations of the local ministerial associations, the board also empowered the county superintendent of schools to act as a censor whose duty it was to rid all school libraries of "books on evolution." [5] Shortly thereafter, the Alamance County Board of Education took similar action; and Moore County stipulated that evolutionists and "non-believers" were to be denied teaching positions in its schools.[6] Several municipalities, including Durham and Charlotte, initiated elective courses in Bible study. Undoubtedly, many local school agencies throughout the state censored books and eliminated teachers suspected of the Darwinian heresy without any formal declarations of policy. Teachers who felt

3. *Biblical Recorder*, XC (February 25, 1925), 7.
4. *Union Republican* (Winston-Salem), April 2, 1925.
5. Edgar W. Knight, "Monkey or Mud in North Carolina," *The Independent*, CXVIII (May 14, 1927), 516; *Greensboro Daily News*, March 4, 5, 1925; *Graphic* (Nashville), March 12, 1925; Howard K. Beale, *Are American Teachers Free?* (New York, 1936), p. 229.
6. *Durham Morning Herald*, May 26, 1925; *Union Republican*, July 23, 1925.

subtle pressures in numerous ways insured their tenure by omitting all references to evolution.[7]

At any rate, incidents were rare in which a specific teacher was publicly charged with heresy or infidelity. Such accusations were usually shrouded in anonymity, hearsay, and rumor. In 1921 there was some discussion of "a teacher" who "shook the faith" of school children by describing the Book of Jonah as "largely mythical." But even then the name of the teacher remained anonymous. Actually the anti-evolutionist crusaders had little to fear from the public school personnel: most of the teachers and administrators subscribed to an orthodox theology, and many of them possessed little more intellectual sophistication than a majority of the ordinary citizens. Hundreds of the state's public school teachers did not even qualify for a high school diploma; many had never heard of Charles Darwin or evolution, and as far as they were concerned, these names might well belong to "a cigarette or a pugilist." Certainly academic freedom was not the kind of issue on which they would take a strong stand; few understood the meaning of the term, and even fewer were willing to jeopardize their jobs by defending it.[8]

The tendency of the individual teacher to accommodate the anti-evolutionists was reflected in the role played by the North Carolina Education Association, the statewide teachers' organization. The Association sought safety through silence: it managed to avoid any open discussion of the issues involved in the evolution controversy during its annual sessions in the 1920's. Its press organ, the *North Carolina Teacher*, published only one pertinent editorial and that was a masterpiece of fence-straddling. Actually the state teachers' association manifested far greater enthusiasm for incorporating Bible study into the public schools than for opposing legislation designed to prohibit the teaching of evolution.[9]

To determine the full impact of the evolution controversy upon public schools is no easy matter. Much of what was accomplished by the anti-evolutionists on the local level was not recorded. Theirs was

7. *Charlotte Observer*, April 21, 1926; *Presbyterian Standard*, LXVI (September 23, 1925), 1.

8. *Biblical Recorder*, LXXXVI (December 21, 1921), p. 6; Knight, "Monkey or Mud in North Carolina," p. 523.

9. *North Carolina Teacher*, II (December, 1925), 116–17.

a quiet success achieved by the subtle manipulation of local political strings and public opinion. Too much publicity, as in the case of the Poole Bill, might create unexpected snares. Occasionally, however, the evolution issue was bandied about freely in local school politics. Such was the case in Johnston County during a special school tax election in July, 1925. One observer noted that "the school sentiment has suffered fearfully from this agitation about evolution." The agitation had been acute in Johnston County largely because evangelist Ham had waged one of his most successful crusades in Smithfield. During the election the anti-tax forces argued that the schools were already honeycombed with evolutionists and that Christian taxpayers ought not to be forced to pay higher taxes to sustain such infidelity. Although the campaign involved other factors, evolution played a significant role in bringing about a school tax reduction in Johnston County.[10]

During the spring and summer of 1925, the anti-evolutionist agitation in general appeared to increase in tempo. Early in April a newspaper story erroneously announced that Wolfgang Kohler, of the University of Berlin, had been scheduled to lecture at the University of North Carolina on "the Intelligence of Anthropoid Apes," but that the University had canceled his appearance through fear of antagonizing the anti-evolutionists and had officially denied that Kohler had ever been scheduled to speak. Howard Odum assured his friends in the North who clamored for verification of the story that it was totally fictitious. Regardless of these denials, the damage had been done. Many appeared so ready to believe the story that they waited neither for the denials nor listened to them when they were made. Instead the zealots capitalized on the story as another evidence of the state-supported colleges' determined effort to poison young minds with the Darwinian heresy.[11] Sylvester J. Betts, a Baptist minister from Raleigh and an outspoken critic of Poteat, seized upon the Kohler incident as an occasion to denounce all "ape psychology" and blame evolution for the "immoral wave" engulfing the nation. "We must get rid of every teacher, professor, and

10. *Greensboro Daily News,* July 6, 7, 1925.

11. *News and Observer,* April 6, 1925; *Greensboro Daily News,* April 8, 13, 1925; John M. Mecklin to Howard W. Odum, April 8, 1925, Howard W. Odum to John M. Mecklin, April 21, 1925, Odum Papers.

president of our colleges who teaches evolution," he declared with great urgency.[12]

Public expressions of similar sentiments by men prominent in various fields kept the agitation at a high pitch. Though less active in North Carolina after 1925, the nationally-known evangelists who had helped to initiate the controversy occasionally returned to the state to assist the anti-evolutionist cause. During May and June, 1925, Billy Sunday enthralled crowds in High Point, Winston-Salem, and Raleigh with his attacks upon modernists, evolutionists, and "other infidels." Preaching at Wesley Memorial Methodist Church in High Point as the guest of the city ministerial association, Sunday thundered: "I don't believe the talk about evolution. If you believe that you came from a monkey, then take your ancestors and go to the Devil." In Raleigh he described modernists as "theological bootleggers" who ought to be treated in the same way as other dealers in illicit merchandise.[13] Shortly afterward, on June 12, 1925, Mordecai F. Ham was enthusiastically received at the Silver Jubilee session of the Baraca-Philathea Association in Raleigh. His sermon, characterized by virulent invective, concentrated upon modernism and education. He claimed that modern education, with which Christians were so preoccupied, frequently impeded the search for God because it was amoral. Education encouraged evolution, modernism, and other infidelities which "came right from Russia and Germany." To prove the existence of this sinister relationship between education and atheistic doctrines from Europe, Ham asserted that the legal war being waged against Tennessee's anti-evolution law was "financed by the anti-Christ communists." Clergymen far less famous than Ham or Sunday, but no less effective in their collective influence, appeared in pulpits throughout the state to champion the "faith of William Jennings Bryan" as the "only hope of a new day in religion." [14]

Prominent jurists, too, utilized their positions as platforms for stating their anti-evolutionist sentiments. Superior Court judges Thomas J. Shaw and Albion Dunn in particular used the bench as a rostrum for denouncing evolution and "other modernistic teachings."

12. *News and Observer*, May 10, 27, 1925.

13. *Biblical Recorder*, XC (May 13, 1925), 6; *News and Observer*, May 14, June 3, 1925.

14. *News and Observer*, May 6, 25, June 13, August 17, 1925.

In charging a grand jury in Cleveland County early in August, 1925, Judge Shaw discussed at length the effects of the modern college upon youth. He stated that over 40 per cent of the students who graduated from universities had, in the process of their college careers, forsaken Christianity for agnosticism and atheism. Some who heard his remarks believed that his statistics referred specifically to the University of North Carolina, but when officials in Chapel Hill challenged the jurist, he claimed that his statistics concerned universities in general rather than any particular institution. Shaw finally admitted that his remarks had been prompted by a reading of M. H. Duncan's *Modern Education at the Crossroads* and James H. Leuba's *Belief in God and Immortality,* two books frequently quoted by anti-evolutionists.[15] Early in September, 1925, Shaw's colleague on the bench, Judge Albion Dunn expressed his disappointment over the failure of the Poole Bill in a statement that was ostensibly a charge to a Pitt County grand jury. Dunn insisted that the choice of subjects to be taught in public schools was a decision for the people to make through their duly elected representatives rather than "some expert of learning" who was likely to substitute study of the age of rocks for the religion of the rock of ages. "It is the right of the people," he declared, "to prohibit the teaching of theories in contradiction to the Holy Bible, for without the Bible we could not exist, and even this court today would have been unable to open but for its belief in Him above and in the use of the Bible." [16]

Another jurist whose name emerged briefly in connection with the evolution controversy was Judge Isaac M. Meekins of the United States District Court. Appearing as a stout defender of intellectual freedom, Meekins incurred the wrath of the anti-evolutionists for a public address in which he supposedly slurred the good name of William Jennings Bryan by classifying him as a "demagogue who preaches that the world is round or flat according to the sense or nonsense of the district school." Although Meekins claimed that his address had been misquoted, his remarks about Bryan created considerable discussion. Many North Carolinians concluded that the

15. *Greensboro Daily News,* July 31, 1925; *News and Observer,* August 4, 10, 1925; Louis R. Wilson, *The University of North Carolina, 1900–1930: The Making of a Modern University* (Chapel Hill, 1957), pp. 520–21.
16. *News and Observer,* September 2, 1925.

judge's views were motivated more by his Republican party affiliation than by any love for academic freedom.[17]

Anti-evolutionists continued to flood the newspapers with letters-to-the-editor in which they demonstrated a preoccupation with the kinship between men and monkeys. Many disapproved of evolution ostensibly at least on the grounds that it impugned man's ancestry, denied his uniqueness, and stripped him of dignity, reducing him to the level of a mere animal. Although their objections were usually religious in nature, the frequent references to the theory's heretical implications regarding man's ancestry suggested that much of the anti-evolution sentiment may have been related to traditional concepts of race held by a majority of the citizens in the state. In spite of its progress in racial affairs, North Carolina remained a white man's land where the assumption of a superior ancestry by whites undergirded their belief in the innate superiority of the white race. Thus, the idea that all men sprang from a common animal ancestor was, for many North Carolinians, as disturbing to their notions of race as it was to their theological concepts. It probably was no mere coincidence that the anti-evolutionists leveled their bitterest and most persistent attacks against those defenders of evolution who also held advanced views on the race question: Poteat headed the state Inter-Racial Commission, Odum and Keister were sociologists who dared to probe into this sensitive area, and Chase was a "damn Yankee." [18]

In the midst of these sporadic interchanges between protagonists in the evolution controversy, the attention of North Carolinians focused upon Dayton, Tennessee, where a legal contest over the state's anti-evolution law was attracting international interest. The proximity of Dayton served only to heighten public interest in the trial among North Carolinians. The detailed coverage of the affair in newspapers, large and small, provided full accounts of the strange happenings in Tennessee which climaxed in the death of Bryan. Both opponents and supporters of anti-evolution legislation in North Carolina attempted to capitalize on the trial.

17. *News and Observer*, June 6, 7, 1925.

18. See *News and Observer*, May 16, 1922, April 17, 1923, June 25, 1925; *Charlotte Observer*, January 11, 1925; Wilbur J. Cash, a student at Wake Forest College at the height of the evolution controversy, later wrote: "One of the most stressed notions which went around was that evolution made a Negro as good as a white man—that is, threatened White Supremacy." See his *Mind of the South* (New York, 1941), p. 339.

Speaking for the opposition, President Chase of the University described the Scopes case as a shameful affair produced largely by the educational backwardness of Tennessee where "self taught" natives could only conceive of science and evolution as instruments for destroying their cherished beliefs.[19] Walter Murphy, the Rowan legislator who had vigorously opposed the Poole Bill in 1925, characterized the trial as "damn inconsequential"; N. C. Newhold of the State Department of Public Instruction declared that North Carolina must bear some of the responsibility and stigma of the Dayton performance because Tennessee was part of the South.[20] The *Chatham Record* held the fundamentalists responsible for making "a bugaboo" of evolution and predicted that the theory would "have ten times as many adherents because of the assaults of the Bryans, Sundays, Hams, and others who had so little judgment as to insist upon making the denial of a sheer scientific principle fundamental to Christianity." [21] The Rocky Mount *Evening Telegram* and the *Greensboro Daily News* viewed the avid interest in the Scopes case as "morbid, rather than wholesome." It was "rooted in religious disputatiousness." [22] While most newspapers heaped extraordinary eulogies upon Bryan at his death, most also agreed that his performance at Dayton smacked of the midway and that both he and Darrow were largely responsible for turning the Scopes Trial into what was variously called a spectacle, a farce, and a "catfight."

Nor was the unfavorable reaction to the Dayton trial limited to the secular press. *Charity and Children* considered Bryan the "giant" and Darrow the "pigmy" of the Dayton affair, but denounced the extremism of both. Archibald Johnson maintained that the Scopes trial merely proved that the Baptists "had been right all these years in contending for absolute separation of church and state." He urged his fellow churchmen to learn well the lessons taught by the trial and to forget "the Dayton foolishness" in order to return to "the real work" of the church.[23] The *North Carolina Christian Advocate*, the

19. *Evening Telegram* (Rocky Mount), July 21, 1925.
20. *News and Observer*, July 17, 1925.
21. *Chatham Record* (Pittsboro), May 29, 1925; see also *Mission Herald* XXXIX (June, 1925), 8.
22. *Evening Telegram*, May 18, 23, 1925; *Greensboro Daily News*, May 8, 1925.
23. *Charity and Children*, XL (June 11, 1925), 4; *ibid*. XL (July 30, 1925), 4; *ibid*., XL (August 6, 1926), 4.

Methodist paper that pursued a similar approach to the Scopes Trial, provoked a ripple of excitement in Methodist circles by publishing an article entitled "Mr. Bryan Goes to Bat and Strikes Out." Written by L. B. Hayes, director of the Methodist youth organization known as the Epworth League, this article depicted Bryan as the "King of Talk" whose "grandstand play at Dayton" would have been "ludicrous had it not been so pathetic." The significance of the article lay in the fact that the editors of the *Advocate* allowed it to appear as a guest editorial and that its appearance failed to produce anything more than a mere ripple of agitation.[24]

In the hands of those opposed to anti-evolution legislation, the Scopes Trial became a propaganda device for utilizing, in behalf of their cause, the heady pride which North Carolinians possessed in their reputation for recent progress. Their exaggerated emphasis upon the differences between Tennessee and North Carolina neither made adequate allowance for their similarities nor conveyed a realistic view of the socio-intellectual climate of either state. And to credit North Carolina with a greater degree of "enlightenment" because of its defeat of an anti-evolution law was to ignore the fact that the intense agitation and local pressures had achieved in the state many of the aims implicit in Tennessee's statute. Actually those aware of the situation had reason "to think that the Scopes Trial might have taken place in North Carolina." Citizens whose sensibilities had been shocked by the Dayton spectacle were therefore rather easily persuaded that a similar fiasco east of the Great Smokies would nullify the state's claim to being "the Wisconsin of the South." Even those concerned with little more than the state's economic development hesitated to risk tarnishing its new reputation in this field by the passage of a "monkey law." A prominent attorney in the state observed:

There is a large body of opinion in North Carolina which objects to the whole theory of evolution upon religious grounds. But—because we have the reputation of being the most progressive of the Southern states; because our people are justly proud of this reputation; because public opinion generally is more enlightened and fair-minded than that in Tennessee (for example); because with the action of that

24. *N.C. Christian Advocate*, LXX (July 16, 1925), 2; see also *ibid.*, LXX (July 30, 1925), 2, 7; *ibid.*. LXX (August 27, 1925), 5.

state before us, even our convinced Fundamentalists hesitate to make this state also a laughingstock; . . .—for these reasons there is little likelihood that any anti-evolution statute will be passed.[25]

Certainly the specter of a monkey trial as damaging to the public image of North Carolina as the Scopes Trial had obviously been to Tennessee helped to bring about a gradual shift in public opinion regarding the feasibility of anti-evolution statutes. It was no accident that during and immediately after the Dayton trial prominent individuals including editors, educators, and clergymen, hitherto silent or neutral, took clear-cut stands against the anti-evolutionists.

Perhaps the most notable example of such individuals was President Eugene C. Brooks of North Carolina State College who finally made known his position in a public address before the summer school of 1925. He viewed the whole conflict over evolution as a part of the postwar social cataclysm in which perspectives were undergoing rapid changes. But he reminded his audience that extreme license in thought and conduct inherent in the very nature of democracy usually became more pronounced in periods of adjustment. At one point he declared: "Academic freedom is as dear to the college teacher as religious tolerance ever was to the Protestant churches. It is well recognized in college circles that academic freedom, even as individual liberty, has its metes and bounds, and does not presuppose that a college teacher has license to propagate any noxious doctrine that may dribble from an unwholesome mind." [26] Since both modern education and "the simple faith of our people" contained truths necessary for the good life, Brooks urged closer co-operation between teachers and ministers as a means of providing youth with the "proper intellectual development." [27]

Even before Brooks became president of North Carolina State College, the anti-evolutionists had come to suspect the institution of harboring "infidels." The very nature of the college as a technological school meant that it emphasized science and contained a sizable science faculty. A formal declaration by some of these faculty members and the Riley-Metcalf debate in 1922 tended to confirm the

25. Quoted in Shipley, *The War on Modern Science*, p. 108.
26. E. C. Brooks, "The Need of Cooperation Between Ministers and Teachers," June, 1925, Brooks Papers.
27. *Ibid.*

anti-evolutionists' suspicions about the existence of infidelity on its campus. By their outspoken opposition to the Poole Bill in 1925, Professors Metcalf and Wells in particular had aroused the ire of the measure's advocates. By the end of that year another State College professor had become the prime target of the anti-evolutionists' criticism.[28] He was Carl C. Taylor, a sociologist, whose liberal views occasionally caused him to run afoul of the more conservative elements in the state. Taylor also had the disadvantage of not being a native North Carolinian. But he attracted the attention of the anti-evolutionists primarily because of his sponsorship of the Raleigh Religious Forum, an annual symposium on contemporary issues held at the Christian Church. In December, 1925, the Forum was devoted to a discussion of the conflict between science and religion; and some of the participants made observations which aroused the anger of the fundamentalists. Dr. W. M. White of Raleigh's First Presbyterian Church, who waged a verbal war on the Forum, engaged in a bitter exchange with Professor Taylor over the purposes of the institution. The *Biblical Recorder* declared that most of the Forum speakers were "free thinkers" who sneered "at the old doctrines of grace." [29] Other critics more zealous in their drive to eliminate infidelity from the state colleges brought pressure on President Brooks to cleanse his institution of such obvious heretics as Wells, Metcalf, and Taylor. But their efforts were of no avail. Those who accused Brooks of assuming an equivocal attitude toward the anti-evolutionists sometimes mistook his moderation and diplomacy for weakness. Actually his politic methods proved to be quite effective in protecting academic freedom at the college.[30]

The active opponents of the monkey law in North Carolina combined their skillful use of the Scopes Trial with other tactics designed to allay the fears of that considerable body of uncommitted citizens regarding public educational institutions. During the two years following the close of the legislature of 1925, they carefully

28. See above, p. 16.

29. *News and Observer*, January 4, 1926; *Biblical Recorder*, XCI (December 23, 1925), 7; see also Gatewood, *Eugene Clyde Brooks*, pp. 224, 229, 242–243.

30. *News and Observer*, April 2, 1926; "Annual Report of the President of the College, 1925–1926," *State College Record*, XXV (May, 1926), 11–12; Brooks's most hostile critic was columnist Nell Battle Lewis who characterized his position in the evolution controversy as that of an "agile" politician; see *News and Observer*, June 27, 1926.

avoided acts and utterances likely to arouse hostility and availed themselves of opportunities to restore public confidence in tax-supported schools. For example, President Harry Chase prevailed upon Professor Collier Cobb to postpone the publication of his book on evolution in order to avoid antagonizing the orthodox populace. On April 16, 1926, Chase wrote Cobb:

> I felt that I ought . . . to say just how I felt about the University Press publishing your manuscript. My feeling is simply this—we know that a very difficult struggle lies just ahead of us, a struggle which will be a real test of our ability to maintain proper conditions for the freedom of teaching and research. It is inconceivable that the University, when this crisis comes, should not speak out plainly and should not use every bit of its strength to resist restrictive legislation. Our friends all over the state are of that mind, but they are also of the mind that if we are to emerge victorious from this struggle the load which they are to carry must not be made heavier by any act of ours. The importance of the victory is so great that I think we can well afford for the moment to refrain from doing anything, when no matter of principle is involved, that tends to raise the issue in any concrete form, or which might add to the perplexities of those who will have to be on the firing line for the University during these next few months. I am trying to keep in mind the overwhelming importance of the objectives for which we are working. For the tone and temper of your book there can be only the highest praise. At the same time, as regretful as I am to say so, I believe that the publication of the book by a member of the University faculty at this moment, through the official channel of the University Press, which deals with evolution would be regarded by our enemies as a challenge thrown down to them, by our friends as an unnecessary addition to their burdens. It is almost inconceivable that such a state of affairs should exist in a civilized community in the twentieth century, but it does exist. If we can win this victory during the next twelve months, I believe that it is just about going to stem the tide in the South. It is tremendously important that it should be won. To this, for the moment . . . we should sacrifice all small battles. I have felt that I should make such a statement, which would indicate my feeling at this point.[31]

A little later Chase wrote a friend that "the wise strategy" for the University to pursue in the evolution controversy was "to set back and saw wood." He calculated that given the limelight long enough

31. Harry W. Chase to Collier Cobb, April 16, 1926, University Papers.

the fundamentalists would probably talk themselves quite to death. He understood the public mind well enough to know that in time it wearied of the agitator, no matter how worthy his cause.[32]

All the while, Chase as well as representatives of other state colleges sought to combat the idea that their institutions were hostile to the precepts of the Christian faith. Without compromising his earlier position, the University president assured civic and alumni groups throughout the state that his institution was "loyal to both religion and science." [33] President Brooks of North Carolina State College told his trustees in 1926: "There is no attempt at State College to undermine the faith of anyone." Brooks also organized a short course at the college for high school science teachers in the summer of 1925 which was designed to eliminate some of the misunderstanding about the relation of science and religion that apparently existed in the public schools.[34]

The task of restoring the tarnished image of state-supported colleges was by no means borne entirely by college executives. Faculty members actively participated in efforts to remove blemishes from their institutions' reputations. Frank P. Graham, a young instructor in history at the University who was studying in Europe at the time of the legislative debate over the Poole Bill, had written a highly publicized letter pleading with North Carolinians to rally to their university in the name of tolerance and liberty.[35] Upon his return to Chapel Hill, he busied himself during the winter and spring of 1925–1926 with speeches in various sections of the state in which he defended freedom of teaching and discussion as the surest means of avoiding doubt and cynicism among students. Howard W. Odum, another University professor, sought to repair the damage caused by articles in his *Journal of Social Forces.* His direct contacts with individual clergymen and ministerial associations in 1925 and 1926 contributed significantly to the allaying of clerical fears. Odum, Graham, and numerous other faculty members of state colleges who hit the speech-making trail in behalf of their institutions carefully

32. Harry W. Chase to Edwin Mims, May 14, 1926, University Papers.
33. *News and Observer,* September 19, 1925.
34. *News and Observer,* July 3, 1925; "Annual Report of the President of the College, 1925–1926," *State College Record,* XXV (May, 1926), 11–12.
35. For the complete text of this famous letter see Appendix D.

omitted remarks and references likely to alienate fundamentalists. Odum, for example, got advice from some of his friends among the clergy regarding strategy and speech topics.[36]

The efforts of the faculty were complemented by the activities of chaplains and directors of Young Men's Christian Associations on state college campuses. Articles about the religious life of students appeared so frequently in the press that the *Greensboro Daily News* wondered whether the colleges were going too far in their self-defenses. North Carolina College for Women categorically denied any "irreligious atmosphere" on its campus and took great pains to describe its elective course in Bible, the activities of the YWCA, and the "well-organized work" of the various denominational organizations on its campus. In a similar vein Harry F. Comer, general secretary of the YMCA at the University, sought to dispel notions of religious infidelity on the Chapel Hill campus. Such efforts undoubtedly helped to counterbalance the blasts of the anti-evolutionists.[37]

Some of the journalistic allies of the University and the state colleges were unable to abide by such mild tactics. Nell Battle Lewis diverged sharply from the *News and Observer*'s editorial policy by returning in kind the bitter assaults of the fundamentalists whose crusade against evolution she described as "thoroughly contemptible." She wrote about the anti-evolutionists in a manner worthy of Mencken and called upon all self-respecting North Carolinians to drive out these insidious, latter-day "barnstormers" simply by regaining their usual sense of proportion. For a while early in 1926 her columns were devoted to a question-answer game that she dubbed "the ABC of Evolution Contest." Each week the person who answered correctly her twenty questions about Darwin and evolution received a copy of Hendrick van Loon's *Tolerance*.[38] No less drastic in his handling of the anti-evolutionists was William O. Saunders,

36. *News and Observer*, November 2, 1925; *Charlotte Observer*, June 12, 1926; Howard W. Odum to William F. McCorkle, September 25, 1925, Howard W. Odum to A. S. McGeachy, May 7, 1926, Thomas F. Opie to Howard W. Odum, May 13, 1926, Howard W. Odum to Thomas F. Opie, May 14, 1926, Odum Papers.

37. See *Greensboro Daily News*, August 6, 1925; *News and Observer*, August 5, 9, 1925, February 21, 1926.

38. *News and Observer*, February 15, 22, 1925, February 21, March 7, 1926.

the irascible editor of the Elizabeth City *Independent,* who ascribed the whole evolution controversy to the existence of a large number of "mis-informed, religious-minded people" in North Carolina.[39] But the *Greensboro Daily News* as usual surpassed all others in its hostility toward the fundamentalist crusade. It passionately defended Poteat and Chase, heaped scorn upon their detractors, and persistently leveled its devastating satire and ridicule upon the anti-evolutionists and their cause.[40] As the controversy increased in tempo, lesser lights in North Carolina journalism such as the *Chatham Record,* the *Mount Airy News,* and the *Hamlet News-Messenger* launched editorial attacks upon "overly zealous" anti-evolutionists.[41]

The Scopes Trial stimulated activities among the anti-evolutionists which were no less important than those of their opponents. By the death of Bryan the anti-evolutionists lost a leader, to be sure. But in death, even more than in life, Bryan became the rallying point for the anti-evolutionists in North Carolina. Martyred in behalf of a noble cause, the Great Commoner from his grave breathed new life into the anti-evolutionist crusade in North Carolina by enhancing the cohesiveness of the movement and by strengthening its determination to outlaw evolution as a means of avenging his death. S. F. Conrad, a Baptist minister active in anti-evolution circles in Charlotte, published at his own expense a twenty-page pamphlet that contained the "highlights" of Bryan's utterances on the "bloody doctrine of evolution" delivered at Dayton.[42] Meeting on September 15, 1925, at Black Jack Church, the state convention of the Free Will Baptists mourned the loss of Bryan, "the greatest champion of Christian America," and resolved to "carry on . . . the work he was doing" in propagating "the truths of the Bible." [43]

The relatively small splinter-group of Methodists, known as Methodist Protestants, sought to carry on Bryan's work by placing their denomination on record as opposed to evolution. The anti-

39. *Independent* (Elizabeth City), January 9, 16, February 6, March 31, 1925.

40. *Greensboro Daily News,* May 8, August 6, 17, 1925.

41. *Chatham Record,* May 29, 1925; *Mount Airy News,* March 4, 1926; *Hamlet News-Messenger,* February 18, 1926.

42. S. F. Conrad (compiler), *Force and Love Meet Again Face to Face: Hard Science and Faith in Jesus Christ* (Charlotte, 1925), 20 pp.

43. *Minutes of the Thirteenth Annual Session of the State Convention of the Free Will Baptists of North Carolina, 1925,* p. 10.

evolutionist element had long been active within the church when the martyrdom of Bryan created an atmosphere in which their aims could be more easily attained. Meeting in High Point at its newly established college on November 4, 1925, the annual conference of the Methodist Protestant Church discussed at length various doctrinal issues involved in the modernist-fundamentalist dispute. Although the conference disclaimed any intention of prescribing "pedagogical policy" for its "institution of higher learning," it did state quite specifically those doctrines to which all Methodist Protestant agencies ought to adhere. Following its reaffirmation of faith in the fundamental doctrines "formulated by our fathers a century ago," the body then adopted a resolution prepared by J. A. Burgess, one of the denomination's most persistently vocal anti-evolutionists. The resolution read: "This Conference places itself on record as being in opposition to any theory being taught in any of the schools of our State, which are supported by taxation, that unites man by blood to the lower animals." [44] By placing their denomination officially within the anti-evolutionist camp the Methodist Protestants diverged sharply from their brethren in the Methodist Episcopal Church. Their resolution, which implied support for an anti-evolution law, closely resembled the statement adopted by the convention of the Original Free Will Baptists in 1926.[45]

The *Presbyterian Standard* marshalled the greatest eloquence in behalf of Bryan's role at Dayton, and agreed that the stand taken by the Methodist Protestants was the best means of completing his unfinished task. The paper had heartily endorsed the passage of the Tennessee anti-evolution law and, with equal vigor, joined Bryan, "that ripe product of Presbyterianism," in championing its constitutionality. Clergymen who disagreed with this position were scorned as "small fry of the ministry" attempting to gain stature among "the intellectuals by proclaiming their belief in their animal ancestry." The *Standard* quite naturally reserved its most venomous adjectives for Clarence Darrow, whom it labelled as "narrow, unscrupulous, unforgiving" and "living for this world." He was "a big city infidel" lionized by a host of "small fry ministers" best known for their

44. *Journal of the N.C. Conference of the Methodist Protestant Church, 1925*, pp. 34, 47, 92.

45. *Minutes of the Thirty-First Annual Session of the Eastern Convention of the Original Free Will Baptists, 1926*, p. 5.

shallowness and hypocrisy.[46] And when the Great Commoner laid down his life for the cause of "the Old Time Bible," the *Standard* declared: "The time has come when those of us who love the old Book should stand together." All men, clergy and laity alike, were called upon to make their positions clear—either accept evolution or Genesis, for there were no other alternatives. Certainly there was "no room for theistic evolutionists," who, according to the *Standard,* were cowardly souls trying to carry water on both shoulders. In effect, the Presbyterian paper issued a call for fundamentalists to close ranks in order to carry the fight begun by Bryan to a successful conclusion.[47] A similar call for unity and action appeared in the editorial columns of such rural weeklies as the *Nashville Graphic,* the *Mooresville Enterprise,* and the *Union Republican.*[48] These papers made it clear that the followers of the dead Bryan were obligated to continue the crusade of their "fallen leader." "The spirit of Bryan must survive," the *North Carolina Lutheran* proclaimed, "or antiChrist will prevail against us in our goodly land." [49] By late summer, 1925, even the language of the anti-evolutionists had assumed a martial quality; they spoke as soldiers of ancient Israel girding themselves for a struggle with the enemies of Jehovah.

One such fighter was William P. McCorkle, the fiery Presbyterian clergyman who continued his attack on modernism and evolution in state institutions. Long after the close of the legislature in 1925, he was still crusading against Keister, the *Journal of Social Forces,* and the "modernistic" McNair lectures.[50] Nor was McCorkle fighting alone. Throughout the spring and summer of 1925 his cause was not only championed by the *Presbyterian Standard* but also by a sizable

46. *Presbyterian Standard,* LXVI (July 8, 1925), 1; *ibid.,* LXVI (July 15, 1925), 2; *ibid.,* LXVI (July 29, 1925), 2; *ibid.,* LXVI (August 5, 1925), 1; *ibid.,* LXVI (August 19, 1925), 1; *ibid.,* LXVI (August 26, 1925), 1.

47. *Presbyterian Standard,* LXVI (July 29, 1925), 1; *ibid.,* LXVI (August 19, 1925), 1.

48. *Graphic* (Nashville), July 23, 1925; *Mooresville Enterprise,* July 30, August 6, 20, 1925; *Union Republican* (Winston-Salem), July 23, August 27, 1925.

49. *North Carolina Lutheran,* III (August, 1925), 4.

50. William P. McCorkle to Howard W. Odum, September 19, 1925, William P. McCorkle to Howard W. Odum, September 23, 1925, William P. McCorkle to Howard W. Odum, September 28, 1925, William P. McCorkle to Howard W. Odum, September 30, 1925, Odum Papers; William P. McCorkle, *Anti-Christian Sociology As Taught in the Journal of Social Forces* (Burlington, 1925), 32 pp.

group of prominent Presbyterian ministers whose attacks on evolution became increasingly bitter. Some, like the Reverends W. M. Sykes and W. R. Coppedge concentrated upon "the weaknesses" of the evolutionary hypothesis which they described as "a guess" resting "on the false assumption of spontaneous generation of life." Others such as Reverends W. I. Sinnott, Albert S. Johnson, and A. R. Shaw devoted their attention to the evil "fruits" of the evolution theory and repeatedly linked it to German militarism, the First World War, and Soviet Bolshevism. Left unchecked, the "pernicious doctrine" would produce equally disastrous results in America.[51]

The strength of this anti-evolutionist faction of Presbyterians became apparent at the meeting of the North Carolina Synod on October 16–18, 1925, in the "Presbyterian town" of Mooresville, a center of anti-evolutionist agitation. It was also the home of Representative Zebulon V. Turlington, who had already announced his decision to fight for the passage of an anti-evolution law in the legislature of 1927. The atmosphere of Mooresville undoubtedly strengthened the hand of the anti-evolutionists in the Synod meeting. At any rate, they succeeded in electing as moderator H. B. Searight of Washington, one of the most vocal critics of evolution, and in passing resolutions which in effect placed the Synod on record as opposed to the teaching of Darwinism. Four ministers, Shaw, Coppedge, McCorkle, and J. E. Robinson, presented papers that condemned the prevalence of evolutionary and other "modernistic teachings" in tax-supported institutions. Outspoken fundamentalists dominated the special committee created to consider these papers, and, after "long and hard" deliberations, the committee proposed several lengthy resolutions that were adopted by the Synod. One of these condemned the articles in the January issue of the *Journal of Social Forces* and called upon the University to prevent the use of its agencies for the dissemination of "radical and dangerous theories." Other resolutions called for "a closer supervision to prevent teaching anything" in public schools which contradicted "Christian truths as revealed in the Word of God," demanded the removal of teachers found guilty of teaching evolution "as a fact," and reaffirmed the

51. *Presbyterian Standard,* LXVI (February 11, 1925), 3; *ibid.,* LXVI (September 9, 1925), 7, 10; *ibid.,* LXVI (September 16, 1925), 10–11; *ibid.,* LXVI (October 28, 1925), 1.

Synod's faith in the historic creeds of Presbyterianism. Stated in the form of a "Declaration of Principles," these resolutions were dispatched to each college in the state with the request that it be read to the faculty. By the end of the Synod session the anti-evolutionist faction appeared to be in full ascendancy; and, under the leadership of Searight, the Synod could be expected to assist in a more aggressive anti-evolution crusade.[52]

Certainly the activities of some Presbyterians following the Synod session indicated that their zeal had been rekindled. By the spring of 1926 they had become deeply involved in the establishment of a statewide organization to foster sentiment for an anti-evolution law. So active were the Presbyterians in this effort that some of their brethren became alarmed lest their denomination be responsible for unleashing a wave of religious hysteria. Presbyterian ministers such as David Scanlon of Durham, Charles Coble of High Point, and R. Murphy Williams of Greensboro sought to stem the tide of what they considered the excesses of "rabid" fundamentalism. Although no evolutionist, Coble admitted that he was shamed by the "unjust, uncharitable, and hence unChristian" acts and accusations of his anti-evolutionist brethren whose presumptuousness he loathed and whose motives he sometimes questioned.[53] Alfred M. Scales, the prominent Presbyterian layman, used the opportunity afforded by his commencement address at Davidson College on June 2, 1926, to warn his fellow churchmen of the dangers inherent in their crusade against a scientific theory. Such voices helped to restore equanimity within the Presbyterian ranks.[54] Even the *Presbyterian Standard* had begun to find editorial topics other than evolution and modernism by the summer of 1926.

Despite the reaction against them, the anti-evolutionists in the Presbyterian church, led by Searight and McCorkle, continued to battle "infidelity" in the publicly supported schools. They concentrated their fire on the University and the McNair lectures. Searight admonished the University for importing a New Englander and a

52. *Presbyterian Standard,* LXVI (October 28, 1925), 1; Declaration of Principles Adopted by the Synod of North Carolina, October 16, 1925, Odum Papers; *Minutes of Annual Session of the Synod of North Carolina, 1925,* p. 491.

53. *News and Observer,* May 25, 1926; R. Murphy Williams to R. R. Clark, October 20, 1926 (copy), University Papers.

54. *Statesville Landmark,* June 7, 1926.

modernist, Professor Charles R. Brown of Yale University, to deliver the lectures in 1926. He blamed the selection on Chase, another Northerner whom he described as a "homeless liberal" [55] attempting to make modernism "the official religion of the state." McCorkle still busied himself with efforts to right what "was wrong with the McNair Lectureship." He engaged in a lengthy correspondence with President Chase in which he frankly stated that the McNair indenture had been violated by the University because the lectures had not been used to provide a "foundation for the conservative defense of the Christian religion." McCorkle strongly advised Chase to include fundamentalists on the roster of lecturers and to seek the advice of clergymen in filling the appointments in the future.[56] Although the anti-evolutionist ardor had cooled considerably by the meeting of the Synod in October, 1926, McCorkle and Searight were determined to press for some action on the McNair lectureship. As moderator, Searight opened the meeting with a strongly-worded sermon that called upon Presbyterians to "wage a great fight for the Faith against the numerous subtle and insidious forces." On the last day of the Synod session, after many delegates had returned home, McCorkle introduced a memorial relating to the lectureship which, over the strong objections of David H. Scanlon, was adopted. At the same time a committee was appointed for the purpose of transmitting the document in person to the proper University officials. The lengthy memorial, in essence, criticized the University for selecting modernists, Darwinian apologists, and Northerners to fill a position created to foster evangelical Christianity. In a final passage the document censured the *Journal of Social Forces* and challenged the University to live up to the trust placed in it by "this conservative Christian commonwealth." [57]

McCorkle headed the committee chosen by the Synod to present

55. *News and Observer*, March 30, 1926; *Charlotte Observer*, May 2, 1926; William P. McCorkle to Harry W. Chase, September 22, 1926, University Papers; see also Charles R. Brown, *A Working Faith* (Chapel Hill, 1928).

56. William P. McCorkle to Howard W. Odum, May 7, 1926, William P. McCorkle to Howard W. Odum, May 13, 1926, Odum Papers; William P. McCorkle to Harry W. Chase, September 22, 1926, William P. McCorkle to Harry W. Chase, October 18, 1926, William P. McCorkle to Harry W. Chase, November 3, 1926, University Papers.

57. William P. McCorkle to Harry W. Chase, October 18, 1926, University Papers; *News and Observer*, October 16, 1926; *Statesville Landmark*, October 18, 1926; *Minutes of the Annual Session of the Synod of North Carolina, 1926*, pp. 623–27.

the memorial to the University. He immediately wrote President Chase requesting a special meeting of the faculty in order to "lay the facts" before it. Chase's polite refusal to convene a general faculty meeting for such a purpose led McCorkle to conclude that he was a "persona non grata to quite a few of the professors." He then distributed copies of the memorial to the faculty and trustees and requested an audience with the executive committee of the board of trustees. Finally, after much ado, McCorkle's group was received by President Chase, and its views which Chase communicated to the trustees prompted a resolution by the board in January, 1927, which amounted to little more than an acknowledgement of the Synod's concern about the lectureship.[58] But the University did not dismiss the matter so lightly as the resolution would indicate. Chase was clearly worried about the repercussions of the Synod's action, and after considerable deliberation, he decided to forgo the McNair lectures in 1927.[59] In the following year, Thornton Whaling, a former president of Columbia Theological Seminary and Professor of Systematic Theology and Ethics at the Louisville Presbyterian Seminary, was appointed McNair lecturer. A self-styled "orthodox theologian who makes no secret of the fact that he is an undisguised Augustinian and Calvinist," Whaling delivered three addresses collectively entitled "Science and Religion Today," which constituted a rather sophisticated statement of the fundamentalist position. Some of those who had demanded changes in the McNair lectureship complained about the superficial quality of Whaling's performance and even requested that his lectures remain unpublished. On the other hand, the mere fact of his appointment was satisfying to many fundamentalists, particularly among the Presbyterians. For McCorkle and his group, it indicated that their efforts had not been in vain.[60]

In the meantime, the Baptists were waging their own battles in the evolution war. Unlike the Presbyterians, whose efforts centered upon

58. William P. McCorkle to Harry W. Chase, November 3, 1926, Report of the Synod Committee Visit to the University, November 11, 1926, William P. McCorkle to Harry W. Chase, November 10, 1926, William P. McCorkle to Harry W. Chase, November 22, 1926, University Papers; see also Wilson, *The University of North Carolina*, pp. 494–95.

59. Harry W. Chase to A. M. Scales, January 20, 1927, University Papers.

60. Thornton Whaling, *Science and Religion Today* (Chapel Hill, 1929), 74 pp; Howard Mumford Jones to the author, June 22, 1962; W. T. Couch to the author, May 22, 1963.

ridding the state-supported schools of the various manifestations of the "Darwinian heresy," the Baptists devoted their energies to driving unorthodoxy from their own denominational ranks. To be sure, many individual Baptists were among the most ardent advocates of anti-evolution legislation, and along with some of their Methodist brethren they were severely critical of the "infidelity" preached by Professor Keister and by the *Journal of Social Forces*. But the Baptist emphasis upon the separation of church and state acted as a deterrent to official denominational involvement in activities designed to regulate teaching in state institutions. So, while the Presbyterians were attacking the "infidelity" of the University, a vocal minority of Baptists were wrestling with Wake Forest and its president. Poteat's triumph at the State Convention in 1922 had brought only a brief respite, and within a year the college president was as much a target of criticism as ever. As usual Poteat refused to retreat when under fire; instead he delivered papers and speeches on evolution before audiences throughout the state. During the spring and summer of 1925, following his McNair lectures in Chapel Hill, unusually large crowds flocked to hear his addresses in Asheville, Greensboro, and Raleigh. Always his central theme was the same: qualified scientists universally accepted the principle of evolution and disagreed only "on the mode of operation of this principle." Poteat frankly stated that questions about the validity of evolution could under no circumstances be assigned to "mass meetings" or legislative bodies. He reprimanded those whose fear about the safety of religion led them to wage war on science and education since the very security of the religion that they held so dear depended for its survival upon intelligence.[61]

Scarcely less disturbing to zealous fundamentalists were the pronouncements of Richard T. Vann, one of the most beloved Baptist leaders in North Carolina. From the beginning of the evolution controversy, Vann had actively opposed moves among Baptists to place restrictions upon curricula of denominational colleges. He had defended Poteat and had provided Connor with a bill in 1925 which was designed to reinforce religious liberty. Although he spurned such labels as modernism and fundamentalism, his theology rather clearly

61. *News and Observer*, May 20, 22, June 6, September 23, 1925; *Greensboro Daily News*, July 18, 1925; *Evening Telegram* (Rocky Mount), July 3, 1925.

fitted into the latter category. But his fundamentalism in no way dampened his enthusiasm for religious freedom. He was convinced that the modernist-fundamentalist conflict, with its focus on evolution, had fallen under the direction of swash-buckling extremists more gifted in exciting panic and passion than in leading Christians to a common ground of understanding.[62]

His ideas were forcibly presented to the Southern Baptist Educational Conference in February, 1925, in an address entitled, "What Have Baptist Colleges To Do With Fundamentalism and Modernism." Appearing later in a pamphlet edition, this address stirred considerable discussion in North Carolina. It was clearly a plea for moderation. Vann pointed out that evolution was frequently denounced but seldom defined; it served primarily as a convenient weapon with which partisans inflamed the prejudices of just-minded men in their own camp against good men of the other side. A great deal of the bitterness had resulted from confused terminology, indiscriminate generalization, and lack of definitions. In his opinion, the controversy over evolution represented a highly dangerous mating of zeal and ignorance. An example of this "unhappy combination" was the resolution passed by a Baptist association in North Carolina in 1924 denouncing "the damnable theory of *revolution*." Vann further reminded his brethren to avoid the error of confusing theology with religion, especially "the Old Time religion" with the "old time theology." "Systems of theology are not divine revelations," he wrote, "but only men's interpretations of such revelation, so that we cannot condemn offhand one whose theology differs from ours." A recognition of these distinctions would go far toward eradicating the hostility between modernists and fundamentalists.

Vann's bold statement of his views regarding the Bible undoubtedly elicited many objections in fundamentalist quarters. He maintained that much of the Bible could "not be taken literally and never was meant to be so taken." In interpretating the Scriptures one had to consider "the fact that the revelation from God was first given thousands of years ago, to an immature race, differing widely from us in respect to time, race, intelligence, habits, and language." Then

62. See Richard T. Vann, "Academic Freedom," *Biblical Recorder*, XC (April 8, 1925), 11; Edwin Mims, *The Advancing South: Stories of Progress and Reaction* (Garden City, 1926), p. 14.

Vann attempted to explain how God's revelation "was and is progressive" and to demonstrate the absurdity of blind literalism. Regardless of one's ideas of divine inspiration of the Scriptures, he could not believe that "our present English Bible" was inspired without believing that some relatively modern scholars and translators were "equally inspired with the Sacred Writers." Vann contended that ill-informed defenders of the faith had induced men to adopt such foolish and unreasonable arguments to protect truth as they see it. Such methods were tantamount "to an effort to confine living and expanding truth into an iron mould" and would result in forcing man to surrender the "power to decide for himself." Baptists could subscribe to such tactics only by openly repudiating the most distinctive tenets of their heritage.[63]

Therefore, Vann urged Baptist colleges to steer clear of both factions in the evolution controversy in order to pursue their real purpose—the unimpeded search for truth in all areas. He warned his Baptist brethren of the grave dangers involved in denominational restrictions on this search. He wrote: "Let the colleges urge the right and the duty of emphasizing the fundamentals of Scripture, illuminated by the researches of science. There may be differences without discord. Of the nearly four million Southern Baptists today, there are nearly four million varieties. And yet, certain vital principles hold them together." [64] Not only was the Baptist college to teach science, it was to have the subject taught by qualified scientists, rather than priests or prophets; and the scientists must be "allowed absolute freedom of research." A limitation on the freedom of the laboratory in a Baptist college was "unthinkable" for a denomination that prided itself on the freedom of the pulpit. Vann assured Baptists that they had far more to fear from emotional defenders of the faith than from dedicated scientists. To follow the counsels of the former the denomination jeopardized the very existence of Baptist colleges.[65]

Although the assertions by Vann and Poteat aroused admiration in some quarters, they served only to prod fundamentalist zealots to more extreme action. Anonymous letters and broadsides demanding Poteat's immediate resignation appeared with increasing frequency.

63. Richard T. Vann, *What Have Baptist Colleges To Do with Fundamentalism and Modernism* (n.p., 1925), pp. 6–14.
64. *Ibid.*, p. 9.
65. *Ibid.*, p. 18.

Unsigned circulars entitled "The Creation of Man," distributed on the Wake Forest campus late in May, 1925, urged students to "take action" against the college president. At the same time rumor whispered that Poteat would resign during the commencement of 1925. Indeed the matter seemed to have been discussed by the trustees at their meeting early in June, but according to the press accounts, the trustees again pledged their loyalty to Poteat and indicated that his "resignation would not have been accepted," even had he tendered it. The faculty signed a statement urging him to remain at the helm of the institution; friends pleaded with him to avoid any step "that would appear as a surrender" to the anti-evolutionists.[66]

Having failed again to achieve the dismissal of Poteat by action of the trustees, the anti-evolutionists prepared to take their fight to the convention once more. There they would attempt to gain control of trustee appointments and to force the elimination of Poteat. Preparations for the attack in the convention took place during the summer and fall of 1925 while the martyrdom of Bryan still held advantages for those continuing the fight that he had begun. Under pressure from the anti-evolutionists, editor Livingston Johnson reopened "with regret" the columns of the *Biblical Recorder* to discussions of evolution on June 17, 1925. He stipulated that only judicious articles by North Carolinians would be published, and he reserved the right to close the discussions at any time. Much of the anti-evolutionist material that dominated the *Recorder* during June and July was aimed at Poteat. Finally, on August 5, 1925, Johnson terminated the evolution discussions in his paper once and for all ostensibly to allow adequate space for "more important" matters.[67]

One charge brought against Poteat was that his evolutionary views had caused a decline in Baptist revenues. Appearing first during a meeting of the education and mission boards in May, the charge became so widespread that by August 24, it was the principal topic of discussion at a gathering of Baptist leaders in Raleigh. J. Frank Norris's *Searchlight* reveled at the prospect of "an empty treasury"

66. *News and Observer*, May 2, 19, June 4, 1925; *Greensboro Daily News*, May 2, 1925.

67. *Biblical Recorder*, XC (June 17, 1925), 6; *ibid.*, XC (July 15, 1925), 8; *ibid.*, XCI (August 5, 1925), 6.

forcing Poteat's resignation. Certainly the marked decrease in Baptist contributions to general denominational funds for education, missions, and charities provided significant ammunition for the anti-evolutionist critics of Poteat. They were quick to point out that contributions to individual churches had shown an increase during the same period. This fact, they argued, demonstrated the unpopularity of Poteat's views. Under the statewide denominational budget system, a deficiency in any one of the several funds was made up from the others. Therefore, the only way a Baptist could make sure that he did not contribute to the denomination's educational fund, hence to Wake Forest and Poteat, was to restrict his donations solely to the local church. The argument about Poteat's responsibility for the Baptist's "empty treasury" became a basic part of the anti-evolutionists' strategy to solidify sentiment against him in the association meetings before the opening of the state convention.[68]

One of the first and most important associations to meet was the Buncombe County Association. Led by Dr. R. J. Bateman of the First Baptist Church of Asheville, the opponents of evolution triggered "fierce forensics" by their attacks on Poteat because the official representative from the state convention's board of missions, Dr. Charles Maddry, refused to let them go unchallenged. Maddry's eloquent defense of Poteat and Wake Forest, supported by "an almost solid phalanx" of Wake Forest alumni at the meeting, secured the withdrawal of a resolution demanding Poteat's immediate dismissal. In its place the association passed a resolution requesting the convention to investigate the teaching of evolution in Baptist schools.[69]

Friends of Poteat who represented the state convention at the meetings of other associations were unable to achieve comparable successes. On September 16, 1925, the Mecklenburg-Cabarrus Association urged all Baptist schools to "discard the theory of evolution"; on September 23, the Chowan Association went on record as "being unalterably opposed" to the teaching of evolution in any school, state or denominational. One of the most sweeping resolutions against the evolutionary hypothesis was enacted by the Gaston County Associa-

68. *News and Observer,* June 4, August 26, 1925; *Searchlight,* May 22, June 19, 1925.
69. *News and Observer,* August 14, 1925.

tion in mid-October under the direction of the Reverend W. C. Barrett, a Gastonia minister. The Gaston group not only demanded the elimination of the evolutionary "influences" in Baptist schools but also devised plans whereby pressure could be exerted upon them to achieve this aim. First, local churches were to be allowed to designate funds for a specific statewide project "without supporting the whole program." This would mean that churches could withhold financial aid to Wake Forest without jeopardizing the programs for missions and benevolences. Second, the Gaston Association suggested that the Wake Forest trustees be elected directly by the state convention "so that they might be amenable to the convention and through it to the Baptist people." In addition to these group actions, individual Baptists such as James R. Pentuff and Sylvester J. Betts continued their relentless fight against Poteat, evolution, and modernism. From Fort Worth, the irascible J. Frank Norris threatened to invade the arena of North Carolina Baptists because Wake Forest had employed Dr. O. C. Bradbury, a biologist whom Norris claimed to have driven from Baylor University.[70]

Early in the autumn of 1925 it became obvious that the annual session of the Baptist State Convention in November would be the scene of another battle over Poteat's views on evolution. No one was more aware of the impending crisis than Poteat himself, but he still preferred to be defeated by the anti-evolutionists than to surrender to their demands. He was supported in this view by a host of influential individuals and organizations. Josiah W. Bailey, a prominent Baptist layman and politician, counseled his brethren to consider their Baptist heritage when they contemplated restrictions on conscience and conviction. Clarence Poe, the trustee of Wake Forest College who had persistently defended Poteat, offered similar advice through the columns of his influential *Progressive Farmer*. In fact, some observers considered Poe's discriminating editorials as a decisive factor in shifting rural sentiment against the anti-evolutionists.[71] *Charity and Children*, in September, 1925, charged that "extreme

70. *News and Observer*, August 14, 26, September 17, 18, October 2, 23, November 13, 1925.

71. *News and Observer*, November 30, 1925; see also Josiah W. Bailey to E. Y. Mullins, June 16, 1926 (copy), Poteat Papers; *Biblical Recorder*, XCI (August 12, 1925), p. 7; Clarence Poe, *My First Eighty Years* (Chapel Hill, 1963), pp. 123–24; Mims, *The Advancing South*, p. 76.

fundamentalists" employed "violent and abusive" tactics because they were "either ignorant or ambitious." The Baptist paper concluded: "This element of misguided brethren is bringing reproach upon the cause they advocate. Their intemperate and bitter utterances discredit all of us who oppose the views of the so-called scientists concerning the origin of man and the integrity of the scriptures. They make it hard for those who believe the Bible including the part of the Sermon on the Mount which says: 'Judge not that ye be not judged.' " [72] The secular press was no less severe in its treatment of Poteat's critics; and several associations such as the Central and Little River Associations either tabled resolutions against evolution or lauded Wake Forest as a "training ground for soldiers of the Cross." Poteat meanwhile sought to rally the alumni by assuring them that nothing less than the "respectability" of their alma mater was at stake. He urged them to eliminate him if need be, but to "stand by the college." [73]

By the opening of the Baptist State Convention in Charlotte in November, 1925, the lines had been drawn. The showdown was imminent. Armed with a written statement of Poteat's "radical" views in the McNair lectures and with a creedal statement adopted by the Southern Baptist Convention earlier in the year, the fundamentalists were optimistic about the possibility of avenging the faith of the deceased Bryan. Sylvester Betts boasted that he had in his pocket a resolution designed to muzzle permanently the teaching of evolution at Wake Forest. A greater threat, however, came from R. J. Bateman of Asheville. Supported by his powerful association, he was ready to sponsor such a resolution. Also backed by his association, W. C. Barrett of Gastonia was prepared to introduce a measure that would change the method of electing Wake Forest trustees and allow the fundamentalists to direct the destiny of the college if they could control the state convention. Wake Forest alumni, hostile to such measures, also converged on Charlotte in order to participate in what many believed to be the most crucial hour in the history of the college. Speaking to these alumni between sessions of the convention, Poteat declared: "The time for conciliation and compromise has passed. Our critics make demands and accept nothing short of submission. We can-

72. *Charity and Children*, XL (September 10, 1925), 4.
73. *News and Observer*, September 17, October 2, November 13, 1925.

not compromise and we cannot straddle." He refused "to be whipped out of a position" which involved "the respectability and opportunity" of Wake Forest. He insisted that the fundamentalists demanded of the college nothing less than the abject surrender of its most precious possession—"hospitality to truth" from every source.[74]

Poteat's display of resolution and the appearance of increasing numbers of Wake Forest alumni as delegates who agreed with him induced the anti-evolutionists to modify their stand. Furthermore, a gift of $100,000 to Wake Forest from Benjamin N. Duke considerably strengthened Poteat's hand against those who threatened financial reprisals against the institution for as long as it retained an evolutionist as president. Under these circumstances Bateman stated his resolution in such a way that it was passed by an overwhelming vote. It contained no mention of evolution and required no dismissals of evolutionists from college posts; rather it followed closely the statement of the Southern Baptist Convention and emphasized belief in the divinity of Jesus, "the fact of creation by God," and the "supernatural elements in Christianity." The friends of Poteat and Wake Forest were "gratified at the moderateness and reasonableness of the statements." So moderate were they that Poteat himself readily subscribed to them.[75]

Immediately following the consideration of the Bateman resolutions, the convention turned to a closely related issue concerning the method of selecting the boards of trustees of Baptist colleges. Fundamentalists disappointed with the Bateman statement might hope to eliminate evolution from the colleges by giving the convention the power to appoint their governing boards. W. C. Barrett, a Wake Forest alumnus and Baptist minister, had for a dozen years spearheaded a movement to tighten the convention's control over its educational institutions. At his insistence in 1912 the self-perpetuating boards of trustees of Wake Forest and Meredith colleges were required to sub-

74. *Biblical Recorder*, XCI (October 21, 1925), 8; *ibid.*, XCI (November 25, 1925), 7; *News and Observer*, November 19, 1925; *Greensboro Daily News*, November 19, 20, 1925; for the *Biblical Recorder*'s vehement opposition to the adoption of a creedal statement by the Southern Baptist Convention, see *Biblical Recorder*, XC (May 20, 1925), 6; *ibid.*, XC (May 27, 1925), 1–4.

75. *Biblical Recorder*, XCI (November 25, 1925), 7; George W. Paschal, *History of Wake Forest College* (Wake Forest, 1943), III, 129–31; Suzanne C. Linder, "William Louis Poteat and the Evolution Controversy," *The North Carolina Historical Review*, XL (April, 1963), 151–52.

mit the names of new trustees to the convention for confirmation. The tendency of church-related colleges to sever their denominational ties, coupled with the current protests over objectionable doctrines being taught at Wake Forest, seemed to make the session of 1925 the propitious moment to achieve Barrett's long-standing aims. Therefore, he introduced a resolution requiring trustees of all Baptist colleges to be elected directly by the convention. Much to the dismay of many, Bernard W. Spilman, a close friend of Poteat, seconded Barrett's measure; but, then Spilman proceeded to take "the sting out of it" by having the matter referred to a committee and by allowing trustees to nominate persons to fill vacancies on their boards. The most significant changes to be inaugurated, therefore, were in permitting nominations directly from the convention floor and in giving that body the authority to remove a trustee at any time.[76]

The various factions in the Baptist dispute emerged from the Charlotte convention claiming victory, a circumstance that completely confounded the *Presbyterian Standard*.[77] The fundamentalists had diluted their demands considerably; the difference between the actions of the Buncombe and Gaston Associations and the resolutions of the convention which emanated from those quarters attested to the Baptist ability to compromise. But at least the fundamentalists had succeeded in obtaining a written creedal statement regarding the Genesis account of creation and a modification of the method of choosing college trustees. On the other hand, Poteat had successfully withstood the pressures of the "mass meeting" without, in his opinion, compromising his conscience or convictions. Evolution had not been banished from the Wake Forest campus, and the new procedure for the election of trustees would go into effect about the time he voluntarily retired from the college presidency. After the Charlotte convention, evolution was a "settled" issue for the remainder of the decade within official Baptist circles.[78] Unquestionably, the accord reached by the Baptists late in 1925 had a profound effect upon the evolution

76. C. Sylvester Green, *B. W. Spilman: The Sunday School Man* (Nashville, 1953), pp. 128–29; *News and Observer*, November 19, 20, 1925; *Biblical Recorder*, XCI (November 25, 1925), 7; Paschal, *History of Wake Forest College*, III, 131–32, 238–41; Linder, "William Louis Poteat and the Evolution Controversy," pp. 151–152.

77. *Presbyterian Standard*, LXVI (November 25, 1925), 1, 2.

78. See *Charity and Children*, XL (November 25, 1926), 4.

controversy in North Carolina. The mere fact that the state's largest denomination refused either to fire an evolutionist as the head of one of its institutions or to exclude unequivocally the theory of evolution from its own ranks presaged the failure of the anti-evolution crusade against state schools. Having failed to cleanse their own household, Baptist anti-evolutionists were hardly in a strong position to undertake similar chores elsewhere.

7 ∽ A MARTYR'S CAUSE

"Extreme orthodoxy betrays by its very frenzy that the poison of skepticism has entered the soul of the church; for men insist most vehemently upon their certainties when their hold upon them has been shaken. Frantic orthodoxy is a method of obscuring doubt."

—REINHOLD NIEBUHR

By the end of 1925 the anti-evolutionists could claim several significant achievements in spite of their failure in the legislature of that year. Morrison's elimination of certain textbooks, the actions of local school boards, and the agitation among some denominational groups went far toward achieving the aim implicit in a statewide anti-evolution law. Yet, opponents of evolution continued to insist upon such legislation as a necessary means of combatting the "malignant theory." Poole had already indicated his intention to renew the fight in 1927. Then, Zebulon V. Turlington, the legislator from Iredell County who had championed Poole's bill, announced in August, 1925, that he would gladly participate in another struggle for the measure. He claimed he had first realized the "full gravity of the situation" when Chase declared during the legislative debate that the teaching of atheism by a University professor was "purely a matter of conscience." In the face of Chase's repeated denials of ever having made such a statement, Turlington replied that he had heard it with his "own ears."[1]

Turlington's criticism of Chase was indicative of the shift that had taken place in the anti-evolutionists' attack: ever since Chase's address to the legislature, the University president had replaced Poteat as the chief target of their assaults. The usually tolerant *Charity and Children* criticized Chase's indifference to public sentiment and blamed his active opposition to the Poole Bill for keeping the controversy over evolution alive. The *North Carolina Lutheran* described his discourses on freedom of speech as "dangerous subterfuges" behind which the University attempted to hide teachings "antagonistic" to the religious beliefs of a majority of North Carolinians. With obvious reference to the University and its president, the *News and Observer* asserted that college professors who screamed loudest about intolerance and infringements on academic freedom were the very ones most prone to sneer at those who disagreed with them by rejecting the theory of evolution.[2]

The failure of the anti-evolution bill in the legislature of 1925 only served to enhance the drive for some means of thwarting the spread of "infidelity" on the University campus. It was not surprising therefore that even before the legislature adjourned proposals began anew for the inclusion of Bible instruction in the University curriculum. In 1923 Chase had in effect rejected a plan similar to the procedure used at the University of Texas whereby elective credit would have been given for nonsectarian instruction in Bible given by the various churches in Chapel Hill. Negotiations between the denominational spokesmen and University officials continued to explore the various possibilities for some type of Bible instruction at the state institution. In 1926, at the suggestion of the Reverend Walter Patten of the Chapel Hill Methodist Church, the various denominations in the University town pooled their resources to create the School of Religion

1. *Mooresville Enterprise*, August 20, 1925; *Greensboro Daily News*, August 16, 1925; *News and Observer*, August 16, 1925; *Charity and Children*, XL (August 27, 1925), 4.

2. *Charity and Children*, XL (February 19, 1925), 4; *North Carolina Lutheran*, III (March, 1925), 1; *News and Observer*, September 20, 1925; the religious press frequently complained about the "arrogance" of the state college officials, and the *Presbyterian Standard* maintained that they viewed all public criticism "as the empty vaporizing of an ignorant mob." *Presbyterian Standard*, LXVII (January 20, 1926), 1.

at Chapel Hill with Mims T. Workman, a seminary graduate, as dean and only faculty member. The School possessed no official connection with the University, although Harry F. Comer, secretary of the University YMCA, was one of its incorporators.[3]

Dean Workman persisted in attempts to gain University credit for his courses but without success. Chase and the University officials still maintained that such an arrangement would violate the principle of separation of church and state. The difficulties of the School of Religion were compounded by the position taken by Presbyterians who came to oppose the whole enterprise largely because Workman was suspected of being "a modernist and higher critic." This complication, coupled with small enrollments, led to the dissolution of the School of Religion in 1928. But the experiment and the agitation that spawned it were not without tangible results. Shortly after the demise of the School of Religion, the University trustees took action that ultimately resulted in a full-fledged curriculum in "the history and literature of religions" including studies in the Bible.[4]

By the beginning of 1926, President Chase was under fire from various quarters. The continued pressure from religious sources and the prospects of another anti-evolution bill in the next session of the legislature were serious impediments to the building of "a truly great University," the task to which he had dedicated himself. The harassment and frustrations took their toll; those close to Chase began to notice signs of weariness and irritation alien to his personality. By February 1, 1926, he had become seriously interested in an invitation to accept the presidency of the University of Oregon. When he went to Oregon to investigate the proposition, North Carolinians suddenly became aware that the prolonged strife over evolution might indeed "dismantle" their University. Chase's warning to this effect earlier

3. Louis R. Wilson, *The University of North Carolina, 1900–1930: The Making of a Modern University* (Chapel Hill, 1957), 544–46; Mims T. Workman to Harry W. Chase, October 13, 1926, Minutes of the Joint Committee of Deans of the University and the Curriculum Committee of the School of Religion of Chapel Hill, November 9, 1926, Alfred E. Lawrence to Harry W. Chase, November ?, 1926, Henry M. London to Harry W. Chase, November 24, 1926, Harry W. Chase to Henry M. London, November 27, 1926, University Papers; *Statesville Landmark*, August 16, 1926.

4. *Presbyterian Standard*, LXVII (September 1, 1926), 1; *ibid.*, LXVII (October 13, 1926), 1–2; *ibid.*, LXVII (October 20, 1926), 1; *Biblical Recorder*, XCII (October 29, 1926), 6; Wilson, *The University of North Carolina*, pp. 545–46.

when distinguished faculty members began to leave the institution had failed to impress them. But the serious possibility of his own resignation provoked a great deal of soul-searching. The general belief that Chase's consideration of the Oregon office was a direct result of the anti-evolutionist, fundamentalist crusade led to a reappraisal of the whole agitation. The consensus was that the controversy had lasted long enough and that unless it were terminated, North Carolina would suffer irreparable damage as well as humiliation in the eyes of the civilized world.[5]

By the time that Chase returned from his trip to Oregon, the clamor for him to remain at the University of North Carolina was emanating from every corner of the state. The *Greensboro Daily News* and the *News and Observer* led the editorial chorus by pleading with him to "continue his valuable leadership in North Carolina." Expressing the sentiment of many journals, the *Hamlet News-Messenger* claimed that his resignation would virtually annihilate the state's recently acquired reputation for progress. The Methodist and Baptist papers joined the secular press in pleading with Chase to remain at his post.[6]

News of his trip to Oregon created profound concern among the University faculty, many of whom despaired at the thought of his resignation. R. D. W. Connor, a distinguished historian on the faculty, wrote Chase: "We are crossing a stream, and we have followed you to the middle of the current. You mustn't leave us here. You must land us high and dry on the other side. Then, you can do whatever you like—provided you like to stay here. Those of us who know you well know that you are not running away from the fight—but what about those on the outside? Will they know what we know?" [7] Professor Odum also believed that Chase's departure would create the impression that "fundamentalism pushed him out," and that the University "was not therefore a good place for big men." [8] Following a stir-

5. Harry W. Chase to Governor A. W. McLean, February 1, 1926, University Papers; *News and Observer*, February 5, 1926.

6. *News and Observer*, February 13, 14, 1926; *Greensboro Daily News*, February 14, 16, 1926; *Hamlet News-Messenger*, February 18, 1926; *N.C. Christian Advocate*, LXXI (March 11, 1926), 2; *Biblical Recorder*, XCI (February 17, 1926), 7.

7. R. D. W. Connor to Harry W. Chase, February 20, 1926, University Papers.

8. Howard W. Odum to E. S. Conklin, March 9, 1926, Odum Papers.

ring address by Professor Frank P. Graham on February 12, 1926, the faculty unanimously passed resolutions pledging Chase its full support and urgently requesting him to remain at the University. The University president could hardly have failed to be impressed by such display of loyalty and affection.[9]

Shortly thereafter the board of trustees and numerous chapters of the alumni organization officially expressed similar sentiments. President Eugene C. Brooks of North Carolina State College assured Chase that the state institutions would successfully ride out the temporary storm over evolution which had made the people "somewhat excitable." "Criticism always stings," Brooks wrote, "but after all that is the price we must pay for the opportunity to work for the public." [10] President Julius I. Foust of North Carolina College for Women joined Brooks in urging Chase to remain in North Carolina. Foust admitted feeling guilty about his "unavoidable" absence from the hearings on the Poole Bill and about Chase's bearing the brunt of the battle for the state colleges. He promised to participate actively in the fight if the measure were reintroduced.[11]

Despite the plaudits showered upon the University president, many of those who had objected to his activities against the anti-evolution bill refused to be saddened by the prospect of his departure from the state. Some actually expressed delight at the idea. The *Charlotte Observer*, in commenting on Chase's trip to Oregon, stated that "the impression need not get out that the University would go to wreck if he should leave it." The Newton *News-Enterprise* chose the moment of Chase's threatened resignation to insist upon "a check on some of these foreigners to see that they do what they are supposed to do—and not be allowed to destroy the faith in the religion of the fathers and mothers of those they teach." [12] H. B. Searight, moderator of the Presbyterian Synod, embarrassed some of his brethren by statements that were tantamount to encouraging Chase to accept the Oregon appointment. On February 20, 1926, while Chase's decision still hung in the balance, James R. Pentuff, the Baptist minister from Concord who had been a spokesman for the anti-evolutionists in the debates

9. *News and Observer*, February 13, 1926.
10. E. C. Brooks to Harry W. Chase, February 11, 1926, University Papers.
11. Julius I. Foust to Harry W. Chase, March 8, 1926, University Papers.
12. *Charlotte Observer*, February 14, 1926; Newton *News-Enterprise* quoted in *News and Observer*, February 15, 1926.

on the Poole Bill, staged what he called "the opening gun" of a drive for a similar measure in the legislature of 1927. Immediately after he had delivered two "rousing" addresses in Fuquay Springs, a mass meeting of the town's citizens passed resolutions requesting legislators to enact an anti-evolution law at their next session.[13]

In spite of these discouraging prospects, Chase announced early in March, 1926, that he would remain at the helm of the University of North Carolina. Apparently the display of loyalty and support by so large a contingent of North Carolinians had impressed him. Possibly, he, like Poteat, also decided to accept the challenge of the anti-evolutionists because he preferred total defeat to abject surrender. At any rate, the threat of his resignation helped North Carolinians to regain that "sense of proportion" that Nell Battle Lewis had long called for. Many considered his departure merely as the first in a series of calamities to befall the University; for them the whole episode was a sobering experience that took its toll upon the anti-evolutionist cause. The prospect of a "dismantled" University had a particularly significant impact upon the passive supporters of the anti-evolution movement, causing many to desert it altogether. On the other hand, the anti-evolutionists who viewed Chase's refusal to leave the University as another defeat became convinced that further delay in the renewal of their campaign for a statewide anti-evolution law would seriously jeopardize its chance of success. A note of urgency appeared in their new call for all Christians to rally to the support of "the Old Book" and "Old Time Religion." In marshalling their forces for a second bid to outlaw evolution, they initiated the most acrimonious phase of the controversy in North Carolina.

By late February, 1926, various rumors about an impending anti-evolution crusade began to take shape. Pentuff claimed that he was initiating such a crusade in Fuquay Springs. L. D. Bass, a Baptist minister in Madison, announced that "some of the biggest anti-evolution guns in the country" including John Roach Straton, William B. Riley, and T. T. Martin, would invade the state during the spring and summer to give the "liberals and modernists a thorough shelling."[14] During the Scopes Trial, Martin, who was field secretary

13. *News and Observer*, February 21, March 30, 1926; William P. McCorkle to Harry W. Chase, September 22, 1926, University Papers.

14. *News and Observer*, February 21, 1926; see also *North Carolina Lutheran*, III (December, 1925), 4.

of the Anti-Evolution League of America, had warned Odum that his organization would "move in on North Carolina next." [15] From Washington, Jonathan Daniels of the Raleigh *News and Observer* reported rumors to the effect that North Carolina fundamentalists were perfecting their organization for the purpose of forcing an anti-evolution plank into the platform of the state Democratic party. He also claimed that, according to some sources, former governor Morrison would spearhead the crusade. While none of these rumors was completely true, their widespread circulation indicated that something was in the wind.[16]

The anti-evolutionists believed that the most propitious moment to launch their new campaign for an anti-evolution statute was the period immediately before the Democratic primaries early in June. Victory in the primary was tantamount to election in solidly Democratic North Carolina; therefore, the anti-evolutionists had to initiate their crusade in time to force the hands of candidates for the legislature on the evolution question during their campaigns. The aims of the anti-evolutionists were to make evolution the central issue of the campaign and to elect enough candidates sympathetic to their cause to insure passage of a bill outlawing Darwinism in the schools. Politicians, who had shied away from the issue, now feared for their future. Many agreed with the observer who remarked, "If a candidate came out for the teaching of evolution, he wouldn't have as much chance as a Catholic." [17]

The first steps toward the creation of a statewide anti-evolution organization took place secretly early in April, 1926. Public notice of these efforts first occurred on April 16, when thirty-two ministers and laymen representing various denominations met in the First Baptist Church of Charlotte. Their announced purpose was to launch an organization to combat "all influences in the schools that tend to destroy the faith of the people in the Bible as the Inspired Word of God." Among the most active participants in the proceedings were: Judge Walter S. Neal of Laurinburg, a prominent Methodist layman and chairman of the State Board of Elections; Dr. Albert Sydney Johnson, pastor of the First Presbyterian Church of Charlotte; Dr.

15. *Greensboro Daily News*, July 17, 1925.
16. *News and Observer*, April 25, 1926.
17. *Ibid.*

A. A. McGeachy, pastor of the Second Presbyterian Church of Charlotte; Dr. W. C. Barrett, a Baptist minister from Gastonia; Dr. James R. Pentuff, a Baptist minister from Concord mentioned earlier; W. E. Price, a well-known Presbyterian layman from Charlotte and a candidate for the legislature; Dr. Luther Little, pastor of the First Baptist Church of Charlotte; and Zebulon V. Turlington of Mooresville, a legislator and Presbyterian lay leader. Judge Neal acted as chairman of this preliminary session.[18]

The major accomplishment of the group was an agreement on a plan of action which embodied blueprints of the Committee of One Hundred, a statewide anti-evolution organization. The committee was to be directed by native fundamentalists in the one hundred counties of the state. The group also passed a series of resolutions expressing its opposition to the union of church and state and its support of efforts to eliminate all doctrines from public schools which "tended to discredit the Bible as the authoritative Word of God." By the close of this session it was apparent that Presbyterians, primarily from the Piedmont region of the state, would dominate the new campaign and that Charlotte, the city of "roaring factories and snorting fundamentalists," would be its headquarters.[19]

On May 4, 1926, the same day that the Episcopalians officially denounced efforts to restrict freedom of teaching, over three hundred anti-evolutionists gathered in Charlotte "to fight the teaching of anti-Bible doctrines in the schools." When the Chamber of Commerce denied this group use of its building on the grounds of "propriety," the gathering convened in the auditorium of the Carnegie Library where, after singing "How Firm a Foundation," it officially launched the Committee of One Hundred. The crusade was to be waged under the motto, "Make Our Schools Safe For Our Children." Shortly after his election as permanent chairman, Judge Neal assured the audience, "We are going to organize the state from stem to stern and anyone who thinks otherwise is badly fooled. Sentiment is against us in some of the large towns but in the rural sections it is all the way and we are going to organize every county and stir them up." [20] After transferring its proceedings to the more spacious quarters of the Second Pres-

18. *Charlotte Observer*, April 17, 1926; *News and Observer*, April 17, 1926; *Greensboro Daily News*, April 17, 1926.

19. *Charlotte Observer*, April 17, 1926; *Goldsboro News*, April 17, 1926; *Statesville Landmark*, April 22, 1926.

20. *News and Observer*, May 6, 1926.

byterian Church, the committee agreed upon a fundamentalist credo that was written into the organization's lengthy platform. This document disavowed any intention of uniting church and state, then proceeded to insist upon barring from all public educational institutions teachers whose religious beliefs deviated substantially from the conservative theology embraced by a majority of the Christian taxpayers of the state. This so-called "moral suasion" platform was designed to serve as a basis for a "direct treaty" to be negotiated by the committee with each state-supported college. If the college refused to accept this procedure or failed to react "properly," the committee promised "to take the matter directly to the legislature." Obviously, the organization would concern itself primarily with the state colleges rather than the public schools; perhaps the latter had been, or were being, sufficiently cleansed of the heresy by the local activities of the anti-evolutionists. At any rate, the committee hoped to force colleges in line by threatening another legislative fight over evolution.[21]

Despite its threats and promises, the Committee of One Hundred was permanently injured by the intemperance and disorder of its opening session. The wild applause, inflammatory addresses, and abusive attacks upon Chase, Keister, and the *Journal of Social Forces* appeared strangely inconsistent with the words of the hymn, "All Hail the Power of Jesus' Name," which the assemblage had just sung. The whole atmosphere precluded calm deliberations. The Reverend William Black, a Presbyterian evangelist, concluded a lengthy speech with the declaration: "Evolution is the blackest lie ever blasted out of Hell." Others used language which was even less appropriate for a church sanctuary. So intemperate did some of the speakers become that the chairman had to remind them that they were "in a House of God." The proceedings, however, became utterly rowdy when a group of self-styled "friends of the University" appeared in the midst of this fundamentalist gathering. The leader of this contingent of "interlopers" was Charles W. Tillett, Jr., a young Charlotte attorney who had persuaded several civic leaders from various parts of the state to join him in an effort to stifle in its infancy this new anti-evolutionist drive. While the resolutions committee was in session elsewhere, the floor was opened for general discussion. Robert Lassiter, one of Tillett's cohorts, immediately raised the question whether all those present

21. *Charlotte Observer*, May 4, 5, 1926; *News and Observer*, May 5, 6, 7, 1926; *Greensboro Daily News*, May 5, 6, 7, 1926.

would enjoy the privileges of the floor. After some deliberation, the chairman agreed to extend the rights of speaking and voting to all present, an action that gave Tillett and his followers legal standing in the session. During the lunch hour this group, which then included E. D. Broadhurst, a Greensboro attorney and an outspoken critic of anti-evolution legislation, plotted its strategy for a showdown with the fundamentalists at the afternoon session.[22]

The proceedings during the afternoon were marked by a mounting resentment of the intruders, flaring tempers, and angry outbursts. When Tillett criticized efforts by churchmen to gag scientific research, H. B. Searight suggested that "those who are not in sympathy with us might go elsewhere and form an organization of their own." But William Shaw, Paul Ranson, Frank McNinch, and William T. Shore, all young civic leaders and University alumni, remained to pose embarrassing questions and to engage in heated exchanges with official spokesmen of the committee. Shaw described the "absurdity" of any effort to make orthodox Christianity a test for membership on a state college faculty. He reminded the audience that such restrictions would automatically eliminate all Jews and Catholics. Thomas R. Glasgow, a Charlotte businessman who had joined Tillett's group, followed Shaw and discussed in considerable detail the implications of the Committee's attempt to make a religious creed a prerequisite for holding a "civil office." [23]

These remarks triggered a general uproar among the anti-evolutionists who, disagreeing among themselves over the interpretations of their ultimate aims, were soon bogged down in bitter arguments with one another. E. D. Broadhurst finally managed to gain the floor only to deliver a brief speech that reduced the proceedings to utter pandemonium. He claimed that the "bitter-tongued" orations of the ministers during the session were sufficient to destroy the laymen's respect and reverence for the clergy. Then he concluded by saying: "Don't make this a church war. You're a lot of scared preachers gathered together. I've listened to your voices and seen your actions today and I tell you I'm discouraged. I'm going to ask you not to start things with which you have no concern. Go home to your churches

22. Robert W. Winston, *Horace Williams: The Gadfly of Chapel Hill* (Chapel Hill, 1942), pp. 211–13; *Charlotte Observer*, May 5, 6, 1926; *News and Observer*, May 5, 6, 7, 1926; *Statesville Landmark*, May 6, 10, 1926.

23. *Charlotte Observer*, May 5, 6, 1926; *Greensboro Daily News*, May 5, 6, 1926; Winston, *Horace Williams*, pp. 212–13; *Goldsboro News*, May 5, 1926.

and preach the Word of God. Let the school boards do their work. I've got to tell you again you're scared preachers, and I'm bitterly disappointed." [24] At this juncture, the Reverend McKendree Long, a Presbyterian preacher, exclaimed: "My God shall not be murdered in His own house!" Walter West, a young, broad-shouldered Methodist minister from Lincolnton, shucked off his coat, doubled up his fists, and charged toward the altar to deal with "this modernist interloper from Greensboro." The spectators who restrained West prevented fisticuffs in the church. This extraordinary episode was the climax of the meeting and overshadowed the remainder of the session. The unfavorable publicity given the initial meeting of the Committee of One Hundred irreparably damaged its reputation and lent credence to the prediction that North Carolina was destined for "a Kulturkampf." [25]

At the same time that native fundamentalists were organizing the Committee of One Hundred, outside forces poured into the state to lend their aid to the anti-evolution cause. True to his promise during the Scopes Trial, T. T. Martin headed the contingent of anti-evolutionists from outside the state who invaded North Carolina in the spring of 1926. Since the death of Bryan the national anti-evolution movement had lacked a single individual to fill the Great Commoner's position; the leading contenders for the Bryan mantle included John Roach Straton, William B. Riley, and Charles F. Washburn, a wealthy Florida realtor. Washburn's Bible Crusaders of America, which had been established to continue Bryan's anti-evolution crusade, was one of the most militant organizations of its kind. Its personnel was composed of many veteran anti-evolutionist campaigners. By 1926 T. T. Martin had become Director-General of Campaigns of the Bible Crusaders while retaining his post in the Anti-Evolution League of America.[26]

Fresh from the field of victory in his native Mississippi, which had enacted an anti-evolution law, the Blue Mountain evangelist arrived

24. Quoted in Maynard Shipley, *The War on Modern Science: A Short History of the Fundamentalist Attacks on Evolution and Modernism* (New York, 1927), p. 102; see also *News and Observer*, May 5, 1926; *Charlotte Observer*, May 5, 1926.

25. Winston, *Horace Williams*, p. 214; *Charlotte Observer*, May 5, 1926; *Greensboro Daily News*, May 6, 1926.

26. For the origins of the Bible Crusaders of America and its decision to launch a campaign in North Carolina, see Stewart G. Cole, *The History of Fundamentalism* (New York, 1931), pp. 270–75; *The Crusaders' Champion*, I (December 25, 1925); *North Carolina Lutheran*, III (December, 1925), 4.

in Charlotte on April 28, 1926, and established headquarters in the Clayton Hotel. He immediately announced plans for a whirlwind campaign throughout North Carolina in an effort to pave the way for the passage of an anti-evolution statute by the next legislature. Martin and other representatives of national anti-evolution societies who joined him emphasized the crucial significance of the state in their nationwide campaign and insisted that a North Carolina statute against evolution would "be decisive." They clearly indicated that "if North Carolina could be won, the nation could be won" and federal legislation to banish Darwinism could be enacted. V. T. Jeffreys of New Jersey, an official of the Anti-Evolution League who had also arrived in Charlotte, acted as Martin's chief lieutenant. Jeffreys characterized the South as "the saving power of the nation" since the North had become "so polluted with foreigners and anti-Christ doctrines." [27]

Both Martin and Jeffreys publicly expressed a desire to work with the Committee of One Hundred and hoped to co-ordinate the campaigns of the local and national organizations. Martin exerted every effort to ingratiate himself with the committee by adjusting his own plans to coincide with those of the local organization. Jeffreys had announced upon his arrival that William Louis Poteat would be one of the main targets of his attack. When this statement prompted spokesmen for the committee to disclaim any intention of seeking to oust the Wake Forest president, Martin "corrected" Jeffreys' remark and insisted that their efforts would be concerned solely with tax-supported institutions. The irony of Martin's decision lay in the fact that he waged a relentless war on Poteat from afar for six years, only to abandon it when he arrived in Poteat's own domain. But, undoubtedly, Martin had come to appreciate Poteat's strength in North Carolina and preferred not to jeopardize the success of his new crusade by further entanglements with the Baptist biologist.[28]

Martin persisted in his attempt to establish a liaison between his forces and the Committee of One Hundred. He conferred with Dr.

27. *Charlotte Observer*, April 29, May 1, 1926; *Goldsboro News*, April 29, 1926. According to one authority, the battle cry of Crusaders was: "North Carolina holds the key to the Nation. As it goes, so goes the Nation." Harbor Allen, "The Anti-Evolution Campaign in America," *Current History*, XXIV (September, 1926), 895.

28. *Goldsboro News*, April 29, 1926; *Greensboro Daily News*, May 3, 1926; *Charlotte Observer*, April 29, 1926; *News and Observer*, April 29, 1926.

A. R. Shaw, a Presbyterian minister prominent in the Committee, but utterly failed to establish the desired contact. He did not even obtain an invitation to attend the committee's opening session on May 4. In fact, the organization consistently snubbed him. Reasons for this attitude are not difficult to find. In addition to being suspicious of "foreigners" in general, the committee undoubtedly realized that Martin's rather notorious reputation among North Carolinians would hardly enhance its cause. Moreover, since the organization was seeking to influence a state election, aid from outside forces would be a liability rather than an asset. Thus, the committee sought desperately, albeit in vain, to prevent any identification of its crusade with that of the Martin entourage.[29]

Although disappointed by this turn of events, Martin nevertheless proceeded with his plans for a statewide campaign under the direction of representatives from various national anti-evolution groups. Like a military general about to launch an offensive, he divided the state into districts and designated one or more of his lieutenants to supervise the campaign in each district. District headquarters were maintained in Charlotte, Hendersonville, Winston-Salem, and Raleigh. Among the most notable members of Martin's task force were Dr. Andrew Johnson of Kentucky, Jeffreys, and three Texas evangelists, Raleigh Wright, J. F. Hailey, and W. E. Hawkins. The essential task of these district commanders was to arrange public debates on evolution, distribute anti-evolution posters and literature, and organize local anti-evolution societies to be affiliated with a national organization.[30]

Martin sounded the keynote of his campaign in a well-advertized address delivered in Charlotte on May 9, 1926. A massive, flag-draped portrait of Bryan filled the rear of the stage from which he spoke. His address, characterized by invective and sensationalism, was largely a reiteration of anti-evolution themes that he had expressed on many earlier occasions, especially in his tract, *Hell and the High Schools*.[31] At one dramatic point in his speech Martin declared:

> Think for yourselves, ladies and gentlemen: I employ a man to educate my boy; he drills into my boy Tom Paine's *Age of Reason*. I object; then the state comes in and sells my home and with the

29. *Charlotte Observer*, May 1, 6, 1926.
30. *Charlotte Observer*, May 4, 6, 9, 1926; *Greensboro Daily News*, May 3, 6, 8, 1926.
31. *Charlotte Observer*, May 11, 1926.

money pays the teacher and says to me: 'You shall pay the teacher's salary and allow him to drill Tom Paine's *Age of Reason* into your boy!'

That is exactly the issue, except that evolution is far worse than Tom Paine's *Age of Reason.* God's word says that God created great whales; evolution teaches that that is a lie; that whales used to have legs and walked around on the earth and got to going into the water more and more and after millions of years evolved into whales; here it is in school books. . . .[32]

He then read a letter written by "a mother's son" whose Christian faith had been destroyed by evolution during his college days. A promising young Christian's life had been "wrecked" by the atheistic evolutionists teaching in colleges supported by Christian taxpayers. "Our only hope," Martin cried out, "is to carry the fight to the people and drive every evolution teacher and every evolution book out of every tax supported school in America." As he closed his address, he pointed to the picture of Bryan and shouted: "There is the greatest statesman that was ever draped with the American flag. The picture was taken while Mr. Bryan and I were at Dayton." The outburst of applause which followed was disproportionate to the small crowd that attended his performance.[33]

While Martin busied himself with publicity, a few addresses, and the general co-ordination of the campaign at his headquarters in Charlotte, a battery of anti-evolutionists were mounting the stump in towns and villages throughout the state. Like the Committee of One Hundred, Martin's forces clearly aimed at influencing the outcome of the Democratic primaries. Andrew Johnson of Kentucky was one of the most indefatigable members of Martin's following. Introduced in Hendersonville as a "cohort of the fallen Bryan and one of the foremost scholars, authors, and preachers in the South," the Kentucky evangelist characterized all evolutionists as "baboon boosters" and promised a fight against them in the next legislature which would be "the worst known since Hector was a pup." Arriving in Raleigh on May 9, 1926, Johnson addressed a crowd of about three hundred on

32. Quoted in William N. Crow, "Religion and the Recent Evolution Controversy with Special Reference to the Issues in the Scopes Trial" (Bachelor of Divinity thesis, Duke University, 1936), p. 69.
33. *Charlotte Observer*, May 11, 1926.

the topic, "Man or Monkey, or Evolution Outlawed by Science." Amid a chorus of "amens" he discussed at length the "fatal gaps in Darwin's theory." Arch T. Allen, the State Superintendent of Public Instruction, attended the lecture out of curiosity and was greatly embarrassed when the evangelist made much ado over his presence, giving the impression that Allen approved of the anti-evolutionists' efforts.[34]

The approach of the Democratic primary quickened the sense of urgency and desperation among the anti-evolutionists. The verbal assaults of the crusaders were hurled indiscriminately in all directions; their shots were so widely scattered, in fact, that evolution appeared to have become less of a target and more of a weapon for eliminating all varieties of unorthodoxy. Therefore, various individuals were subjected to the anti-evolutionists' attacks for reasons other than their views on evolution. One of these was Professor Carl Taylor, the North Carolina State College sociologist who was assailed ostensibly because of his activities regarding the Raleigh Religious Forum; actually, however, his classification as a "foreigner" and as a liberal on social issues was the real basis for the hostility. Another "foreigner" who incurred the wrath of the fundamentalists was Dr. Edmund D. Soper, the Dean of the newly-established School of Religion at Duke University. A recognized authority on comparative religions, Soper had hardly arrived in Durham from Northwestern University when he was labeled a "modernist"—a dangerous man to be watched closely. In his frequent addresses and sermons throughout the state, he did not hesitate to describe the disturbance over evolution as "last year's bird nest" and to suggest that the religious controversialists might find psychology a much more fertile area for dispute than biology. But Soper's theology was actually viewed with less alarm than his views on race, particularly when it was rumored that he advocated racial intermarriage. Although the theologian flatly denied these reports, his views on "the race question" provoked considerable discussion in the spring of 1926 and appear to have been the real reason for the hostility toward him.[35]

34. *Hendersonville Times,* May 5, 12, 1926; *News and Observer,* May 10, 13, 1926.

35. *News and Observer,* July 5, November 16, 1925, March 7, May 4, November 10, 1926; see above pp. 000; Edmund D. Soper, *What May I Believe?* (New York, 1927), pp. 43–56.

On May 12, 1926, the Anti-Evolution League of North Carolina, an affiliate of the national society of which Martin was field secretary, was incorporated by three North Carolinians. Two of the incorporators were citizens of Charlotte who had not played conspicuous roles in the anti-evolutionist agitation. The third, however, was James R. Pentuff. Actually, the Anti-Evolution League was controlled by Martin, but for purposes of publicity it was an organization of native vintage. Its purpose was to attract greater support among North Carolinians and to provide Martin with a liaison between outside and native anti-evolutionists. At any rate, some of the more zealous opponents of evolution such as Sylvester J. Betts of Raleigh were quick to endorse the League and to assist Martin's crusade. Apparently hoping to devote full time to League activities, Pentuff promised to publish a magazine, *The Citizens' Review,* which would serve as the organ of the organization. Although subscriptions to the proposed publication were sold at the anti-evolution rallies held by Martin's speakers, the magazine was never published. Subscriptions probably did not indicate success for such a journal. In fact, the anti-evolutionists found it increasingly difficult to arouse enthusiasm or to raise cash at their rallies. The size of the audiences, small in the beginning, continued to dwindle. On several occasions the crowd dispersed before the orators had concluded their addresses.[36]

The leaders of the crusade, and especially Martin, were keenly aware of the apathetic response. For this reason the World's Christian Fundamentals Association dispatched Dr. Arthur I. Brown, a Canadian physician turned evangelist, to assist Martin. A veteran anti-evolutionist whose impressive academic pedigree received careful attention in Martin's publicity, Brown delivered addresses in various sections of the state in which he assailed Poteat and Richard Vann, proclaimed the "end of time was close at hand," and described all evolutionists as atheists. The *Greensboro Daily News* regretted that the Vancouver surgeon had "quit medical doctoring for divinity doseing." But even that hostile newspaper conceded that he possessed "far more sense, scholarship, personality, and platform ability than most of the agitators." Brown ultimately went to Charlotte in order to assist Martin in bolstering the sagging fortunes of the crusade.[37]

36. *Greensboro Daily News,* May 12, 1926; *Evening Telegram,* May 13, 1926; *News and Observer,* May 13, 1926.

37. *News and Observer,* May 18, 21, 1926; *Greensboro Daily News,* May 16, 17, 24, 1926; *Raleigh Times,* May 18, 1926.

But it was left for Martin himself to stage the spectacle that presumably would accomplish such ends. He announced his intention to debate evolution in public with some well-known atheist approved by the American Association for the Advancement of Atheism. His choice of a protagonist was H. L. Mencken; but when Mencken ignored his challenge, he agreed to debate with Howell S. England of Detroit, a representative of the Association. The atheistic society had been formed in November, 1925, and within six months it claimed members in forty-two states and listed seventeen branches. One of its "fundamentals" was belief in evolution. The Association's application for incorporation in North Carolina had been rejected by the attorney general.[38]

No sooner had Martin made known his plan to debate England than an avalanche of criticism descended upon him. The mayor of Charlotte rejected his request for use of the city auditorium, and the Mecklenburg County commissioners denied him use of the county courthouse. Nor was he able to rent Wearm's Baseball Field. The city's ministerial association, usually so quick to assume a definite stand in such matters, refused to take sides in the growing controversy over Martin's activities. All of the churches in the city refused to allow him use of their sanctuaries for his debate. The Charlotte Ku Klux Klan announced its vehement opposition to the presence of an atheist in their city and promised to give England "a quick send off" if he dared to enter Charlotte.[39]

Distressed by this unexpected turn of events, Martin claimed that his proposed debate had been "grossly misunderstood." He tried desperately to correct the widespread impression that the debate was to deal with "atheism versus Christianity" rather than Genesis versus Darwin. But his plan to demonstrate the link between evolution and atheism by debating the theory with an atheist proved to be disastrous. Indeed, the Klan had misunderstood his purpose, and because of its misunderstanding it had decided to prohibit the debate in a manner comparable to Martin's proposed restrictions on evolutionists. Those who perceived the irony of Martin's complaints about the lack of respect for freedom of thought and speech in Charlotte believed

38. *Mooresville Enterprise*, October 29, 1925; LeRoy Johnson, "The Evolution Controversy During the 1920's" (Ph.D dissertation, New York University, 1954), p. 155.

39. *Charlotte Observer*, May 23, 24, 1926; *Greensboro Daily News*, May 24, 1926.

that the crusader had run afoul of the same kind of intolerance that he had so long preached. Certainly the Klan's argument that a "nonbeliever" should be prohibited from defiling their "church-going community" was similar to that employed by the evangelist against evolutionists. Martin, however, never appreciated the irony in his new role as a defender of "free speech." [40]

Finally, after two weeks of negotiations, he rented a dance pavilion in Lakewood, a suburb of Charlotte located outside the city limits. Here, in such unimpressive surroundings, Martin and England staged their debate on May 31, 1926. Their topic was entitled, "Should the teaching of evolution, that man descended from a lower order of animals, be excluded from tax-supported schools." England used a monkey named "Genesis" to illustrate his arguments, while Martin reached a new high in his use of invective against evolutionists. Although the debate possessed many features of a vaudeville performance, it was "a listless affair" attended by fewer than two hundred people. The presence of the Charlotte Klansmen who objected to an atheist's being so near their city undoubtedly dampened the enthusiasm of many prospective curiosity-seekers. Disheartened by the series of disasters which climaxed in the debate, Martin retired from North Carolina, leaving the native anti-evolutionists to continue the fight.[41]

The press had played a key role in bringing about the failure of Martin's crusade. Many newspapers refused to distinguish between Martin's forces and the Committee of One Hundred; both were characterized as extremist organizations talented in the fostering of hatred and dissension. The *Greensboro Daily News*, manifesting its usual hostility for such groups, depicted Martin and his associates as "saviors from without" sent to North Carolina to provide "a crutch for crippled Christianity." The paper appealed to all patriotic North Carolinians to reject this "unwanted" assistance and suggested that if Martin were so interested in debating, he ought to return to Mississippi where lynching would be an appropriate topic for public discussion. But its severest criticism was reserved for the saviors from within, the Committee of One Hundred, which the *Daily News* accused of

40. *Charlotte Observer*, May 22, 23, 26, 1926.

41. *Charlotte Observer*, May 27, 30, June 2, 1926; *Greensboro Daily News*, June 3, 1926.

"starting a religious war." [42] The Rocky Mount *Evening Telegram,* the Wilmington *Morning Star,* and the *Goldsboro News* agreed that the "unwanted foreigners" were stirring up the state "needlessly." [43] The *Asheville Times,* in a wholesale denunciation of the Committee of One Hundred and the Martin forces, likened their activities to those of the hysterical witch-hunters of Salem. "There is no way yet found to increase knowledge," the *Times* declared, "without shocking somebody's belief." [44] The *Lexington Dispatch* and the *Statesville Landmark* echoed this sentiment and also insisted that the anti-evolutionists were attempting to establish a union of church and state in North Carolina.[45] Although the influential Raleigh *News and Observer* still opposed anti-evolution legislation, it blamed the "unfortunate" display of passions at the opening session of the Committee of One Hundred upon "the uncalled-for attacks" by Tillett and Broadhurst.[46] But the press generally exhibited a strong aversion toward the anti-evolutionists and, by publicizing their more extreme actions, helped to create a public revulsion for the whole movement.

The denominations steered clear of any identification with either Martin or the committee. Baptist papers criticized both; most other religious papers remained silent. The Presbyterian church was most closely identified with the Committee of One Hundred because Presbyterians dominated the organization. On May 4, 1926, the very day of the committee's opening session in Charlotte, the Episcopal Diocese of East Carolina which was meeting in Tarboro went on record as "deploring and opposing all efforts to limit freedom of thought, freedom of teaching and discussion, and freedom of research to ascertain the truth in any branch of knowledge." [47] President William Preston Few of Methodist-related Trinity College, which had recently become Duke University, reminded his fellow

42. *Greensboro Daily News,* May 4, 6, 24, June 3, 1926.

43. *Evening Telegram,* May 13, 1926; Wilmington *Morning Star* quoted in *Greensboro Daily News,* May 7, 1926; *Goldsboro News,* April 25, 1926.

44. *Asheville Times,* May 6, 8, 10, 27, 1926.

45. *Lexington Dispatch* quoted in *Goldsboro News,* April 25, 1926; *Statesville Landmark,* May 10, June 7, 1926.

46. *News and Observer,* May 6, 9, 1926.

47. *Greensboro Daily News* (May 12, 1926) maintained that since other denominations avoided involvement in the revived anti-evolution movement in 1926, "the burden of saving the faith will fall on the Presbyterians"; *Mission Herald,* XL (May, 1926), 8.

Methodists that Saint Paul had ceased his heresy hunting after seeing the light on the road to Damascus. A year later Few led the movement within the General Conference of the Methodist Church which squelched an attempt to include an anti-evolution article in the church's *Discipline*.[48]

The academic forces were willing for the most part to follow the example of President Chase of the University. His strategy was to allow the anti-evolutionists to convict themselves by their own actions rather than to challenge them with an organized movement of academicians. Chase confided to a friend that the meeting of the Committee of One Hundred had branded the fundamentalists in North Carolina with an "intolerance, bigotry, and fanaticism" from which they would never recover.[49] The apparent inactivity of the college communities did not indicate any lessening of their hostility to the anti-evolutionist cause. Both Brooks and Foust had rather quietly aligned their institutions with the University; William Louis Poteat continued to combat what he called "the widespread obscurantism which identified the new learning with heresy." [50] The North Carolina Academy of Science at its twenty-fifth annual session on the Wake Forest campus in May, 1926, endorsed "most emphatically" the "stand of Dr. H. W. Chase and Dr. W. L. Poteat on the freedom of thought and teaching." Another resolution by the Academy stated: "It is absolutely and unqualifiedly necessary that all those hypotheses, theories, laws, and facts which constitute the legitimate content of any field of study may be dealt with any time by any teachers." [51]

The opposition to anti-evolution legislation appeared among college students as well as faculty members. At Duke University students organized a society called *Schola Caveat* shortly after the establishment of the Committee of One Hundred. The avowed aim of this semi-secret society was "to foster freedom of schools in North Carolina." According to rumors, similar groups were being estab-

48. *N.C. Christian Advocate,* LXXI (April 22, 1926), 1; *News and Observer,* February 11, 1927; Edwin E. Slosson, "Legislation Against the Teaching of Evolution," *The Scientific American,* XXIV (May, 1927), 477.

49. Harry W. Chase to Edwin Mims, May 14, 1926, University Papers.

50. *News and Observer,* May 16, June 27, 1926; *Asheville Times,* May 16, 1926.

51. Shipley, *The War on Modern Science,* pp. 99–100; *News and Observer,* May 2, 1926; *Greensboro Daily News,* May 1, 1926.

lished on other campuses in the state. During the commencement season of 1926 college students heard a host of visiting dignitaries including Walter Lippmann and Douglas Southall Freeman laud North Carolina for rebuffing attempts to "reinstate the Inquisition."[52]

The gathering momentum of the opposition to legal restrictions against the teaching of evolution clearly placed the anti-evolutionists on the defensive. Martin, for example, found himself more concerned with fighting the charge that he was a "paid propagandist from out of state" than with battling Darwinism. "I have not one dime back of me," he claimed, "and I have gone over $10,000 in debt in this fight against evolution." Moreover, Martin could not understand why he had "been singled out" as a "foreigner and interloper" when North Carolinians allowed "a foreign evolutionist" to head their state university. But this reference to Chase did little to bolster Martin's prestige among natives.[53]

When Martin's crusade failed to win the endorsement of the Committee of One Hundred and appeared to be collapsing, his superior in the Bible Crusaders, Charles F. Washburn of Clearwater, Florida, sought to save face for his organization. In a lengthy announcement regarding the termination of Martin's crusade in North Carolina, he stated: "The Bible Crusaders fight like Spartans for principles and measures, but rarely for men and candidates. We could not enter into politics in North Carolina and contend for candidates directly . . . because later we will appear before many of these and ask them as a legislature to pass an anti-evolution bill in North Carolina just as we did in Mississippi." Although Washburn recognized the "many antagonisms" that confronted the crusaders in North Carolina, he was unwilling to admit that Martin's campaign had failed. Instead, he made it appear that the crusaders had merely staged a strategic retreat and would return to reap victory when the legislature met.[54]

52. Hersey E. Spence, *"I Remember": Recollections and Reminiscences of Alma Mater* (Durham, 1954), p. 81; *News and Observer,* May 15, June 4, 8, 1926; the faculty sponsor of the *Schola Caveat* was Dr. Edmund D. Soper, Dean of the Divinity School at Duke University. Soper had already aroused considerable discussion for his "heretical" ideas on race as well as on evolution. *News and Observer,* March 8, 1926; *Asheville Times,* May 15, 1926.

53. *Charlotte Observer,* May 23, 26, 1926.

54. *Charlotte Observer,* May 22, 1926.

The departure of Martin and his corps of crusaders meant that the burden of the fight fell upon the Committee of One Hundred. But even the native fundamentalists were in serious trouble. The turbulence of the committee's original session had clearly taken its toll. Shocked by the unbecoming behavior of their cohorts, some of the most active and valuable supporters began to desert the organization. Dr. Archibald A. McGeachy, a well-known Presbyterian clergyman whose church was the scene of the stormy session, resigned immediately; and, although he still agreed with the original aims of the committee, he was "entirely out of sympathy with the spirit" in which it "was now attempting to accomplish them." "I am assured," he declared, "that they are not a body to whom can safely be entrusted any education or legislation."[55] W. E. Price, the first secretary-treasurer of the committee who was a candidate for the legislature, abandoned the organization before the primary; the warm endorsement of the fundamentalist movement by Julian Miller in his *Charlotte Evening News* turned into utter contempt following the tumultuous session of the Committee on May 4. Other desertions took place within a few months, and even Judge Neal, ostensibly because of "ill health," left the organization before the end of the year.[56]

Not only was the anti-evolution campaign beset with these desertions, it was also troubled by internal theological dissensions. The attempt by the committee to write a platform acceptable to all fundamentalists proved to be unsuccessful; instead the platform triggered internal disputes that weakened the organization. Sylvester J. Betts, who described himself as a "one hundred per cent fundamentalist," disagreed with several points in the platform, particularly the resolution requiring teachers to "hold" certain views as a prerequisite for employment. He maintained that such a requirement was a clear-cut infringement of the freedom of thought and demanded that the word "teach" be substituted for "hold." Dr. W. M. White, of Raleigh's First Presbyterian Church, a prominent figure in the committee, supported Betts's contention and blamed

55. A. A. McGeachy to Howard W. Odum, May 8, 1926, Odum Papers; McGeachy declined Odum's invitation to visit Chapel Hill in order to inspect the University at first hand on the grounds that such action would "be misconstrued and misrepresented as the act of a traitor to principles." *Ibid.*

56. *Greensboro Daily News*, May 6, 1926; Winston, *Horace Williams*, p. 216; *Statesville Landmark*, November 8, 1926.

Tillett's "interlopers" for pushing the committee to such extremes. Betts's persistent airing of his objections not only touched off a dispute within the committee but also aroused the ire of such Baptist spokesmen as Livingston Johnson and Dr. Charles H. Durham, who characterized his defense of the faith as "a nauseating spectacle." Despite its depleted ranks and internal dissension, however, the committee continued to exist and promised to wage a vigorous fight against evolution and modernism.[57]

Martin's sensational tactics and the fiasco of the committee's original session shocked the sensibilities of North Carolinians in general and disillusioned many who still believed that evolution ought to be barred from the classroom. Few were willing to risk the "good name" of the state in a Scopes Trial; many were beginning to weary of the whole discussion. Even the *Charlotte Observer*, one of the most persistent friends of fundamentalism, believed that the anti-evolution crusade under Martin had degenerated "into a cheap show of the common order." By June 2, 1926, the *Observer* had become convinced that "the state has had enough of this monkey business for quite a spell." [58]

For a while, however, the political campaigns before the primaries on June 5, 1926, failed to reflect this waning interest. The anti-evolutionists had entered the political arena with the avowed purpose of electing men to the legislature who sympathized with their aims. Although the State Democratic Convention late in April was "the most pacific of gatherings," in which evolution was not mentioned,[59] the politicians were by no means certain of such harmony in the primaries. And events during May indicated that their anxiety was well founded. By June, *Charity and Children* was lamenting: "Religion and politics are mightily mixed these days. Preachers will take a larger part in the campaign than usual this season, and politicians will misquote more of the Bible than ever before." [60] Most people agreed that evolution was an issue in the campaigns; some believed it was the "paramount" issue. The *Greensboro Daily News*

57. *News and Observer*, May 9, 13, 14, 22, 23, 1926.
58. *Charlotte Observer*, June 2, 1926.
59. *News and Observer*, April 28, 30, 1926.
60. *Charity and Children*, XL (June 3, 1926), 4.

was convinced that "the monkey has replaced the donkey in Tar Heel Democracy." [61] Certainly the anti-evolutionists, especially the Committee of One Hundred, were urging all candidates for the legislature to state publicly their stand on the evolution question. The *Stanly News-Herald*, which urged its readers "to vote as you pray," maintained that such a declaration was mandatory in view of the "vital" issues at stake in the evolution controversy. The Junior Order of United Mechanics recorded its opposition to the teaching of evolution in tax-supported institutions and sent out questionnaires to all candidates for the legislature to determine their positions on the question. But a revolt by a faction within the Order largely destroyed whatever results such a device might have achieved.[62]

The candidates were by no means oblivious to the pressure, and in some contests the issue of evolution played a crucial role. D. Scott Poole, unopposed in the Hoke County primary, again assumed the lead in the matter of anti-evolution legislation by promising to introduce such a bill in the next legislature. With a note of regret the *Charlotte Observer* editorially warned Poole that by 1927 neither the people nor his colleagues in the legislature would "be so greatly interested" in evolution as they had been two years earlier.[63] Be that as it may, the announcement by Poole was the signal for candidates to align themselves on the evolution issue. In Stanly County, where the local newspaper ardently championed an anti-evolution statute, the primary designated as the county's legislator Luther H. Bost, a Methodist steward and chairman of the local board of education who shared the editor's views. Richmond County was the scene of a particularly heated legislative race involving candidates for both the Senate and the House. After an intense fight in which evolution received a thorough airing on the political stump, the candidates who ran on the "Anti-Poole Bill Platform" were victorious. In Wilson County the Ku Klux Klan and anti-evolutionists tried in vain to unseat veteran legislator Henry Groves Connor, Jr., largely because of his opposition to the Poole Bill in 1925. A similar effort to defeat Nat A. Townsend of Harnett County also failed. Dr. J. C. Braswell, the

61. *Greensboro Daily News*, June 9, 1926.
62. Shipley, *The War on Modern Science*, p. 94; *Charlotte Observer*, June 6, 1926; *Greensboro Daily News*, June 4, 1926.
63. *Charlotte Observer*, May 20, 26, 1926.

Nash County physician and outspoken champion of anti-evolution legislation, was "a clear-cut casualty" in the primary fight over Darwinism. He was defeated by a young Baptist and Wake Forest-trained lawyer, Otway B. Moss of Spring Hope. Another Baptist and Wake Forest alumnus, Walter J. Matthews, ran on an anti-Poole Bill platform in Scotland County, the home of Judge Walter Neal and a center of anti-evolutionist agitation. Matthews roundly defeated the incumbent Angus D. Currie, a Presbyterian who had voted for the Poole measure in 1925.[64]

The politics of evolution provoked widespread excitement in Wake and Pasquotank counties. In Wake County, the site of the state's capital city, the anti-evolutionists received a stunning defeat in spite of their vigorous efforts in behalf of Sherwood Upchurch. They flooded the county with handbills adorned with pictures of Upchurch pointing to a monkey and exclaiming, "I may look like him but I refuse to claim kin." [65] No less spectacular was the campaign in Pasquotank County waged by William O. Saunders, whose repertoire of invective had long been directed at fundamentalist evangelists, William Jennings Bryan, and the Committee of One Hundred. Running on an "anti-Ku Klux Klan and anti-Fundamentalist platform," Saunders was overwhelmingly defeated by J. Kenyon Wilson, a corporation lawyer supported by the county politicians. Although Saunders characterized the primary results as a victory for "Isaac, Jacob, and Abraham," it is doubtful whether the Pasquotank voters were registering their support of anti-evolution legislation as much as they were disapproving the election of so controversial a figure as Saunders.[66]

Of all the primaries the one in Mecklenburg County, by now considered the mecca of fundamentalism, promised to be the most turbulent. Two Presbyterians, J. Clyde Stancill and William E. Price, were elected. Although Price had resigned his position in the Committee of One Hundred before the primary, he was still in favor of an anti-evolution law. The real fracas, however, took place in the

64. *Greensboro Daily News*, June 9, 15, 1926; *Charlotte Observer*, July 7, 1926; *Statesville Landmark*, July 5, 1926.

65. *News and Observer*, June 8, 9, 1926; see Suzanne C. Linder, "William Louis Poteat and the Evolution Controversy," *The North Carolina Historical Review*, XL (April, 1926), 153.

66. Keith Saunders, *The Independent Man* (Washington, 1962), pp. 91–93.

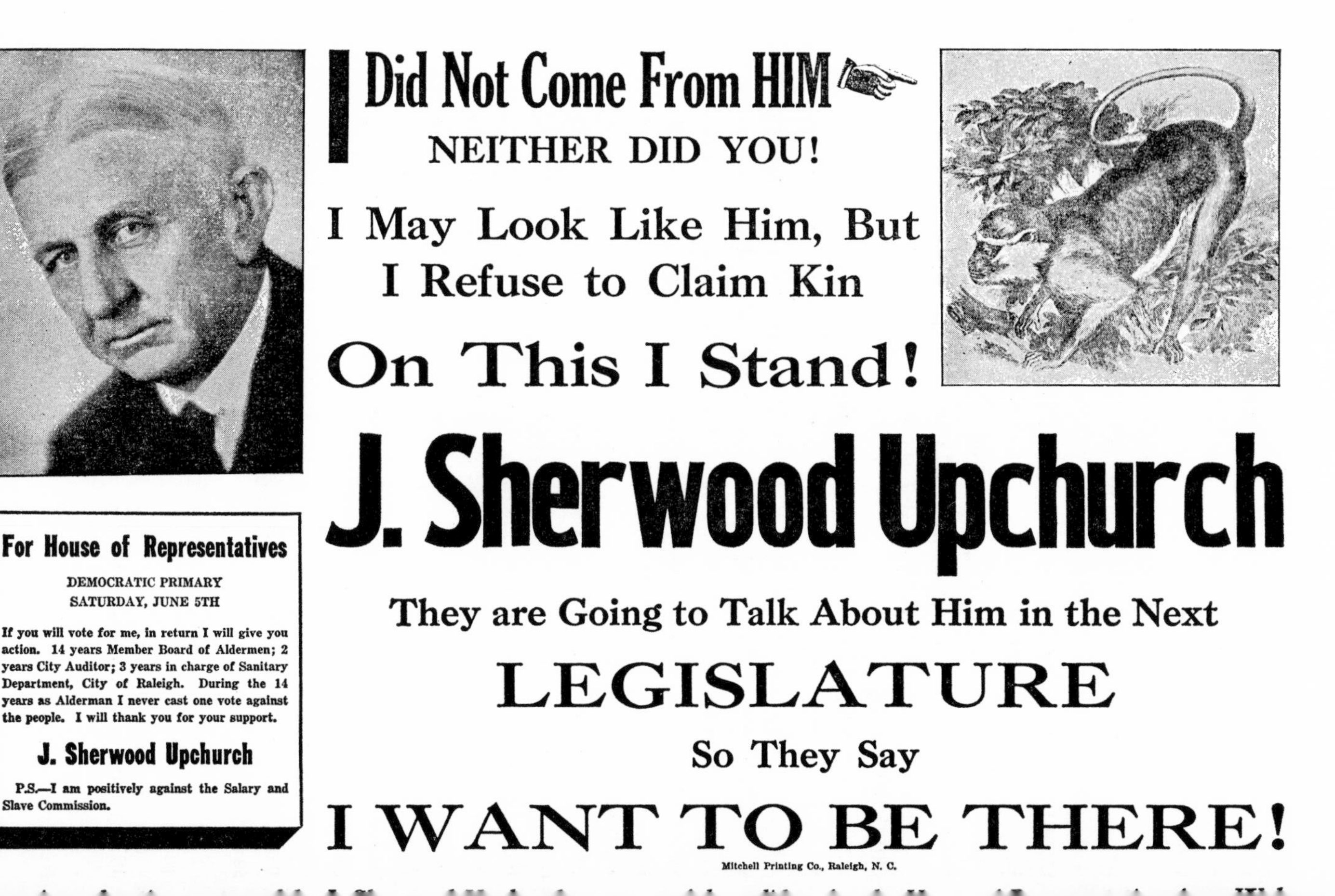
I Did Not Come From HIM
NEITHER DID YOU!
I May Look Like Him, But
I Refuse to Claim Kin
On This I Stand!
J. Sherwood Upchurch
They are Going to Talk About Him in the Next
LEGISLATURE
So They Say
I WANT TO BE THERE!
For House of Representatives
DEMOCRATIC PRIMARY
SATURDAY, JUNE 5TH
If you will vote for me, in return I will give you action. 14 years Member Board of Aldermen; 2 years City Auditor; 3 years in charge of Sanitary Department, City of Raleigh. During the 14 years as Alderman I never cast one vote against the people. I will thank you for your support.
J. Sherwood Upchurch
P.S.—I am positively against the Salary and Slave Commission.
Mitchell Printing Co., Raleigh, N. C.

run-off primary between two female aspirants for the House, Julia Alexander and Carrie MacLean. Julia Alexander, the incumbent, was a Presbyterian closely identified with the Committee of One Hundred and a staunch supporter of anti-evolution legislation; Carrie MacLean was a Baptist and well-known attorney who publicly decried efforts to restrict freedom of speech. Miss MacLean's victory was interpreted as "a definite and positive defeat" for the anti-evolutionists. In the legislature of 1927 she was appointed to the Committee on Education where her vote against a second Poole Bill negated the vote of her colleague from Mecklenburg, William E. Price.[67]

Unquestionably the evolution issue loomed large in the political campaigns in the spring of 1926. Henry M. London, the state's legislative reference librarian, considered the issue significant enough to make it the basis for a portion of his analysis of the primary results. London calculated that less than 24 per cent of the legislators who supported the Poole Bill in 1925 were renominated, while over 37 per cent of those opposed to the measure retained their seats. According to his analysis the only legislator defeated for renomination who had opposed the Poole Bill was Frank C. Brinson of Pamlico County. He had been replaced by Vestor C. Banks, a clerk in the Free Will Baptist Church which officially endorsed anti-evolution legislation. In the general election in November, 1926, a Republican unseated veteran Democratic legislator Will W. Neal of McDowell County, presumably because Neal's "fundamentalist constituents never forgave him for opposing the Poole Bill" in 1925. Nevertheless, the public generally interpreted the outcome of the primaries as a serious, if not disastrous, setback for the anti-evolutionists. A sizable segment of the press agreed with the contention of the *Greensboro Daily News* that the primaries offered irrefutable proof of North Carolina's refusal "to canonize the faith savers."[68]

67. *Charlotte Observer*, July 5, 1926; *Greensboro Daily News*, June 4, 14, 1926; Shipley, *The War on Modern Science*, pp. 97–98.
68. *News and Observer*, June 16, 1926; *Statesville Landmark*, November 22, 1926; *Greensboro Daily News*, June 15, 1926.

8 ~ THE LAST STAND

"Let those who rejoice in the defeat of this effort to save our Bible from final rejection and our children from unbelief remember that 'he laughs best who laughs last.'"

—THE PRESBYTERIAN STANDARD

The defeat of the anti-evolutionists in the Democratic primaries did not end the agitation over evolution in North Carolina. Newspapers continued to be swamped with letters-to-the-editor on the subject, and a virtual war of printed words was underway by the summer of 1926. From the beginning of the controversy citizens had employed their pens freely in producing essays, pamphlets, tracts, and verse to express their sentiments on the evolution issue. Those opposed to the propagation of the theory were far more productive than their adversaries. And by early 1927 they could claim a "fundamentalist novel" among their literary efforts. Written by Luther Little, pastor of the First Baptist Church in Charlotte, and published by the Presbyterian Standard Company, this "thrilling romance" entitled *Manse Dwellers* was a fictional account of the trials and joys of a fundamentalist minister in a small city. A portion of the book described the heretical sermons preached in the absence of the minister by the assistant pastor. This young heretic held a graduate degree from the denominational college in the state where he had forsaken the "old-time religion" for "naturalistic philosophy."

His heresy lay in his refusal to accept the plenary inspiration of the Scriptures. The author, a prominent member of the Committee of One Hundred, used the "thrilling romance" as the vehicle for criticizing "both Christian and state education" for "exposing the minds of the young people to such serious errors" as naturalistic interpretations of the Bible.[1]

More characteristic of the anti-evolutionist literature than Little's volume was a thick pamphlet entitled *The Bible and Evolution,* by Kenneth S. Wuest, a professor of Bible in the Free Will Baptist Seminary in Ayden. His basic theme was that science "has trespassed upon the ground which belongs solely to the church, and as a result has brought forth the theory of evolution to explain, first man's origin, second, the purpose for which man exists, and third, man's destiny." After thirty-two pages of text to demonstrate the inherent dangers of evolution, Wuest concluded: ". . . let it be said that because evolution is destructive of the vital elements of Christianity, because it is unscientific in its methods, because of its unwarranted and unproven claims, and because of its inconsistent position with regard to Jesus Christ, therefore evolution has no place in the Christian church nor in schools endowed by Christian people." [2]

Although the anti-evolutionists were far more prolific in the production of polemical literature than their opponents, they by no means monopolized this sphere of activity. Those hostile to the anti-evolution crusade occasionally produced serious discussions of the issues at stake in the controversy. Rather typical of this type of literature was a tract by the Reverend E. C. Murray of St. Pauls entitled *Does the Bible Teach Natural Science?* which roundly criticized anti-evolutionists for using the Bible as a textbook in science and for confusing the "scientific theory of evolution" with a "radical rationalistic philosophy of evolution." [3] But adversaries of the anti-evolutionists generally produced literature marked less by its profundity of argument than by its ridicule and taunting caricatures. Two such pamphlets appeared in 1926: *The Book of Ham,* by William O. Saunders, which was aimed at the anti-evolutionist evangelist Mordecai F. Ham, and *Ginger and Pepper: Evolution and*

1. Luther Little, *Manse Dwellers* (Charlotte, 1927), pp. 143–49.
2. Kenneth S. Wuest, *The Bible and Evolution* (n.p., 1926), pp. 4–7, 32.
3. E. C. Murray, *Does the Bible Teach Natural Science?* (Lumberton, n.d.).

Reminiscences in which author Charles W. Tillett poked fun at Judge Neal, Luther Little, William Black, and others active in the Committee of One Hundred. Newspapers such as the *Greensboro Daily News* and the *Raleigh Times* employed the same tactics against the anti-evolutionists with the aim of pointing up the "ridiculousness" of their position.[4]

A strange little book by George Ezekiel Hood of Goldsboro entitled *The Origin of Man* appeared in mid-summer of 1926. It occupied a unique niche in the literature of the evolution controversy largely because it posed a novel theory to explain man's origin. The theory included elements from the thought of both Darwinians and fundamentalists. Hood maintained that "God made us by degrees" and that "we came the species route, not from cells, but from cross drops of blood." [5] Summarizing his "blood" hypothesis, he wrote: "We read in Genesis from one end to the other that the blood was used for many and varied purposes, and last, but not least, for the remission of our sins. My theory is that all of us were once mighty powerful animals, and the blood and minerals upon which these fed were so tremendously powerful, we originated from a cross in a male drop of blood with a female drop and by Nature's process we were evolved from one stage to another until we were fully developed into matured men and women." [6] The distinctive character of man lay in the peculiar quality of his blood which accounted for his rationality, intelligence, and superiority over all other creatures. Hood believed that his special evolution theory could be accepted by the religiously orthodox without compromising their orthodoxy. He carefully explained how his "blood" theory substantiated the divinity of Christ and the idea that God created man in His image. His little book is noteworthy primarily as an example of the bizarre literature that emerged during the conflict over evolution. Its influence was negligible; protagonists in the controversy apparently ignored altogether its effort to mediate the dispute.

Another dispenser of strange ideas was Charles F. Bluske of

4. *Goldsboro News*, March 3, 1926; Charles W. Tillett, *Ginger and Pepper: Reminiscences* (Charlotte, 1926); *Greensboro Daily News*, June 3, 14, August 6, 1926; *Raleigh Times*, May 18, June 15, 1926.

5. George Ezekiel Hood, *The Origin of Man* (Goldsboro, 1926), 111 pp.

6. *Ibid.*, p. 5.

Asheville, the "inventor of the New Science of Power." This belligerent fundamentalist and mechanical tinkerer attempted to refute the validity of evolution by a curious mixture of theology and mechanics. He claimed to be the inventor of an apparatus for bicycles which exerted "one hundred per cent more power" upon the pedals "than there is put into it by your foot." According to his new principle of mechanics, "angularity motion is so constructed that a 'straight' in conjunction with counteraction does not equal an 'Angle' in opposition to collect power." Convinced that his "new discovery" disproved accepted principles of leverage, Bluske then assumed that evolution was another "scientific boob" taught as truth by "ignorant" scientists.[7] In other words, if there was one scientific error, all science was false. In one of his anti-evolutionist pieces he wrote:

> This [his new discovery] shows a mistake of the ignorant scientific world in figuring; then these weak-minded scientists try to tell you about evolution? It's a nutty bunk. Scientists and modernists stop the way of progress and are a laughing stock to the intelligent mind, for we now can create invisible energy by invisible leverage, and the unproven theory of evolution of the ignorant scientists is now overthrown, because we now can create a power above our strength and beyond our reach, by long motion confined to short motion, showing that God could in the beginning put man together in His image by THE ELECTRICAL FORCE OF NATURE, for when Christ raised the dead to life it proved that God could create instantly by the Power of His Voice.[8]

Rising to new heights of intemperance, Bluske described a scientific evolutionist as a combination of "a jackass, a hog, and a skunk." Intellectuals were evolutionists; therefore they constituted "an insane set of educated fools" teaching "lies in the Universities." Only the "common people" through their "common-sense" were capable of comprehending the ultimate realities; intellectuals and scientists were "a lot of whiners" possessing "rotten, silly notions" and unable to understand truth. Evolution was manifestly false because it violated the principle that "lesser life cannot create greater life." The common man knew he was not "like an animal" because he could not "eat grass like a horse." Evolution, then, was merely the means

7. Charles F. Bluske, *A New Discovery—A Challenge to the Scientific World* (circular, n.d., n.p.).
8. *Ibid.*

by which "weak-minded" intellectuals carried on their unChristian, Bolshevistic assault upon the high standards of American morality. Bluske suggested that the whole "Evolution Monkey Gang" be exiled "out of the country." [9]

The Asheville "expert on the Law of Applied Power" was not one to hide his light under a bushel. He managed to achieve a good deal of notoriety by spreading his ideas abroad. His letters appeared in *Harper's Magazine* and the *American Mercury* as well as in newspapers throughout North Carolina. His pink circular, which contained a picture of him beside a bicycle equipped with his new invention, was widely distributed. In it he dared "any scientist in the world" to accept an invitation to debate evolution in public in order to prove his claim that all scientists were "cowards." He promised to pay twenty-five dollars in gold to any scientist who could endure such a debate without being made "a laughing stock." After an abusive lashing of William Louis Poteat, Bluske challenged him directly and offered him the choice of debating or "bare fist" fighting as means of settling their differences over evolution. Poteat, of course, ignored the invitation and dismissed the Asheville inventor as a noisy crank. The public also refused to take Bluske seriously; nevertheless, his crude rantings tended to substantiate the charge that the anti-evolutionist crusade was the bluster of fanatics.[10]

By the late summer of 1926, the storm over evolution had abated considerably. The secular press manifested less interest in it, and of the church papers only the *Presbyterian Standard* continued to be concerned. Other church papers ignored the issue altogether. Although the Presbyterians at their synod meeting in the autumn of 1926 offered some comfort to the fundamentalists, the only church body to give official sanction to the anti-evolutionist cause that year was the the Eastern Conference of the Original Free Will Baptists.[11] Even the admonitions of Billy Sunday, Cyclone McLendon, and

9. *Ibid.*

10. *Ibid.*; Maynard Shipley, *The War on Modern Science: A Short History of the Fundamentalist Attacks on Evolution and Modernism* (New York, 1927), pp. 95–96, 100; Charles F. Bluske to William Louis Poteat, September 17, 1925, Poteat Papers.

11. *Minutes of the Annual Session of the Eastern Conference of the Original Free Will Baptists*, 1926, p. 5.

Mordecai F. Ham, all of whom paid brief visits to the state during the summer of 1926, failed to elicit enthusiastic responses. Evangelist Gipsy Smith, Jr., who conducted a "giant crusade" in Goldsboro, soon found that his sermons against evolution had far less appeal than other topics.[12] Another indication of the cooling of passions was the fact that Henry L. Mencken, the high priest of irreverence in the eyes of the orthodox, visited the University of North Carolina at the invitation of Professor Odum without creating a sensation.[13] In surveying the status of the evolution controversy in the South, Frank Kent of the *Baltimore Sun* reported in July, 1926, "As things stand today in North Carolina, the anti-evolution movement is no longer a serious threat." Although the public in general manifested an increasing indifference toward evolution, it was still a lively enough issue to ignite disturbances in some quarters.[14]

On July 1, 1926, such a disturbance erupted at the annual meeting of the Methodist Epworth League. Ralph Simmerson, a "precocious young student from Spencer," created quite a sensation by his fiery championship of a resolution which would have placed the League on record in opposition to the teaching of "any theory which connects the ancestry of man with a lower order of animals." The League president, L. B. Hayes, a young minister characterized by some as an extreme modernist, ruled that the resolution was not pertinent and managed to have it tabled without first having it read to the group. When Simmerson tried to read the measure, he was ruled out of order. Jumping to his feet again, he set off a general uproar by accusing Hayes of undemocratic, high-handed procedures. Order was finally restored, and the resolution remained on the table.[15]

Even more significant was the action of the North Carolina State Federation of Labor during the last day of its annual convention in Salisbury on August 11, 1926. J. S. Upton, a machinist from Salisbury, introduced a resolution in which the organization appealed to the forthcoming legislature to prohibit the teaching of evolution

12. *Goldsboro News*, June 3, August 3, 4, 5, 6, 8, 9, 10, 14, 24, 29, 1926; *News and Observer*, August 10, 1926.
13. Howard W. Odum to H. L. Mencken, August 20, 1926, H. L. Mencken to Howard Odum, October 25, 1926, Odum Papers.
14. *News and Observer*, July 19, 1926.
15. *News and Observer*, July 2, 1926.

in all tax-supported schools and colleges. W. F. Moody of Raleigh, a past president of the State Federation, argued vehemently against any such action by a labor group, but his motion to table the Upton resolution was lost by a decisive vote. Then, President C. P. Barringer of Charlotte attempted to squelch the measure by reading a letter from William Green, head of the American Federation of Labor. The labor leader clearly indicated his belief that anti-evolution laws infringed upon freedom of thought and therefore should not be encouraged by labor bodies. Despite Green's counsel, the State Federation passed the Upton resolution by "an almost unanimous vote." [16]

The action of the Federation undoubtedly boosted the morale of the anti-evolutionists whose fortunes had been waning ever since the spring primaries. In fact, the whole year had been a lean one for them. Even the announcement by Poteat in August, 1926, that he would retire from the presidency of Wake Forest College within a year brought them little comfort. They realized that age was his "sole consideration," [17] that age, and not their efforts to oust him, was the real reason for his decision. For a while, however, it appeared that in the establishment of the School of Religion in Chapel Hill they had scored a victory. But whatever satisfaction they gained from it was shortlived. Not only did the University refuse to grant credit for its Bible courses, but as was stated earlier, Dean Mims T. Workman proved to be far too "liberal" to suit the tastes of the fundamentalist zealots.[18]

Hard on the heels of these disappointments was another setback to the anti-evolutionist cause which resulted from a highly publicized court trial involving one of its most ardent champions. On March 23, 1926, James R. Pentuff initiated a twenty-five thousand dollar libel suit against the *Raleigh Times*. In an editorial describing his anti-evolution lectures in Fuquay Springs, the Raleigh paper had described the Concord minister as "an immigrant ignoramus." Pentuff engaged the well-known anti-evolutionist leader Zebulon V. Turlington as his attorney. Because of the personalities and the issue

16. *Statesville Landmark*, August 12, 1926; *News and Observer*, August 12, 1926; Shipley, *The War on Modern Science*, p. 94.
17. *Biblical Recorder*, XCII (August 4, 1926), 2; *Goldsboro News*, August 4, 1926; *News and Observer*, August 3, 1926.
18. *Biblical Recorder*, XCII (October 29, 1926), 6.

involved, the case attracted a great deal of attention. Unfortunately for the anti-evolution cause, Pentuff was exposed, under cross-examination, as scarcely the type of man to protect Tar Heel Christianity from its enemies. He admitted under oath that he had lived in eight states, had declared bankruptcy in West Virginia, had been arrested twice in Yancey County, and had been involved in a "bad check case" in Morganton. These facts seemed strangely inconsistent with his elaborate academic pedigree and his claims to a distinguished career as an educator. The exposure of his past not only induced the judge to dismiss the libel suit late in October, 1926, but also ended his effectiveness as an anti-evolutionist spokesman in North Carolina.[19]

By the end of the Pentuff trial the press had begun its predictions regarding the major issues to confront the biennial session of the legislature which was to convene in January, 1927. Journalists agreed almost unanimously that anti-evolutionists would be unable to arouse much interest for the cause among legislators. The *Goldsboro News* reminded the die-hard advocates of anti-evolution legislation that "North Carolina is not Tennessee." The *Statesville Landmark* urged the General Assembly to concentrate upon "important" matters while anti-evolution bills were allowed "to sleep the sleep that knows no waking in the Committee." The *Jackson County Journal* reported with obvious elation that the Committee of One Hundred had "dwindled to a mere handful of rabid anti-evolutionists" whose misguided zeal would wreck their chances of success. In Raleigh, Nell Battle Lewis agreed with this interpretation but warned against underestimating the lengths to which the anti-evolutionists would go in order to achieve their goals. While most newspapers opposed another legislative fight over evolution and predicted that such a struggle would be barren of results, they also agreed that the evolution question would again consume much time and energy in the legislature of 1927. On this score their forecasts proved to be correct.[20]

The Committee of One Hundred had by no means forsaken its

19. *Goldsboro News*, April 29, October 29, 1926; *Charlotte Observer*, March 24, 1926; *News and Observer*, April 28, 1926.

20. *Goldsboro News*, December 11, 1926; *Statesville Landmark*, August 30, December 23, 1926; *Jackson County Journal* (Sylva), December 15, 1926; *News and Observer*, November 4, December 20, 1926.

original aims. Its depleted ranks and its semi-secret sessions which went largely unnoticed in the press induced some to pronounce, quite prematurely, the organization's obituary. At the meeting of the committee in Charlotte on November 4, 1926, Judge Neal resigned the chairmanship and was replaced by Dr. A. R. Shaw, a Presbyterian minister. Julia Alexander became temporary secretary-treasurer, and shortly afterward began publication of the *Fundamentalist.* Shaw announced that steps were "being taken to affiliate with a Bible league to embrace every county in the state." He also indicated that the committee would concern itself with such issues as divorce, Sabbath desecration, and law enforcement as well as "the character of teaching in our schools." Whatever the intentions of the organization, it remained primarily interested in outlawing the teaching of evolution and, during the last two months of 1926, concentrated upon preparing for a legislative battle early the next year.[21]

The executive committee met again on December 9, to undertake another administrative reorganization and to adopt a new name. The old Committee of One Hundred became the North Carolina Bible League. In order to enhance its chances of lobbying in the legislature, the League attempted to assume the character of a nonsectarian, citizens' association by broadening the scope of its aims as previously indicated by Shaw and by substituting laymen for clergymen in the executive offices. Shaw resigned as president so that Zebulon V. Turlington, legislator-elect from Iredell County, could assume the post. Two other laymen were also elected: Julia Alexander became secretary; and J. D. Call, a Charlotte businessman, was chosen treasurer. The only clergyman given an office was W. C. Barrett, the Baptist minister of Gastonia and an arch foe of evolution, who became vice-president. The Bible League concluded its initial session by appointing a committee to retain "a capable Christian lawyer" as the organization's chief lobbyist and legal consultant regarding "the proposed legislation looking toward outlawing evolution." [22]

Shortly before the next meeting of the League, president-elect Turlington issued a lengthy statement explaining the aims and

21. *Statesville Landmark,* November 8, 1926; *News and Observer,* November 5, 1926; *Fundamentalist,* I (December 9, 1926).

22. *News and Observer,* December 10, 1926; *Statesville Landmark,* December 13, 1926; *Goldsboro News.* December 11, 1926.

purposes of the new organization. He declared that the League stood "for truth and all search for truth" and that it heartily supported research. Although the League rejoiced "when truth has been discovered," it was unalterably opposed to the teaching "of a thing as truth that remains in the realm of hypothesis." Turlington then gave specific examples of scientists known to have "falsified" data in order to justify their unproved and unprovable hypotheses. He clearly implied that a great deal of false information about evolution was being taught in North Carolina schools by men who were more propagandists than teachers. Turlington also maintained that the League's proposal to eliminate evolutionists from schools supported by Christian taxpayers was merely a modern version of Thomas Jefferson's fight to free dissenting sects from being taxed to support an established church whose doctrines were repugnant to them. "It is tyrannical," the Iredell legislator declared, "to compel the people of the State to contribute their money for the purpose of teaching conceptions of religious things in which they heartily disbelieve, even though it be done under the guise of teaching science." According to Turlington's interpretation, the Bible League was engaged in a mighty struggle for "religious liberty and for the separation of church and state." Its fight was an expression of "the highest form of patriotism."

His statement to the press also attempted to refute two charges often leveled against anti-evolutionists. First, he explained the "regrettable" situation that developed at the May meeting of the Committee of One Hundred as the work of modernist interlopers who ever since had made much ado over the session. For him, this incident was merely another example of the persistent attempts by the "opposition" to "divert the public mind from the real issue." Second, Turlington answered the charge that an anti-evolution law would create in North Carolina the same conditions that existed in Tennessee. He refused to believe that Tennessee was as benighted as a biased press depicted it and reminded North Carolinians that while their educational leaders were preoccupied with a fight for "intellectual freedom," Tennessee had relieved its people of the burden imposed by school book publishers by providing cheaper textbooks for school children. He clearly indicated that the cause of the latter was far more important than the discussions of intellectual freedom in North Carolina, which constituted another device for sidetracking the "real issue." [23]

Turlington's statement elicited a rash of unfavorable comments in the press. Editors who scrutinized it closely were critical of its inconsistencies and scoffed at its attempt to identify the Bible League with Jefferson's struggle for religious liberty in Virginia. Perhaps the most comprehensive critique was a widely reprinted article by Rowland Beasley, editor of the *Monroe Journal*. Although Beasley admitted that the legislature had the actual authority to prescribe in detail the school curriculum, he considered the exertion of such power highly unwise. The legislature, he said, could outlaw evolution in exactly the same way that it would require teachers to teach "that two and two equal five." But it could not legally forbid the teaching of evolution on the basis suggested by Turlington, for the Iredell legislator had assumed that evolution was "a matter of religion," and religion was "the one subject about which the law making body is prohibited from legislating." Furthermore, Beasley considered preposterous the Bible League's claim of being a defender of truth when, without any proof, it was seeking "to legislate evolution as a fake." His conclusion was that the evolution issue could best be settled outside the political arena, because legislative meddling in matters of opinion invariably created more problems than it solved.[24]

The *North Carolina Lutheran* challenged Beasley's argument by maintaining that precisely because evolution was a religious question, it ought to be excluded from all tax-supported schools. First, the *Lutheran* attempted to prove that evolution was not a scientific issue since the theory was neither "verified nor verifiable." Instead, evolution belonged to the religious sphere where "belief in the realm of the unseen" was accepted. Evolutionists "walked by faith, not by sight"; they accepted evolution on faith as religionists rather than on the basis of demonstrated fact as scientists. Like virtually "all religions of the world," evolution attempted to explain the origin of the universe and of man. The *Lutheran* concluded:

The matter of origins is therefore a religious question. It is more distinctly religious than it is scientific. Hence the teaching of organic

23. *News and Observer*, December 27, 1926.
24. *News and Observer*, January 2, 1927.

evolution is teaching religion. The evolutionists who are contending against the anti-evolutionists for a safely guarded separation between Church and State, and accusing the anti-evolutionists of attempting to inject a religious question into State legislation, should take their own medicine first and see that every text-book which teaches the Darwinian theory is withdrawn from the tax-supported schools. So long as such text-books are used . . . the State is teaching religion. There is no refuting this fact. The anti-evolutionists are asking that the State cease to use the tax money to supplant the Bible religion by the Darwinian religion. It is without doubt a reasonable and just demand.[25]

The *Lutheran* clearly indicated that it supported an anti-evolution law as a means of restoring the separation of church and state.

On December 30, 1926, ten days before the opening of the legislature, the Bible League met in closed session in Charlotte. Turlington called the meeting to order, then announced that he could not accept the office of president to which he had been elected on December 9. His reasons for this decision were not made clear, but the fact that he was an elected official of the state and was considered as a "dark-horse" candidate for the House speakership may have figured in his decision. The possibility of a conflict of interests, however, did not deter him from remaining active in the League, in which he served as a director and as a member of its committee on constitutions and by-laws. When Turlington stepped aside, the League apparently forsook its earlier intention to place laymen in the chief official posts and elected R. McKendree Long, a Presbyterian minister and evangelist of Statesville, as president. The son of a well-known Superior Court judge and an artist before entering the ministry, Long was described as a "brilliant all-round champion of fundamentalism." "We expect to wage an aggressive but unacrimonious campaign," he declared shortly after accepting the League presidency, "and believe that our vindication is a blessed certainty." Equally confident, Secretary Julia Alexander proclaimed: "We are going to keep up the fight until we get control of the State and maybe of the nation." [26]

The League met on December 30, presumably to plan its strategy

25. *North Carolina Lutheran*, V (January, 1927), 4–5.

26. *Statesville Landmark*, December 30, 1926; *News and Observer*, December 31, 1926.

for the forthcoming legislative battle, but the secrecy surrounding the proceedings precluded anything more than a vague notion of its actions. Thomas C. Bowie, a prominent political figure and former legislator from West Jefferson, was selected as the "Christian lawyer" to assist the League in presenting its case in the General Assembly where he apparently would work closely with Turlington. The League also elected an impressive roster of directors which included Bowie, Turlington, W. H. Sprunt of Wilmington, the Reverend H. B. Searight of Washington, the Reverend W. M. White of Raleigh, and W. H. Belk of Charlotte. Perhaps the most distinctive feature of the League's personnel at this juncture was the predominance of Presbyterians; but the Presbyterian whose name was conspicuously absent from the League's roll was D. Scott Poole, the Hoke County legislator who had already expressed his intention to introduce another anti-evolution bill in the House. Although Poole had no connection with any organized movement to outlaw evolution, he was willing to co-operate with the League.[27]

More than fifty representatives from seven Piedmont counties attended an extraordinary session of the Bible League held in Statesville at the Vance Hotel on January 6, 1927. These delegates authorized the drafting of an anti-evolution bill that would be presented to the General Assembly in the name of the League. In order to marshal public opinion in a way that would insure consideration of the measure, they decided to circulate numerous petitions that requested the enactment of an anti-evolution law. This display of public approval was to be presented to the legislature along with the League's bill. Then, the session adopted a permanent "platform and constitution," the contents of which were borrowed largely from the "moral suasion platform" of the old Committee of One Hundred and from Turlington's statement to the press in December. The three-fold purpose of the League was: (1) to organize local chapters in every county, township, and community in the state; (2) to "oppose anti-Bible teaching, especially in all our tax-supported institutions of learning"; (3) to promote a statewide "educational campaign along the line of good citizenship." Membership in the League was open to all voters who believed "in the whole

27. *News and Observer,* December 31, 1926; *Greensboro Daily News,* December 31, 1926; *The Charlotte Observer,* December 30, 31, 1926.

Bible as the infallible Word of God and are willing to defend it as such." In its declaration of principles the League maintained that tax-supported schools belonged "to the people," a majority of whom believed in the Bible as the divinely inspired, authoritative revelation of God's will. Since these schools owned by the people allowed the teaching of doctrines "disparaging to the Bible," the people had "every right" to remove from these institutions anything that menaced their religion. In short, "our schools shall be our servants and not our masters." At the same time the declaration recorded the League's opposition to the union of church and state and proclaimed the organization a civic body dedicated to strengthening state schools by inspiring "our people with confidence in said institutions as safe places for our boys and girls." To emphasize the civic, as opposed to the ecclesiastical, nature of the organization, the League disclaimed any concern for denominational schools, proclaimed its belief in "freedom of thought and research," and described itself as a guardian of the Jeffersonian tradition of liberty. "But," the League declaration concluded, "we deny the right of those in charge of our state schools to employ and retain teachers who hold and express views fundamentally contrary to the simple teaching of the Bible, and force tax payers to pay the bills." [28]

On January 5, 1927, the day before the Bible League met in Statesville, the state legislature convened in Raleigh. The ceremony by which House members were sworn into office provided an opportunity "for the insertion into the House record of a suggestion of Fundamentalist doctrine." For the ceremony each legislator was provided a small Bible by the principal clerk, Alex Lassiter, who told the representatives that the Bibles were theirs "to keep as momentoes [*sic*] of this occasion." The House then passed a resolution of appreciation in which the Holy Scriptures were described as "the only true rule and guide of faith." Some observers interpreted this incident as the beginning of the fundamentalist offensive in the legislature.[29]

The organization of the House several days later elicited a mixed reaction among the opponents of anti-evolution legislation who were maintaining a keen interest in legislative events. Richard T. Fountain

28. *News and Observer,* January 7, 1927; see also Appendix B.
29. *News and Observer,* January 6, 1927; *House Journal, 1927,* p. 13.

of Edgecombe County, a moderate on the evolution issue, was elected speaker. Connor returned to his post as chairman of the Committee on Education, and Turlington became head of the powerful Appropriations Committee. There had been speculation that Turlington would receive the post of his choice since he had provided valuable support to Fountain in the contest for speaker. Some assumed that the Iredell legislator would request the chairmanship of the Education Committee as the best position to wage his fight in behalf of the Bible League. At any rate, the prospect of Turlington at the helm of the Appropriations Committee was no less disturbing to those who feared that he would utilize this post to achieve the same ends. Conceivably he might attempt to exert financial pressure upon schools and colleges that manifested hostility toward the demands of the Bible League. Such apprehension was in part offset by the announcement of the membership of the Committee on Education, which had undergone a careful re-shuffling since 1925. Of its thirty-eight members only twelve had previously served on the committee, and of the old members only four, including Poole himself, had voted for the anti-evolution bill in 1925. The composition of the Education Committee reflected a desire of a majority of the legislators to prevent the evolution issue from reaching the floor of the House.[30]

Other forces joined the legislators in an attempt to forestall further controversy over evolution. The major newspapers again appeared in the vanguard of those opposed to "monkey" legislation of any kind. Voicing the theme of numerous journals, the *Asheville Times* warned "sincere Christians" against being seduced by arguments for laws "to force men's consciences and to shackle the freedom to learn and teach." The *Beaufort County News* claimed that "all the fuss about evolution" was "a waste of time and energy" which North Carolinians should expend in lifting their schools to a respectable academic level.[31] Among the civic and professional organizations that publicly opposed any consideration of an anti-evolution bill by the legislature were the Buncombe County Bar Association and the Rocky

30. *News and Observer*, January 5, 1927; *Evening Telegram* (Rocky Mount), January 4, 6, 11, 1927.

31. *Asheville Times*, January 19, 1927; *Beaufort County News*, January 27, February 19, 1927.

Mount Ministerial Association. The Episcopal Church had already voiced its objections; ministers from various denominations began to speak out in opposition to any re-enactment of the political battle over evolution which had occurred two years earlier. The Reverend W. A. Stanbury of the Edenton Street Methodist Church in Raleigh stated publicly that the proposed anti-evolution law represented "the vocal ignorance of the state," rather than any movement by responsible church leaders.[32]

Undeterred by such opposition, the anti-evolutionists persisted in their determination to carry the fight to a finish. Ever since arriving in the capital, Representative Poole had been talking about his forthcoming anti-evolution bill which he claimed would be "quite different" from his measure in 1925. He indicated that he was particularly interested in writing into his new bill restrictions against school books that contained any "slighting" references to religion. When asked to give an example of what he would consider as such a reference, Poole replied that the use of the phrase "Methodist preacher" as a term of reproach would constitute a violation of his projected bill. Apparently he had intended to introduce the bill in the House on January 18, 1927, and when the much heralded measure was not introduced on that date, Poole explained that he had lost his original copy and would have to redraft the bill, which would be introduced in "a day or two." In the meantime, Turlington had been in consultation with him, and Thomas C. Bowie was completing an anti-evolution bill to be offered in the name of the North Carolina Bible League. The executive committee of the League approved Bowie's bill at a meeting on January 22; three days later, Bowie arrived in Raleigh with it. He announced that Poole would sponsor the measure and that Turlington might attach his name to it. By this time, however, Turlington seemed to be nagged by misgivings about the whole project; there were indications that he and Poole had disagreed over the contents of the bill. At any rate, the second anti-evolution bill, like the first, bore only the name of Representative Poole.[33]

32. *Asheville Times*, January 16, 1927; *Charlotte Observer*, January 19, 31, February 8, 10, 1927; *News and Observer*, January 23, 1927.

33. *News and Observer*, January 16, 18, 1927; *Evening Telegram*, January 6, 18, 26, 1927.

The measure, drafted by Bowie and delivered to Poole on January 25, was introduced in the House the following day. The bill stated:

Section 1. That it shall be unlawful for any professor, teacher or instructor to teach in any school, college or educational institution within the State of North Carolina receiving aid from the State, any doctrine or theory of evolution which contradicts or denies the divine origin of man or of the universe, as taught in the Holy Bible.

Provided, however, that nothing in this act shall be construed to prohibit the teaching in said schools, colleges, or educational institutions of all useful arts and sciences, unless the same are taught in a manner as to contradict the fundamental truths of the Holy Bible.

Section 2. That any professor, teacher or instructor violating the provisions of Section 1 of this act shall be guilty of a misdemeanor and upon conviction shall be fined or imprisoned in the discretion of the court, and in the discretion of the court may be disqualified from teaching in such schools, colleges or educational institutions upon such terms and conditions, and for such a time as the court, in its discretion, may order.

Section 3. That this act shall be in force from and after its ratification.[34]

The Poole Bill of 1927 differed from the measure presented two years earlier in two principal ways: it forbade the teaching of *any theory* that contradicted the biblical account of man's origin rather than the teaching of evolution as a fact, and it provided penalties for teachers found guilty of teaching such theories. The *New York Times* described the measure as "most extreme," and Maynard Shipley of the Science League of America called it "the most drastic and far-reaching anti-evolution bill ever presented before a state legislature of this Republic." [35]

The introduction of the Poole Bill provoked a storm of criticism from those who had urged that the evolution issue be dropped altogether. Even the Raleigh *News and Observer* finally took a forthright stand against the bill and its advocates. It gave wide coverage to the defeat of similar measures by the legislatures of West Virginia and New Hampshire and advised North Carolina to follow

34. *News and Observer*, January 26, 1926; see also *House Journal, 1927*, p. 85; the original of the Poole Bill of 1927 with the minority report attached is in the Legislative Papers of 1927, Records Center, State Department of Archives and History, Raleigh.

35. *New York Times*, February 7, 1927.

their example. Editor Daniels assured his readers that an anti-evolution law was unnecessary because neither public school teachers nor college professors were "engaged in any dangerous propaganda" to undermine the Bible.[36] The *Asheville Times* asked: "If the legislature dangles a jail sentence over the heads of biology teachers in the state schools, how long will the rest of the population be free to read and believe what they choose?" [37] The Rocky Mount *Evening Telegram*, another opponent of the Poole Bill, rejoiced at the apathy with which legislators greeted the measure. Nell Battle Lewis considered the bill "utterly uncivilized," but warned academicians to be prepared for another legislative struggle. She especially urged State Superintendent of Public Instruction Arch T. Allen and college presidents E. C. Brooks and Julius I. Foust to avoid those "unforeseen maladies" that prevented them from joining Chase in the legislative fight in 1925. She even struck off a poem entitled "Where Will You Be Boys?" addressed to Chase, Allen, Brooks, and Foust in which she pleaded with them "to speak out" in order that North Carolina might be spared the humiliation of Tennessee. In an effort to ridicule the Poole Bill, Charles W. Tillett, Jr., the Charlotte attorney who "interfered" with the proceedings of the Committee of One Hundred, also resorted to verse and produced "An Ode to the Poole Bill." [38]

The leaders of the educational institutions, following the example of President Chase of the University, decided against appearing at the hearings on the Poole Bill. Chase announced that the position of the University in the matter was already clear and that he could contribute nothing worthwhile by another encounter with the General Assembly. President Brooks of State College advised his faculty to avoid being "drawn into the discussion of the bill" unless "it became absolutely necessary." Both Brooks and Chase were convinced that their allies in the legislature would be able to defeat the measure without their assistance.[39]

36. *News and Observer*, January 24, 27, 1927.

37. *Asheville Times*, January 27, 1927; see also *ibid.*, January 17, 19, 28, 1927.

38. *Evening Telegram;* January 10, 26, February 25, 1927; *News and Observer*, January 23, 1927; see Appendix A.

39. *News and Observer*, February 8, 1927; Minutes of the Faculty Council of North Carolina State College, February 1, 1927, Archives of North Carolina State University at Raleigh.

The Bible League at the same time was busily engaged in marshaling popular support for its cause. President McKendree Long undertook a speaking tour; Secretary Julia Alexander moved to Raleigh to use her influence with her former colleagues in the legislature in behalf of the Poole Bill. Other officials of the League circulated petitions in various sections of the state. By the first week in February, over ten thousand citizens had signed petitions urging the General Assembly to enact an anti-evolution bill. League spokesmen intended to bolster their appeal before the Education Committee with this documentary evidence. Alarmed by the apparent outburst of popular support of the anti-evolution crusade, some observers expressed the fear that the League's strength had been grossly underestimated. But it soon became evident that neither the League's noisy threats nor the display of signed petitions would induce panic among the legislators. Moreover, the League had failed to win the endorsement of a single major daily newspaper and could rely for editorial assistance only upon a few rural, small-town papers.[40]

Although Long was an energetic leader of the Bible League, he had a penchant for impolitic utterances which proved to be a serious liability to his cause. The remark causing the greatest flurry in the press was made in a sermon in Charlotte on January 30, 1927. After denouncing the evolutionists in unusually severe language, Long condemned civic clubs for their emphasis on materialism. At one point he exploded, "Run your civic clubs until you run them to hell where they belong. You never discuss missionaries or anything like that in your civic clubs. You rant on the subject of material wealth and commerce until it has gone so far that moral and spiritual values are the last things to be thought of in North Carolina." Such an indictment scarcely endeared the Bible League president to the hundreds of Rotarians and Kiwanians in the state. The press seized upon his statement as evidence of Long's fanaticism. *Charity and Children* observed that "Mr. Long is an extremist and he abuses things that he does not understand with the zeal of a professional evangelist." The *Greensboro Daily News*, which publicized every *faux pas* of the anti-evolutionists, suggested that if Long considered the influence of civic clubs so malicious, he should have the

40. *News and Observer*, February 6, 1927; *Mooresville Enterprise*, February 10, 1927; *Stanly News-Herald* (Albemarle), February 18, 1927.

legislature pass a law "to prohibit the teaching of any civic club doctrine in the state of North Carolina." Such use of legislative power, according to the *Daily News*, was the normal means by which the "guardians of morality" cleansed society. On the other hand, the *Stanly News-Herald* defended Long and accused the press of exaggerating a minor incident in order to discredit him and "make an ass of the Bible League while the Poole Bill is pending in the legislature."[41]

On the afternoon of February 10, 1927, the Committee on Education opened its hearings on the Poole Bill. Both allies and opponents of the measure were ready to stage another verbal battle before the large audience that packed the galleries. Bowie was the first speaker to address the Committee. In a forty-five minute oration he discussed the constitutionality of the Poole Bill, which was actually his handiwork, and emphasized the existence of ten thousand signatures on petitions advocating its passage. He assured the committee that "a more patriotic body" than the Bible League "never assembled in any state" and that its goal was "to save America from going the way of other civilizations" such as Egypt and Rome, which had succumbed to the insidious influences of paganism. In a short address that followed Bowie's feat of eloquence, John R. Kurfees of Greensboro, an ardent anti-evolutionist whose letters and articles had appeared in newspapers throughout the state, sought to demonstrate the need for the Poole Bill by reading from a zoology textbook used at the University. The third speaker for the anti-evolutionists was William Black, official evangelist of the Presbyterian Synod, whose flowing white hair and beard gave him the appearance of a Hebrew patriarch. Describing himself as "a Christian and Democrat," he assured his audience: "I wouldn't be here but for my love of the old Bible." Then he launched into what amounted to a sermon in defense of the Poole measure.[42]

The climax of the anti-evolutionist argument was an impassioned address by McKendree Long, President of the Bible League. One observer noted that he no sooner began his remarks than he

41. *Greensboro Daily News*, January 31, February 1, 1927; *Charity and Children*, XLII (February 10, 1927), 4; *Stanly News-Herald*, February 11, 18, 1927.

42. *News and Observer*, February 11, 1927; *Greensboro Daily News*, February 11, 1927; *Charlotte Observer*, February 11, 1927; see also John Kurfees, *The Fight Is On! The Issue Is Clearcut!* (n.p., n.d.).

"bounded at once upon a sequoia pedlian summit and every subsequent word was a polysyllable wonder." Long stated virtually all of the usual anti-evolutionist arguments in the course of his address. Occasionally, "when he struck upon anything particularly juicy," he asked for a show of hands by those on the Education Committee "who knew what and whom he was talking about." After several such incidents in which only one or two members of the committee raised their hands, Professor A. P. Kephart of North Carolina College for Women interrupted to suggest that the committee might not appear so ignorant if Long could manage to pronounce correctly the scientific terms he used so glibly. Long bowed graciously toward the professor, explained that his "Southern brogue" rather than his mispronunciation was the source of the difficulty, and proceeded with his lengthy address.[43]

The opposition to the Poole Bill was headed by Theodore Partrick, the Episcopal rector and editor of the *Carolina Churchman,* who had long been an outspoken critic of any legislation to restrict freedom of teaching. Partrick insisted that any faith worth having must be able to subject itself "to the light of advancing knowledge." He charged that those who "feared for the safety of the Christian faith" were "not worshipping truth but the form in which it is expressed." Then, near the end of the three-hour hearings, an unexpected and unscheduled speaker against the bill gained the floor. Without formal introduction, Paul J. Ranson, a law student at the University amazed by his own temerity, jumped to his feet when he could no longer bear to listen to "all this foolishness." He assured the crowd that the University had not destroyed the Christian faith that he had acquired in a pious Presbyterian home, that those who blamed evolution for the immorality of the age were deluding themselves, and that American youth was far more interested in where they were going than "from whence they came." "Ratty" Ranson's impromptu remarks did indeed provide the *coup de grâce* for the Poole Bill. Almost before the applause that followed his statement ended, the Committee on Education adjourned without taking a vote.[44]

43. *Greensboro Daily News,* February 11, 1927; *Biblical Recorder,* XCII (February 23, 1927), 7; *News and Observer,* February 11, 1927.

44. *News and Observer,* February 11, 1927; *Biblical Recorder,* XCII (February 23, 1927), 7; *Durham Morning Herald,* February 11, 1927; Partrick, formerly editor of the *Mission Herald,* became editor of the *Carolina Churchman* in 1926.

At a committee session five days later, Representative Nat A. Townsend of Harnett County moved that the Poole Bill be given an unfavorable report. His motion passed by a vote of twenty-five to eleven. The juggling of the committee personnel had left the anti-evolutionists hopelessly outnumbered, and, as expected, the committee proved to be far more receptive to the arguments of Partrick and Ranson than to those of the Bible League officials. Poole and Turlington, who was floor leader of the anti-evolutionists, announced their intention to bring the measure before the House on a minority report. For a while it appeared that the procedure of 1925 would be re-enacted.[45]

The anti-evolutionists, however, decided to assess their chances of success before filing such a report. Petitions in behalf of the bill continued to come in, and by mid-February, 1927, around fifteen thousand signatures had endorsed the passage of the Poole measure. But the legislative spokesmen for the bill had to weigh this factor against the obvious hostility of the General Assembly toward their cause. Nor could they fail to be impressed by the editorial offensive launched by newspapers to keep the bill buried in the committee.[46] The Rocky Mount *Evening Telegram* typified the reaction of most of the press when it rejoiced at the thought of "the Bowie-Poole Monkey Bill" being "talked to death and asphyxiated by those who claim to be its friends." [47] Turlington and Poole apparently realized that the odds were against them, but after communicating with officials of the Bible League, they filed a minority report which presumably meant that they intended to get the bill before the House.

When the Poole Bill appeared to be headed for a second defeat, its strategists in the legislature began to search for some alternative that might achieve the aims of an anti-evolution bill without antagonizing the legislators. A solution to their problem was offered by James A. Hartness, a so-called "wizard" among the politicians. Hartness was a Presbyterian long active in the Anti-Saloon League and in Democratic politics. He lived in Statesville, the home of McKendree Long, and had been associated with Turlington in Iredell County politics.

45. *News and Observer*, February 16, 1927; *House Journal, 1927*, p. 241.
46. *News and Observer*, February 20, 1927.
47. *Evening Telegram*, February 25, 1927; see also *Durham Morning Herald*, February 16, 1927; *Greensboro Daily News*, February 13, 16, 24, 1927; *News and Observer*, February 10, 16, 1927.

His alternative to the Poole Bill undoubtedly reached the attention of the legislators through Turlington. Hartness' plan was to enact a law making teachers in tax-supported institutions "officers of the state" within the meaning of Article 6, Section 8, of the North Carolina constitution which required a belief in God as a prerequisite for holding a state office. In short, Hartness proposed to subject teachers to a "religious test" with a minimum of new legislation; the additional advantage of such a scheme was that it probably would arouse less opposition than the Poole Bill. Although Hartness drafted a bill to implement his idea which received considerable attention, the anti-evolutionists in the legislature for some reason decided not to sponsor the measure.[48]

On February 23, 1927, Turlington finally announced that, despite the filing of a minority report, the Poole Bill would not be called up for consideration in the House.[49] His action apparently had not been approved by the Bible League. On the day following Turlington's announcement, McKendree Long stated publicly: "From what I can learn . . . the bill is not dead. I personally favor and always have favored a finished fight on the floor of the House so that the people of the state know how their representatives stand. . . . We appreciate what the proponents of the bill in Raleigh may think best but in spite of a prejudiced committee, modernistical gallery demonstrations, the variation of politics and the infidel educators, we will maintain our position to the end." [50] A remnant of the die-hard anti-evolutionists was inclined to join Long in continuing the fight. The *Presbyterian Standard* refused to accept defeat on the evolution question and was convinced that the forces of righteousness represented by the anti-evolutionists would ultimately triumph. In a final editorial on the subject, the paper warned: "let those who rejoice in the defeat of the effort to save our Bible from final rejection and our children from unbelief remember that 'he laughs best who laughs last.' " [51] McKendree Long himself tried desperately to prevent the disintegration of the Bible League. His

48. *Greensboro Daily News*, February 3, 16, 1927; *The North Carolina Manual*, 1929, p. 534; Louis R. Wilson, *The University of North Carolina, 1900–1930: The Making of a Modern University* (Chapel Hill, 1957), p. 522. *News and Observer*, February 15, 1927.

49. *News and Observer*, February 24, 1927.

50. *News and Observer*, February 25, 1927.

51. *Presbyterian Standard*, LXVIII (February 23, 1927), 1.

revival sermons describing the "attempts to do away with the Bible" utterly failed to rekindle interest. Nor were the visiting preachers at Raleigh's Baptist Tabernacle able to arouse enthusiasm by their denunciation of evolution. "Teach a child of ten that he is only a high class monkey . . . ," one such minister declared, "and you lay the foundations for infidelity, pessimism, and suicide." The responses to such indictments indicated the validity of the observation by the *Beaufort County News* that the people of the state were far more interested in business, crops, and taxes than in laws to outlaw a scientific theory.[52]

In spite of the efforts of Long and his cohorts, the possibility of the legislature's passing an anti-evolution law had evaporated. Turlington's announcement on February 23 had been the death knell. Having pushed aside evolution, the North Carolina legislators turned their attention to other business such as a measure "to unmask the Ku Klux Klan." Those legislators formerly so interested in an anti-evolution law including Poole, Turlington, and Price devoted their energies in behalf of legislation officially entitled "an act to prevent sexual immorality." By the spring of 1927 the discussion of evolution had virtually ceased in North Carolina. James R. Pentuff's initiation of a second libel suit against the *Raleigh Times* in March merely reminded the public of his unsavory reputation. Bowie's "severe heart attack" in March sharply curtailed his activities, and Judge Neal's death in May left the anti-evolution movement without a single leader of statewide prominence.[53] Although some observers anticipated a renewed drive to outlaw evolution by the next biennial session of the legislature, such a possibility had disappeared even before the end of 1927. Evolution had by then been replaced by another and more immediate threat to the traditional values of North Carolinians—the possibility of a city-bred, "wet," Roman Catholic as the Democratic candidate for President.[54]

52. *Stanly News-Herald*, March 7, 8, 1927; *Beaufort County News*, February 19, 1927; *News and Observer*, March 21, 1927.

53. *News and Observer*, February 17, 27, March 3, May 24, 1927; *House Journal, 1927*, pp. 52, 173; *Greensboro Daily News*, February 24, 1927.

54. See *Charity and Children*, XLII (March 17, 1927), 4; *News and Observer*, April 7, 11, 1927; *N.C. Methodist Advocate*, LXXII (April 28, 1927), 1; an excellent account of the campaign and election of 1928 is provided in Elmer L. Puryear, *Democratic Party Dissension in North Carolina, 1928–1936* (Chapel Hill, 1962), pp. 3–20.

EPILOGUE

The controversy over evolution which raged in North Carolina throughout most of the decade following World War I was a socio-intellectual disturbance of sizable dimensions. It involved far more than two different reactions to a biological theory or a clash between divergent schools of theology. Basically, the disturbance was caused by a collision between two states of mind that occurred during the first major intellectual confrontation with the twentieth century by North Carolinians. Evolution happened to be the issue on which protagonists decided to wage their major struggle. Although a variety of other issues might have been selected as the focus of the struggle, the choice of evolution was in some ways a natural one, for many North Carolinians related it, in one way or another, to a host of undesirable modern phenomena. Since virtually no distinction was made between the concept of organic evolution, Darwinism, and evolutionary philosophy, many citizens linked evolution with atheism, secularistic trends, immorality, disintegration of the family, "godless education," Bolshevism, and German militarism. In their vocabulary, evolution was a catchall word meaning modern evils in general. Gipsy Smith, Jr., for example, insisted upon spelling it "devilution."

The vast majority of North Carolinians during the 1920's undoubtedly subscribed to a fundamentalist theology in which there was no place for a belief in evolution. Most of them probably preferred to have the subject omitted from classroom discussion. Yet these same North Carolinians refused to heed the pleas of those who demanded an anti-evolution law as a remedy for "modern infidelity." The explanation in part is provided by the fact that there were two varieties of anti-evolutionists in the state. The overwhelming majority belonged to the noncombative type. Although anguished by the march of modernity, they nonetheless remained receptive to the ideas of those who advocated coming to terms with modern concepts and theories, including the evolutionary hypothesis. Their fundamentalism was far more flexible and perhaps more spacious than that of the militant minority. The latter assumed the tactics of embattled, panic-stricken warriors making a last-ditch effort to preserve their historic faith from the onslaughts of the evolutionists, among whom they included scientists, Social Gospelers, and intellectuals in general. The zealots brooked neither ambiguities nor equivocation; they heaped abuse upon those who strayed from the straight and narrow orthodoxy by embracing evolution and sought by whatever means available to stem the tide of defection. Evolution was likened to a graven image of the Old Testament variety which, unless destroyed, would lead society to eternal damnation. The zealots were therefore waging a righteous war designed to clear the right-of-way for the return of godliness. It was not their cause to which the noncombative fundamentalists in North Carolina objected; rather it was their tactics, the shrillness of their clamor, and their inclination to tamper with such principles as religious liberty and separation of church and state. While most North Carolinians agreed with the ends toward which the vigilantes worked, they were disturbed, if not utterly repelled, by the unchristian means employed to achieve the restoration of godliness. The public became disenchanted with the anti-evolution movement in the same degree to which it exhibited extremism. After 1925 the rabid anti-evolutionists hastened their own isolation by their extremist tendencies. Ultimately they sealed the doom of their movement by their own intemperance, sensationalism, and vulgarity.

Therefore, the defeat of the two anti-evolution bills by no means signified a complete victory for evolution or religious modernism. The opponents of the legislation could rarely be classified as either evolutionists or modernists. For the most part they were moderates, often theological fundamentalists, who preferred to have their faith compete in the free marketplace without the aid of legislative props rather than risk a violation of the principle of separation of church and state. Others feared that such legislation would tarnish the state's reputation for progress and make it "ridiculous in the eyes of the civilized world." The notoriety gained by Tennessee as a result of the Scopes Trial increased such apprehension among North Carolinians who otherwise would have taken little interest in the evolution agitation. The most vociferous opponents of the anti-evolution legislation were a few academicians, journalists, and clergymen who considered such statutory restrictions as by-products of ignorance, intolerance, and bigotry. Although a majority of the legislators responsible for defeating such measures seldom shared this interpretation, they did agree that an anti-evolution law would create more problems than it solved. Like their constituents, the legislators never viewed the defeat of the Poole bills as license for radicalism. Their most common reaction was that educational institutions ought to take a critical look at themselves and to avoid flying in the face of orthodoxy.

For obvious reasons, nevertheless, the outcome of the evolution controversy in North Carolina has been hailed as a victory for academic freedom. Certainly, intellectuals figured prominently in the accomplishment of this triumph. Poteat, Chase, Odum, and others refused to relinquish the freedom of the academic cloister or to surrender the college to the control of the mass meeting. Despite the personal vilification by their adversaries, they stood fast against the rising tide of anti-intellectualism. They waged their struggles without the active support of a large segment of the academic community, although academic freedom was an issue at stake. Public school teachers and officials, including the State Superintendent of Public Instruction after 1922, remained silent throughout the agitation. Their silence was all the more remarkable in view of the fact that one major issue in the evolution controversy focused upon the question of whether the teachers or the taxpayers furnished the educational concepts embodied in the public schools. A partial explanation of this reaction is found in the status of public school personnel in North Carolina during the 1920's. Despite rapid progress in the qualification of teachers after World War I, a large percentage of the teachers, principals, and superintendents possessed little more academic training or intellectual sophistication than the majority of their patrons. Their appreciation and understanding of academic freedom was probably no more acute than that of the ordinary layman; and, even if teachers had been aware of the issue, the threat of losing one's job was sufficient to preclude serious dissent. Collective action by teachers in the North Carolina Education Association would have required considerably less courage; but the Association chose to ignore the implications of the evolution controversy except to endorse Bible teaching in public schools. Similarly, the organization's publication sought safety through silence. The thoroughgoing manner in which the public school personnel acquiesed to the wishes of the local school patrons—or at least allowed itself to be intimidated—suggested that even if North Carolina had passed an anti-evolution law, it might have been spared a Scopes Trial for the lack of a defendant. Actually, the battle in which academic freedom loomed so large was waged primarily by the presidents of a Baptist college and the state university and by a few clergymen, editors, and politicians.

Finally, the failure of the anti-evolutionists to achieve a legislative victory in North Carolina had significant consequences beyond the boundaries of the state. North Carolina had been considered "pivotal" by the national anti-evolutionist crusaders who reasoned that "if North Carolina could be won, the nation could be won," and appropriate federal legislation could be enacted. The failure of the second Poole Bill in 1927 was disheartening for those who held such views. But anti-evolutionists in North Carolina and elsewhere rapidly and easily shifted their attention to a new cause—the candidacy of Alfred E. Smith—which embodied many of the same ingredients found in the evolution controversy. A single personality came to replace a scientific theory as the focus of their socio-intellectual and religious prejudices.

APPENDIXES

Appendix A — Contemporary Poems

WHERE WILL YOU BE, BOYS? [1]
by
Nell Battle Lewis

Where will you be boys, where will you be,
When the roll is called up yonder to determine who is free,
Harry,[2] Julius,[3] Archie,[4] and the well-known Eugene C,[5]
Where will you be, boys, where will you be?

Are you coming Dr. Harry, as you did two years ago,
To put the educated in a proud and pleasant glow,
To tell the world with suavity one man, at any rate,
Isn't frightened by fanatics in a literal-Bible state!

Will the Southern bring you swiftly, Dr. Julius to defend,
North Carolina education when it really needs a friend
Will you tell the brethren plainly that the women whom you teach
Have a right to all the knowledge that the years have put in reach?

Will you tell them, Mr. Allen, that the children under you
Shan't be shut by legislation from what Science says is true;
That the business now transacted in the system which you head
Is to teach the truth regardless of Mr. Bryan?

Do you feel them coming on you, creeping on you once again,
Any symptoms of an ailment that would mean a bed of pain?
Reassure a state so anxious for your safety, Dr. Brooks,
For an educator's often so much frailer than he looks.

Will you speak out in meeting when next Thursday rolls around,
Or will you be in hiding with your ears glued to the ground,
And silent, as the spineless were in Tennessee?
Where will you be, Boys, where will you be?

1. From the Raleigh *News and Observer*, February 6, 1927.
2. Harry W. Chase, president of the University of North Carolina.
3. Julius Foust, president of the North Carolina College for Women.
4. Arch T. Allen, State Superintendent of Public Instruction in North Carolina.
5. Eugene C. Brooks, president of the North Carolina State College of Agriculture and Engineering.

AN ODE TO THE POOLE BILL [1]

A Threnody
by
C. W. Tillett

Alas for the Poole Bill
That Zeb [2] *called the "fool bill,"*
It looks like it's mighty nigh dead!
But Mack [3] *is not weeping,*
He says it's just sleeping
And will wake from its Tam Bowie [4] *bed.*

But the monkeys in Siam
Are anxious as I am
To see how it all will turn out;
They are gathering in trees
They are swarming like bees,
And here is what all of them shout.

We hope Mack will win
and prove man's no kin
and never has been,
to any ancestor of ours!

1. From the Raleigh *News and Observer*, March 5, 1927.
2. Zebulon Vance Turlington, representative from Iredell County, an ardent supporter of the Poole Anti-Evolution Bill.
3. McKendree Long, a Presbyterian minister, head of the North Carolina Bible League, the organization that advocated the passage of the Poole Bill.
4. Thomas Bowie, a veteran legislator from Ashe County, employed by the North Carolina Bible League in 1927 as its chief lobbyist in behalf of the Poole Bill.

EVOLUTION[1]
by
Raymond Browning[2]

Back in the dark of intangible nothing,
Billions of years ere the earth gathered form,
Somehow the gloom changed to volume and substance;
Some way came motion, came light, and came storm.

Nebulous fire floated up out of nowhere;
By some strange movement suns rolled from the flame.
Then by the millions came stars, moons and comets,
Found their own courses and rolled in the same.

This tiny earth like a dark lonely dust-mote
Wandered about for some million years more,
Gathered some atmosphere, rivers and mountains,
Made the land stable, set tides on the shore.

Then came the cell, or the small protoplasm,
Perhaps an amoeba—just happened, you know—
Stirred from its shapelessness, took form and motion,
Learned by experience just how to grow.

Thus as the ages dragged by it ascended,
Through all diversified forms that we see,
Till by environment made ape or monkey,
Scratched, grinned and chattered—then climbed up a tree.

Now if some son of an ape will come forward
And kindly remove the mysterious veil,
Perhaps he can tell how his nimble ancestry
Succeeded in shedding the fur and the tail.

This is the weird fable he puts above Genesis,
This gruesome myth of man's climb from the clod;
Maniac's dream in exchange for our Bible;
Nightmare of science instead of our God!

1. From the *News and Observer*, October 18, 1923.
2. A clergyman in Hendersonville, N.C.

Appendix B ∽ Platform, Constitution and By-Laws of the North Carolina Bible League Adopted at Statesville, N.C., January 6, 1927

Name:

The name of this organization shall be The North Carolina Bible League.

Declaration of Purpose:

1. To organize Bible Leagues in every county, township and community in the State.
2. To oppose anti-Bible teaching, especially in all our tax-supported institutions of learning.
3. To promote a State-wide educational campaign along the line of good citizenship.

Membership:

All persons entitled to vote, who believe in the whole Bible as the infallible Word of God, and are willing to defend it as such, are eligible to membership in this League.

PLATFORM

Declaration of Principles:

First. Whereas, the public schools and colleges of North Carolina are supported by taxes levied upon the people of the State; and,
Whereas, all these educational institutions belong to the people of the State; and,
Whereas, we have good and sufficient reasons to believe that things are being taught in some of these institutions that are disparaging to the Bible.
Therefore, Be it Resolved, that we call upon the people in every

county in North Carolina who believe in the whole Bible as the inspired word of God to exercise their rights and privileges as citizens in removing this danger to our homes and to our religion.

Second. (1) We are unalterably opposed to the union of Church and State. This league is not a movement on the part of the Church, but of citizens of the State.

(2) We are likewise opposed to any attacks issuing from any source which tend to discredit the Bible as the authoritative revelations of God's will as our rule of faith and practice.

(3) We are strongly opposed to the State's teaching any doctrine or theory which tends to destroy the faith of our people in the Bible as the authoritative Word of God. This unassailable position we shall maintain despite ridicule or misrepresentation.

(4) We conceive it to be the function or duty of our state-supported schools to serve the *whole people,* and not to serve any mere class of people.

(5) We commend to the consideration of the people of North Carolina the following statement of Thomas Jefferson: "To compel a man to furnish contributions of money for the propagation of opinions which he disbelieves, is sinful and tyrannical." Our State schools shall be our servants and not our masters.

(6) We wish to emphasize the fact that we are not seeking to cripple any of our State schools, but to strengthen them and thereby inspire our people with confidence in said institutions as safe places for our boys and girls.

(7) We want it distinctly understood that this organization, as such, has nothing to do with denominational schools, or those that are privately owned, inasmuch as these are supported by voluntary contributions; and also, that we are standing for principles and not for or against men.

(8) Further, we do not question the right of freedom of thought or research. "We believe in freedom by the truth" and in freedom to search for truth; but we deny the right of those in charge of our State schools to employ and retain teachers who hold and express views fundamentally contrary to the simple teaching of the Bible, and force the taxpayers to pay the bills.

(9) Such questions as divorce evils, Sabbath observance, and others that vitally affect the moral and religious welfare of our people may be dealt with by the League at its discretion.

CONSTITUTION

Organization:

In order to make the foregoing declaration of principles effective, we recommend that the permanent organization of this body be as follows:

Officers:

The officers of the League shall be President, Vice-President, Secretary, and Treasurer. Their duties shall be those that are common to such officers.

Directors:

The number of Directors shall be ten or more, at the discretion of the League.
The President, Vice-President, Secretary and Treasurer shall be ex-officio members of the Board of Directors.

Duties of the Directors:

(1) To organize as rapidly as possible Bible Leagues in every county in the State.
(2) To devise a plan by which the work of the League may be successfully financed.
(3) To serve as a steering committee in making appeals to State and school officials and to the legislature just when and as the League may determine.
(4) It shall be the duty of the Directors to transact the business of the League between general meetings.
(5) To serve as the agent of the League in conducting a State-wide educational campaign along the line of true, worthy citizenship.

BY-LAWS

First:

(1) The League shall meet at least every six months, in December and June.
(2) Should necessity arise, the League will meet at the call of the President.

(3) Any fifteen members duly assembled shall constitute a quorum for the transaction of business.

Second:

(1) The Directors shall meet every three months.

(2) Should the occasion so demand, a meeting may be called by the Chairman of the Board.

(3) Any seven members duly assembled shall constitute a quorum for the transaction of business.

(4) The Officers and Directors shall be elected at the December meeting for a period of twelve months.

AMENDMENT

The constitution and platform of this League may be amended by a majority vote at any regular or called meeting, due notice having been given.

Appendix C ∽ *The Poole Bill and Our Legislators*[1]

During this month the interest of our readers has been divided between the fate of Collins, the Kentucky mountaineer, and the Poole Bill that would forbid the teaching of evolution in our schools. The legislators have expressed their feeling on the subject and many of them have shown that whatever may be their ability as politicians, few of them are experts in logic, and few are capable of fine distinctions in thought.

The President of the University [Harry W. Chase] seemed to be relying upon this confusion of thought in his hearers in his remarks to the legislature. There is a charm about the word freedom that is apt to blind the judgment of nearly all men.

Men forget that there is no such thing as absolute freedom of any kind.

A man is said to be born free; yet from the time he utters the first cry, down to the time when he leaves this world, he is closely hedged about by laws he is bound to obey.

Every man has a right to use his mind and to have his own thoughts; but he is not free to express his thoughts when they infringe upon the rights of others.

The clerk in the village grocery is free in a certain sense; but if he imagines that such freedom gives him a right to run down the value of his employer's goods or estrange his customers, he will soon find out his mistake.

These gentlemen of the University are scholars and they are accustomed to draw close distinctions. They know that they contracted to teach, and they also know that the State can decide what they are to teach. If it is the view of the State that their teaching is injurious to the young men, then the State can put a stop to it.

No one can restrict their thought, not even the State as the employing agent; but some one can restrict expression of their thought, when such expression is undoing all the teachings of mothers and the church. . . .

1. Editorial, the *Presbyterian Standard,* LXVI (March 4, 1925), 1–2.

Appendix D ∽ "Evolution, University and the People," by Frank P. Graham,[1] Associate Professor of History, University of North Carolina

Fragments of news have reached me in a far country that the question of the preaching of "evolution" has suddenly crowded in upon the question of the deficit in our state affairs, and, that corollary to the issue of evolution and President Chase's stand thereon, an attack was let loose upon the University and his administration. Such an attack seemed more threatening in the headlines of the papers than in the minds of the legislators, and, of course, on such a belated issue, was bound to fail in our state. However, as there remain controversial by-products of misinformation, I would like, as they say in Washington, "to make a few remarks with leave to print," in a distant effort to make clear a few facts, which set in their simple relations, may help us to a clearer view. Both the University and its president, on account of their place in our life, call for criticisms and differences of opinion from time to time, but neither of them calls for a defense from anyone and I do not presume to make any defense. "They need none, there they stand." But a little stocktaking even by one who is too far away to have either exact or the latest information, may help to a more complete understanding of the University, its faculty, and its president by the people of the state.

Let us review a few simple facts and consolidate our positions about them so as to keep, whatever be our minor differences, a solid line on all matters that involve the very life and purpose of the University and the colleges. I do not venture to speak for more than myself, but I hazard the guess, based on direct and indirect acquaintance, that the views here expressed, however inadequately, are substantially the opinion of thousands of University and college alumni and scores of thousands of North Carolinians "born and bred." Let us consider the charges—three in number—so far as I have been able to gather them here.

First, it is charged that President Chase is a Northerner. True. He was born a Northerner, who, without sacrifice of that fact or any honest loyalties which it may involve, became a North Carolinian by our invitation and his own choice. He did not invade the South in 1861–5 nor did he invade North Carolina with Northern and

1. *News and Observer*, April 5, 1925.

Western cohorts at any more recent time. Rather, North Carolina invaded his far Northern Home and invited him to come and live and do his day's work among us. He accepted that invitation and so lived and worked that his near neighbor Professor H. M. Stacy, quite essentially a North Carolinian, upon becoming acting President in difficult times, chose Dr. Chase, above all his fellows to be acting Dean and his right hand man. By the circumstance of Mr. Stacy's tragic death, acting dean Chase became acting president of the University.

He was then chosen President in his own right without seeking on his part. As president, he had become so much a part and pivot of our own life that he is in his work and plans more really North Carolinian than those who are louder in the locality and vocality of their patriotism.

As to Mr. Chase being a Republican in politics, I cannot say. He has never obtruded his politics on me nor, I am confident, on any other person. If he is a Republican, he is not more than what are a majority of our fellow citizens in the Republic and some two-fifths of the people of North Carolina. Since the point is raised, I hope that he is, for surely so large a part of our people are not to be begrudged so non-political preferences. As a public man he has represented only one interest; that interest is the continuous will of the people of North Carolina to preserve the spirit of the old and build a structure of a greater University where their children can seek to develop untrammeled by tyranny, their best physical, intellectual, and spiritual selves.

In the promotion and execution of that purpose, President Chase has been neither Republican nor Democrat, neither Northerner, nor Westerner, nor Southerner. He has been North Carolinian and American—as an American president of a North Carolina University. So far from being un-North Carolinian in this role, he is in line with and adds to such a presidential tradition. To be otherwise would be intolerable to himself, to University men, and to the people of whom they are an expressive part. A Democratic, North Carolina, ex-Confederate soldier, without disloyalty either to the section for which he had fought or to the party for which he had campaigned, nominated Dr. Chase for the University presidency, with a sense of the logic of the situation, a view to new times, and with a present loyalty as true as his old. In meeting each occasion in terms of the living issues of that occasion, this soldier representative of the lost cause, forever honored by our people, is more nearly representative of North Carolina than those who would bring into the living present the animosities of a decided past. If we cannot rise to the North Carolina stature of the Confederate soldier, who looks beyond geography and politics, to the man, then untried as an executive, we can, at the very least, remember that President Chase is no more of a Northern Republican than he was when he was called to the presidency, that he is now much more of a North Carolinian in his understanding of local traditions and aspirations and that his fitness for his task has necessarily multiplied with the responsibilities severely placed upon him by the rapid expansion of the economic and educational enterprises of a progressive people.

North Carolinians are not the sort of people who would invite a man into their midst and then fail to accord him all the rights of home. President Chase is not in any real sense an outsider, but the spirit of those who would mark him so is alien to all that is generous and fair in the life of our people. Those who for reasons of honest misconceptions or misguided zeal, would thus misrepresent the people of this state, will, in their truer mood, join in the desire and the effort to keep our life open and free to all who would help build a nobler commonwealth. If not, then we must meet them on the line they have drawn, toe-to-toe and blow-for-blow.

Second, it is said picturesquely that there are too many Northerners and Westerners on the faculty of the University. But there is another side of that picture. Just as, in the mixing of their blood and ideas, the English, Scotch-Irish, Scotch, German, French and the rest, have all made their distinctive contributions to North Carolina folk strain and culture, so the thought and life of the University and the colleges have been enlivened and enriched by the teachers from different sections. The danger is often the other way. Inbreeding of ideas and methods is not good for either the faculty or the students. New contacts, outside points of view, conflict of opinions, comparisons of standards and methods, cross-fertilization of minds—these are essential conditions for wholesome freedom and progress. In the history of mankind, it stands out from time to time that, where the ways and races have crossed and ideas have clashed with ideas, there have been the scenes and the stuff for the rise of great civilizations. The people of North Carolina and the University of North Carolina are so sure of their distinctive life and tradition that they are not afraid of so-called outsiders, but rather, like all truly progressive peoples of the past and the present, are eager for other contacts, methods, and ideas, out of whose clashing vigor and variety comes progress in the means and richness in the meaning of life.

Outsiders were brought to the University by Presidents Caldwell, Swain, Battle, Winston, Alderman, Venable, Graham, and Chase. The "Natives" are and have generally been the largest single group. The proportion of outsiders in the present administration is less, I believe, than it was in the first or the second. The "outsiders" make their distinctive contributions and either soon pass on to other pastures or send their roots down into our soil and become the most local of us all. The local spirit and color and charm of Chapel Hill, the most ancient of its traditions and the very sweetness of its placid tones, have been made richer by the association and the interpretations of those who have brought to their new home the fresh sensitiveness of appreciation of a new old beauty against a background of different traditions and different things. The worth of these reinterpretations of our local values, these other points of view, methods, and ideas would make it salutary to have many outsiders, even if all the most eminent men in all fields of knowledge and all the foremost men in qualities of leadership should be found in North Carolina. But since this is humanly impossible, it is even more vital to the life and progress of the University or any other college anywhere that a good number of its executives and professors be called from the outside.

Strong as is the purely geographical factor in a fresh and various interchange of values, the functional factor is even stronger. The head of the department, who has the deepest sense of his responsibility to provide the best for his students, is justly disposed to choose his staff on a functional rather than on a regional basis. If he is head of a department of electrical engineering, for example, he is concerned with providing the best possible training for the young men who aspire to be efficient technicians and engineer-statesmen as a youthful answer to the hydroelectric challenge of the Piedmont South. In the selection of the teacher-engineer to train these leaders of the new era in our history, the claims of the people of North Carolina to the very best from their sons and the claims of these sons to the very best from the University and colleges are going to outweigh any smaller claim. The regional patriotism of the people of North Carolina is far more involved in the thousands of their own sons and daughters being given the best available teaching than in the choice of any one of their native sons to do that teaching. The esprit de corps of each college department, the pride and standards of all the professional and craft groups in the state, reinforce the regional patriotism of the people in their demand for nothing less than the best as indispensible to the realization of their own truest local life. Professional and functional groups are certainly not less than nation wide, and the choice made in any one of these groups is made when possible, from the best qualified for the particular position in the whole national group. That some of those chosen should happen to come from Massachusetts, Georgia, Alabama, Illinois, Missouri, Dakota, and South Carolina is merely incidental to the wholesome distribution of persons, functions, and institutions in our federal Republic. North Carolina is holding her own at Chapel Hill. North Carolinians are like the rest in the open field of the whole teaching world. and are not at Chapel Hill by benefit of section or by the artificial virtue of a tariff of protective prejudice. On no other basis can there be the self-respect necessary to true teaching. On any other basis there is apt to develop complacency, stagnation, and even deterioration, whether tried North, or South, or East, or West. It goes without saying that the people of North Carolina will not now permit the violations of the local traditions of the University's vigor, variety, and freedom whose springs are in the subsoil of her own life and whose momentum was gathered in another century.

Thirdly, it is said that evolution is taught at Chapel Hill. Evolution was taught at the University by North Carolinians before President Chase was born. Though modified from time to time and with the increase of knowledge, the theory of evolution had moved from conquest to conquest and is now an important part of the teaching of geology, physics, chemistry, biology, psychology and sociology. It is taught in most of the colleges in every civilized nation in the world. It is taught by Christian missionaries in the colleges of Asia and Africa. Today students in many of the high schools in both hemispheres accept the theory as freely as they do the Copernican system and the circulation of the blood. By papal edict it was handed down that the earth did not move around the sun and by solemn law it was enacted that the blood did not circulate through the human body. But fortunately for the human race the earth continued on its celestial course and the blood went on its arterial way. Despite reports to the contrary, ex cathedra in medieval times and ex lege in modern times, the earth revolves and the blood circulates, and life evolves, not only biologically, from simpler to more complex organisms, but also socially, with the restless searchings of men for the Kingdom of God. The great evolutionary process vines its way to acceptance around the world in accordance with laws higher than the constitution, whether joined or opposed by the misconception of men and the laws of states.

The Poole Bill raised issues older than the state of North Carolina. The Inquisition, the Index and the stake are the unclaimed ancestors of the Poole Bill. Bruno chose to be burned to death rather than be saved on ecclesiastical terms. The teachers and the youth of North Carolina today would revolt against this ancient tyranny in its latest form. A tyranny that commanded them to be dishonest with themselves is not their idea of the way to salvation. All honor to President Chase for speaking clearly and standing squarely on the issue raised. May we also salute with equal respect President William Louis Poteat, who by his stand at Wake Forest has been for all the colleges, the buffer state against unreason, the shock absorber of intolerance, and the first line trench against bigotry these many years. President Chase, confronted with the issue, went out to meet it.

"God helping him he could do no other." Then and there he revindicated his leadership and holds more tightly to his side the fighting loyalty of University men. Let us all close ranks solidly about him. He has raised the University standard to be seen by all our people. Freedom to think, freedom to speak, and freedom to print are the texture of that standard. That freedom the great Virginians led the way in writing into the first amendment to the Constitution of the United States. It was one of the conditions of North Carolina's ratification of the Federal instrument. Upon this threefold freedom Thomas Jefferson founded our oldest national political party. It is the cornerstone and motto of the first American university to open its doors in the name of the people—in a little North Carolina village one hundred and thirty years ago.

Lux Libertas is cut with native chisel deep in the stones quarried from local soil. It is written upon the standard that flies its message to the winds that fetch the rains to the farms and sweeps the smoke from the factories of a busy people in a pleasant land between the mountains and the sea. Appropriations may come down for a time, Lux Libertas never! It is a motto inscribed on University emblems, not as a classical gesture to an ancient past but as a profession of her faith by the right of her life. It is a battle cry to which will rally out of all the localities of North Carolina the legions of her sons to stand again about the ancient foundations set upon a hill in the woods of Orange. Against those who have refused the claims of North Carolina youth to room in the colleges, the legions of the schools and colleges gathered, during the hard times of 1920–21, in their towns, villages, and countrysides, and with them the people, to put up more buildings for the boys and girls knocking at the crowded gates of the congested colleges. If need be, they will gather again to stay the hands of those who would tear down the very freedom for which those buildings stand.

The buildings at the University—symbol of all our schools and colleges—are forever treasured of the people because they tell their own story of poverty, struggles, failures, and heroisms. The ancient buildings, clustering under the great oak about the old well, are dearer to University men because of their associations with a great tradition of freedom. The new buildings, rising now where late the wilderness stood, have stirred the imagination of school boys because those buildings promise to open doors to them which shall not close upon any quest for truth.

It is a tradition of our people that they "would have it a place where there is always a breath of freedom in the air . . . and where finally truth shining patient like a star bids us advance and we will not turn aside." To preserve this spiritual possession of the people for the inheritance of their children, North Carolinians will fight against the false fear of truth and foes of freedom whatever be the power.

Appendix E ∽ Evolution—A Religious Question[1]

That evolution is a scientific question, according to the broad use of the term, "Science," must be admitted; for all human knowledge can, in some way, be incorporated in some classification of science. But if we should take the following definition of natural science as given by a scientist himself when he is wont to make his foundation look secure, evolution would be completely ruled out of the domain of science: "Science is that body of knowledge made up of verified and verifiable facts and their relationships which pertain to Nature and her processes, and to man insofar as he is immersed in the physical order." "Science is all verified and organized knowledge (Dinsmore's "Religious Certitude in an Age of Science," Page 11.) This definition coordinates with scientists' repeated claims to deal with "the facts of science." If natural science be so restricted as to deal only with "verified and verifiable facts" and not with theories, then the evolution theory ceases to be within the realm of natural science. If any one disputes this statement let him proceed, in the presence of competent witnesses to "verify" the origin of matter, or the origin of force, or the origin of organic matter, or the origin of life, or the origin of mind, or the origin of and the perpetuation of the numerous living genera. The fact is, no scientist ever has, and we venture to assert, never will "verify" as facts, the theoretic assumptions that these things have come about by evolutionary forces and process. When the materialistic scientist is thus forced to abandon his foundation of "verified or verifiable facts," or empiric science, he then takes refuge under some gorgeous theories, or philosophy, or science. These theories are almost as diverse as the materialistic scientists themselves (almost every one has a theory of his own) and are about as changeable as the phases of the moon. It is only when natural science leaves its field of dealing with facts as found existing in matter, force, life, mind, etc., and enters upon the philosophy or theories of their supposed origins and developments, that evolution can be classed as a scientific subject.

It is not so with religion. Religion is based upon a belief in the realm of the unseen; hence unverified by any laws of physics or of matter. There have always been some materialists who are wont to ignore or deny the reality of the unseen or spiritual kingdom, but they have generally been almost without a dynamic religion. The almost universal voice of strong religionists throughout all ages has

1. *North Carolina Lutheran,* V (January, 1927), 4–5.

been like that of Paul (II Cor. 5:7) "we walk by faith, not by sight." The gorgeous ancient mythologies and the uncultured superstitions, have all been miserable perversions of the true belief and faith in the truly spiritual. And all the prominent religions of the world have had and can have set forth as a prominent feature of their religions their belief in the origin of the universe and of mankind. These theories are now spoken of as cosmogonies. There have been many of them, and they have always been closely associated with the gods. A religion without some such attempt at the explanation of the origin of the universe and of mankind would be a very defective religion indeed.

The Jews have the oldest recorded explanation of the origin of the universe and of mankind that is known in the world. Their records assert that it came to them by the hand of Moses, "The man of God," and is given in the first chapters of Genesis.

Christianity adopted this same Mosaic account of the genesis of all things, mankind included, not only because it is the most satisfying to an intelligent people, but also because Jesus Christ frequently approved of and quoted from the books of Moses. Jesus never saw cause to criticise the books of Moses as being gorgeously fictitious, or mere mythological bed-time stories. To eliminate from Christianity the idea expressed in the first article of the Apostle's Creed, "I believe in God the Father, Almighty maker of heaven and earth" would be to dig from under it its first and great foundation stone. The matter of origins is therefore a religious question. It is more distinctively religious than it is scientific. Hence the teaching of organic evolution is teaching religion. The evolutionists who are contending against the anti-evolutionists for a safely guarded separation between Church and State, and are accusing the anti-evolutionists of attempting to inject a religious question into State legislation, should take their own medicine first and see that every text-book which teaches the Darwinian theory is withdrawn from the tax-supported schools. So long as such text-books are used or such teachers supported, the State is teaching religion. There is no refuting this fact. The anti-evolutionists are asking that the State cease to use the money to supplant the Bible religion by the Darwinian "religion." It is, without doubt, a reasonable and righteous demand.

BIBLIOGRAPHY

Manuscript Sources

Eugene Clyde Brooks Papers	Duke University Library
Governors' Papers	North Carolina Department of Archives and History
Legislative Papers	North Carolina Department of Archives and History
Nell Battle Lewis Papers	North Carolina Department of Archives and History
Minutes of the Faculty Council of North Carolina State University	Archives of North Carolina State University
Howard W. Odum Papers	University of North Carolina Library
William Louis Poteat Papers	Wake Forest College
"Reynolda Scrapbooks"	Presbyterian and Reformed Historical Center, Montreat, North Carolina
Correspondence of the State Superintendent of Public Instruction	North Carolina Department of Archives and History
University of North Carolina Papers	University of North Carolina Library
Robert W. Winston Papers	University of North Carolina Library

Minutes and Proceedings

Eastern Convention of the Original Free Will Baptist Church. *Minutes*. Session of 1926.

House of Representatives of the General Assembly of North Carolina. *Journal*. Sessions of 1923, 1925, 1927.

North Carolina Annual Conference of the Methodist Episcopal Church, South. *Journal*. Sessions of 1920–1928.

North Carolina Annual Conference of the Methodist Protestant Church. *Journal.* Sessions of 1920–1928.
Presbyterian Synod of North Carolina. *Minutes.* Sessions of 1920–1928.
State Convention of the Free Will Baptists of North Carolina. *Minutes.* Session of 1925.
United Daughters of the Confederacy [North Carolina Division]. *Minutes.* Session of 1923.
Western North Carolina Annual Conference of the Methodist Episcopal Church, South. *Journal.* Sessions of 1920–1928.

Pamphlets and Tracts

Betts, Sylvester J. *Criticism of Dr. Poteat's Book Recently Published.* Raleigh, 1925.
Bluske, Charles F. *A New Discovery—A Challenge to the Scientific World.* n.p., n.d.
Cobb, Collier. *Evolution and Christianity.* n.p., 1920.
Conant, J. E. *The Church, the Schools, and Evolution.* Chicago, 1922.
Conrad, S. F. (compiler). *Force and Love Meet Again Face to Face: Hard Science and Faith in Jesus Christ.* Charlotte, 1925.
Durham, E. C. *If Evolution Is True.* New Bern, 1922.
Hassell, Sylvester. *Evolution.* n.p., 1925.
Hood, George E. *The Origin of Man.* Goldsboro, 1926.
Kurfees, John. *The Fight Is On! The Issue Is Clearcut!* n.p., n.d.
McCann, Alfred W. *God—or Gorilla.* New York, 1922.
McCorkle, William P. *Anti-Christian Sociology As Taught in the Journal of Social Forces.* Burlington, 1925.
Martin, T. T. *Hell and the High Schools: Christ or Evolution, Which?* Kansas City, 1923.
Mouzon, Edwin D. *Fundamentals of Methodism.* Richmond, 1923.
Murray, E. C. *Does the Bible Teach Natural Science?* Lumberton, n.d.
Pentuff, James R. *Christian Evolutionists Answered and President W. L. Poteat's Utterances Reviewed.* n.p., 1925.
Porter, John W. *Evolution—A Menace.* Nashville, 1922.
Poteat, William Louis. *Christianity and Enlightenment.* n.p., 1922.
Tillett, Charles W. *Ginger and Pepper: Reminiscences and Recollections.* Charlotte, 1926.
Vann, Richard T. *What Have Baptist Colleges To Do with Fundamentalism and Modernism?* n.p. 1926.
Wuest, Kenneth S. *The Bible and Evolution.* n.p., 1926.

Newspapers and Periodicals: Religious

The Biblical Recorder. Baptist.

The Carolina Churchman. Episcopal.
Charity and Children. Baptist.
Crusaders' Champion. Nondenominational.
The Fundamentalist. Nondenominational.
The Methodist Protestant Herald. Methodist Protestant.
The Mission Herald. Episcopal.
The North Carolina Christian Advocate. Methodist Episcopal.
The North Carolina Lutheran. Lutheran.
The Presbyterian Standard. Presbyterian.
Searchlight. Baptist.
The Western Recorder. Baptist.

Newspapers and Periodicals: Secular

The Asheville Times.
The Beaufort County News. Washington.
The Catawba News-Enterprise. Newton.
The Chapel Hill Weekly.
The Charlotte Evening News.
The Charlotte Observer.
The Chatham Record. Pittsboro.
The Commonwealth. Scotland Neck.
The Concord Daily Tribune.
The Courier. Asheboro.
The Daily Advance. Elizabeth City.
The Durham Morning Herald.
The Evening Telegram. Rocky Mount.
The Fayetteville Observer.
The Fool-Killer. Boomer.
The Franklin Times. Louisburg.
The Gastonia Gazette.
The Goldsboro News.
The Graphic. Nashville.
The Greensboro Daily News.
The Greensboro Record.
The Hamlet News-Messenger.
The Hendersonville Times.
The Hickory Record.
The Independent. Elizabeth City.
The Jackson County Journal. Sylva.
The Lexington Dispatch.
The Messenger and Intelligencer. Wadesboro.
The Monroe Journal.
The Mooresville Enterprise.
The Morning Star. Wilmington.
The Mount Airy News.

The New York Times.
The News and Observer. Raleigh.
The North Carolina Teacher. Raleigh.
The Raleigh Times.
The Smithfield Herald.
The Stanly News-Herald. Albemarle.
The Statesville Landmark.
The Union Republican. Winston-Salem.
The Winston-Salem Journal.

Articles

Allen, Harbor. "The Anti-Evolution Campaign in America," *Current History,* XXIV (September, 1926), 893–97.

Bailey, Kenneth K. "Southern White Protestantism at the Turn of the Century," *The American Historical Review,* LXVIII (April, 1963), 618–35.

Barnes, Harry E. "Sociology and Ethics: A Genetic View of the Theory of Conduct," *The Journal of Social Forces,* III (January, 1925), 212–31.

Benjamin, Paul. "The North Carolina Plan," *The Survey,* XLVIII (September 15, 1922), 705–7.

Bernard, L. L. "The Development of the Concept of Progress," *The Journal of Social Forces,* III (January, 1925), 207–12.

Bryan, William Jennings. "The Fundamentals," *The Forum,* LXX (July, 1923), 1665–80.

Eaton, Clement. "Professor James Woodrow and the Freedom of Teaching in the South," *The Journal of Southern History,* XXVIII (February, 1962), 3–17.

Fosdick, Harry Emerson. "Evolution and Religion," *The Ladies' Home Journal* (September, 1925), 12, 180, 183, 185.

Jackson, W. C. "Culture and the New Era in North Carolina," *The North Carolina Historical Review,* II (January, 1925), 3–18.

Johnson, Gerald W. "Billy with the Red Necktie," *The Virginia Quarterly Review,* XXX (Autumn, 1943), 515–61.

———. "Chase of North Carolina," *The American Mercury,* XVII (July, 1930), 183–90.

———. "Journalism Below the Potomac," *The American Mercury,* IX (September, 1926), 77–82.

———. "North Carolina in a New Phase," *Current History,* XXVII (March, 1928), 843–48.

———. "Saving Souls," *The American Mercury,* I (July, 1924), 364–68.

———. "A Tilt with Southern Windmills," *The Virginia Quarterly Review,* I (July, 1925), 184–92.

Knight, Edgar W. "Monkey or Mud in North Carolina," *The Independent,* CXVIII (May 14, 1927), 515–16, 527.

Lewis, Nell Battle. "North Carolina," *The American Mercury,* VIII (May, 1926), 36–43.

Linder, Suzanne C. "William Louis Poteat and the Evolution Controversy," *The North Carolina Historical Review,* XL (April, 1963), 135–57.

"North Carolina's Negro Program," *The American Schoolmaster,* XV (May 15, 1922), 192–93.

Pearson, C. Chilton, "Race Relations in North Carolina: A Field Study of Moderate Opinion," *The South Atlantic Quarterly,* XXIII (January, 1924), 1–9.

Richardson, William H. "No More Lynchings: How North Carolina Has Solved the Problem," *American Review of Reviews,* LXIX (April, 1924), 401–4.

Riley, William B. "The Faith of Fundamentalists," *Current History,* XXVI (June, 1927), 434–40.

Shipley, Maynard. "The Forward March of the Anti-Evolutionists," *Current History,* XXIX (January, 1924), 578–82.

Slosson, Edwin E. "Legislation Against the Teaching of Evolution," *The Scientific American,* XXIV (May, 1927), 473–77.

Tindall, George B. "The Benighted South: Origins of a Modern Image," *The Virginia Quarterly Review,* XL (Spring, 1964), 281–94.

———. "Business Progressivism: Southern Politics in the Twenties," *The South Atlantic Quarterly,* LXII (Winter, 1963), 92–106.

———. "The Significance of Howard W. Odum to Southern History," *The Journal of Southern History,* XXIV (August, 1958), 285–307.

Villard, O. G. "What the Blue Menace Means," *Harper's,* CLVII (October, 1928), 535–36.

Walker, Stanley. "The Fundamentalist Pope," *The American Mercury,* VIII (July, 1926), 257–65.

Winston, Robert W. "The Noose of Darwin and the Neck of Orthodoxy," *The Journal of Social Forces,* III (November, 1924), 111–17.

———. "North Carolina: A Militant Mediocrity," *The Nation,* CXVI (February 12, 1923), 209–12.

Other Works

Allen, Frederick Lewis. *Only Yesterday.* New York, 1959.

Allen, Leslie H. (editor). *Bryan and Darrow at Dayton: The Record and Documents of the "Bible-Evolution Trial."* New York, 1925.

Atkins, Gaius G. *Religion in Our Time*. New York, 1932.

Ashe, S. A. (editor). *Biographical History of North Carolina*. 5 vols. Greensboro, 1906.

Ayres, C. E. *Science: The False Messiah*. Indianapolis, 1927.

Bailey, Kenneth K. "The Anti-Evolution Crusade of the Nineteen-Twenties." Ph.D. dissertation. Vanderbilt University, 1953.

———. *Southern White Protestantism in the Twentieth Century*. New York, 1964.

Barnes, W. W. *The Southern Baptist Convention, 1945–1953*. Nashville, 1954.

Barr, Walter. *Baxter McLendon: A Biography*. Bennettsville, S.C., 1928.

Battle, Kemp. *History of the University of North Carolina*. 2 vols. Raleigh, 1907.

Beale, Howard K. *Are American Teachers Free?* New York, 1936.

Bird, William E. *The History of Western Carolina College: The Progress of an Idea*. Chapel Hill, 1963.

Brown, Charles R. *A Working Faith*. Chapel Hill, 1928.

Bucke, Emory S. *The History of American Methodism*. 3 vols. New York, 1964.

Cash, Wilbur J. *The Mind of the South*. New York, 1941.

Cole, Stewart G. *The History of Fundamentalism*. New York, 1931.

Connor, R. D. W. *Rebuilding an Ancient Commonwealth*. 2 vols. New York, 1928–1929.

Corbitt, D. L. (editor). *Public Papers and Letters of Angus Wilton McLean, Governor of North Carolina, 1925–1929*. Raleigh, 1931.

———. (editor). *Public Papers and Letters of Cameron Morrison, Governor of North Carolina, 1921–1925*. Raleigh, 1927.

Couch, W. T. (editor). *Culture in the South*. Chapel Hill, 1934.

Crow, William N. "Religion and the Recent Evolution Controversy with Special Reference to the Issues in the Scopes Trial." Bachelor of Divinity thesis. Duke University, 1936.

Dabney, Virginius. *Liberalism in the South*. Chapel Hill, 1932.

Daniels, Jonathan. *Tar Heels: A Portrait of North Carolina*. New York, 1941.

Dillenberger, John. *Protestant Thought and Natural Science*. New York, 1960.

———, and Claude Welch. *Protestant Christianity Interpreted Through Its Development*. New York, 1954.

Dinsmore, Charles A. *Religious Certitude in an Age of Science*. Chapel Hill, 1924.

Dixon, Helen. *A. C. Dixon: A Romance of Preaching*. New York, 1931.

Fosdick, Harry Emerson. *The Modern Use of the Bible*. New York, 1924.

Furniss, Norman F. *The Fundamentalist Controversy, 1918–1931.* New Haven, 1954.
Garber, Paul N. *That Fighting Spirit of Methodism.* Greensboro, 1928.
Gatewood, Willard B., Jr. *Eugene Clyde Brooks: Educator and Public Servant.* Durham, 1960.
Ginger, Ray. *Six Days or Forever? Tennessee v. John Thomas Scopes.* Boston, 1958.
Gobbel, Luther. *Church-State Relationships in Education in North Carolina Since 1776.* Durham, 1938.
Green, C. Sylvester. *B. W. Spilman: The Sunday School Man.* Nashville, 1953.
Greene, John C. *Darwin and the Modern World View.* Baton Rouge, 1961.
Harmon, Nolan B. *Understanding the Methodist Church.* Nashville, 1955.
Hays, Arthur Garfield. *Let Freedom Ring.* New York, 1937.
Henderson, Archibald. *The Campus of the First State University.* Chapel Hill, 1949.
———. *North Carolina: The Old State and the New.* 5 vols. Chicago, 1941.
Hicks, John D. *Republican Ascendancy, 1921–1933.* New York, 1960.
Hobbs, Samuel H. *North Carolina: Economic and Social.* Chapel Hill, 1930.
Hofstadter, Richard. *The Age of Reform: From Bryan to F. D. R.* New York, 1955.
———. *Anti-Intellectualism in American Life.* New York, 1963.
Hordern, William. *A Layman's Guide to Protestant Theology.* New York, 1957.
House, Robert B. (editor). *Public Letters and Papers of Thomas Walter Bickett, Governor of North Carolina, 1917–1921.* Raleigh, 1923.
Johnson, LeRoy. "The Evolution Controversy During the 1920's." Ph.D. dissertation. New York University, 1954.
Johnson, Mary Lynch. *A History of Meredith College.* Raleigh, 1956.
Kendrick, Benjamin B., and Alex M. Arnett. *The South Looks at Its Past.* Chapel Hill, 1935.
Kennedy, Gail (editor). *Evolution and Religion: The Conflict Between Science and Theology in Modern America.* Boston, 1957.
Kitchin, Reed. "The Story of the North Carolina Club," in the *North Carolina Club Year Book, 1924–1925.* Chapel Hill, 1925.
Lawrence, Robert. *Here in Carolina.* Lumberton, N.C., 1939.
Lefler, Hugh T., and Aubrey L. Brooks. *The Papers of Walter Clark.* 2 vols. Chapel Hill, 1950.
———, and A. R. Newsome. *North Carolina: The History of a Southern State.* Chapel Hill, 1963.

Leuchtenberg, William E. *The Perils of Prosperity, 1914–1932*. Chicago, 1958.

Levine, Lawrence. *Defender of the Faith: William Jennings Bryan, The Last Decade*. New York, 1965.

Lingle, Walter. *Presbyterians, Their History and Their Beliefs*. Richmond, 1961.

Little, Luther. *Manse Dwellers*. Charlotte, 1927.

Machen, J. Gresham. *Christianity and Liberalism*. Grand Rapids, n.d.

McLendon, Baxter F. *Defending the Faith and Other Sermons*, Clinton, S.C., 1925.

———. *The Story of My Life and Other Sermons*. Bennettsville, S.C., 1923.

McVey, Frank. *The Gates Open Slowly: A History of Education in Kentucky*. Lexington, 1949.

Mathews, Shailer. *The Faith of Modernism*. New York, 1924.

Mims, Edwin. *The Advancing South: Stories of Progress and Reaction*. Garden City, 1926.

Niebuhr, Reinhold. *Does Civilization Need Religion?* New York, 1928.

North Carolina Manual. Raleigh. (Issues of 1925 and 1927).

Odum, Howard W. *An American Epoch: Southern Portraiture in the National Picture*. New York, 1930.

Ormand, Jesse M. *The Country Church in North Carolina*. Durham, 1931.

Ovens, David. *If This Be Treason*. Charlotte, 1957.

Paschal, George W. *History of Wake Forest College*. 3 vols. Wake Forest, 1943.

Pierce, Alfred M. *Giant Against the Sky: The Life of Bishop Warren Akin Candler*. Nashville, 1948.

Plyler, Marion T. *Through Eight Decades As Minister, Editor, and Author*. Durham, 1951.

Poe, Clarence. *My First Eighty Years*. Chapel Hill, 1963.

Porter, Earl W. *Trinity and Duke, 1892–1924: Foundations of Duke University*. Durham, 1964.

Poteat, William Louis. *Can a Man Be a Christian Today?* Chapel Hill, 1925.

Puryear, Elmer L. *Democratic Party Dissension in North Carolina, 1928–1936*. Chapel Hill, 1962.

Rice, Arnold. *The Ku Klux Klan in American Politics*. Washington, 1962.

Robertson, Archibald T. *That Old-Time Religion*. Cambridge, 1950.

Saunders, Keith. *The Independent Man*. Washington, 1962.

Shipley, Maynard. *The War on Modern Science: A Short History of the Fundamentalist Attacks on Evolution and Modernism*. New York, 1927.

Soper, Edmund D. *What May I Believe?* New York, 1927.
Spence, Hersey E. *"I Remember": Recollections and Reminiscences of Alma Mater*. Durham, 1954.
———. *When Preachers Meet: The Story of the North Carolina Methodist Pastors' School*. Greensboro, 1962.
Tippett, Thomas. *When Southern Labor Stirs*. New York, 1931.
Underwood, Mary E. "Angus Wilton McLean, Governor of North Carolina, 1925–1929," Ph.D. dissertation, University of North Carolina, 1962.
Watson, Richard L. (editor). *Bishop Cannon's Own Story: Life As I Have Seen It*. Durham, 1955.
Weisberger, Bernard A. *They Gathered at the River: The Story of the Great Revivalists and Their Impact upon Religion in America*. Boston, 1958.
Whaling, Thornton. *Science and Religion Today*. Chapel Hill, 1929.
Whitener, Daniel J. *Prohibition in North Carolina, 1715–1945*. Chapel Hill, 1945.
Wilson, Louis R. *Harry Woodburn Chase*. Chapel Hill, 1960.
———. *The Chronicles of the Sesquicentennial*. Chapel Hill, 1947.
———. *The University of North Carolina, 1900–1930: The Making of a Modern University*. Chapel Hill, 1957.
Winston, Robert W. *Horace Williams: The Gadfly of Chapel Hill*. Chapel Hill, 1942.
Woody, Robert (editor). *The Papers and Addresses of William Preston Few, Late President of Duke University*. Durham, 1951.

INDEX

J

K

L

M